A Teacher's Handbook To Inquiry Learning

1201 Ideas to Stimulate Inquiry

by
Dr. Fred Stopsky

AUTHOR:	Dr. Fred Stopsky
EDITORS:	Dr. Ray Ann Havasy
	Eric Patysiak
LAYOUT & DESIGN:	H. Donald Kroitzsh

Copyright ©MMIII by Fred Stopsky. All rights reserved. No part of this publication may be reproduced, stored in a retrieval system or transmitted, in any form, or by any means, electronic, mechanical, recorded, photocopied, or otherwise, without the prior written permission of the copyright owner, except by a reviewer who may quote brief passages in a review.

Printed in the United States of America

Published by:
CSTL Publishing
PO Box 23
Port Washington
New York 11050

Email: trysci@netzero.net
FAX: 516-767-1465

Prepared by:
Five Corners Press
Plymouth, Vermont 05056 USA

A Teacher's Handbook to Inquiry Learning
ISBN: 0-9742574-0-0 $39.00

TABLE OF CONTENTS

CHAPTER 1
    AN INTRODUCTION TO INQUIRY 9

CHAPTER 2
    INQUIRY AND THE ART OF QUESTIONING 15
        INTRODUCTION 16
        ANALYZING CLASSROOM QUESTIONS 19
        RECALL QUESTIONS 20
        ANALYTIC QUESTIONS 21
        DIVERGENT QUESTIONS 22
        DIALOGUE WITH THE TEACHER 23
        IDENTIFYING A CENTRAL IDEA 25
        RETHINKING QUESTIONS 26
        SEEING BUT NOT SEEING 27
        ASSUMPTIONS 28
        TEXTUAL QUESTIONS FOR CRITICAL THINKING 29
        DIALOGUE WITH THE TEACHER 30
        PREAMBLE TO THE CONSTITUTION 31
        DECLARATION OF INDEPENDENCE 32
        GETTYSBURG ADDRESS 33
        DIALOGUE WITH THE TEACHER 34
        ANALYTIC AND DIVERGENT QUESTIONS ABOUT FAIRY TALES 35
        ANALYTIC AND DIVERGENT QUESTIONS ABOUT FAIRY TALES 36
        SONG OF AN UNLUCKY MAN 37
        NURSERY RHYMES 38
        NURSERY RHYMES 39
        DIALOGUE WITH THE TEACHER 40
        THE CHERRY TREE STORY 42
        "A SHOT B AND A DIED" – WHAT HAPPENED? 43
        ADDITIONAL IDEAS TO STIMULATE STUDENT INITIATED QUESTIONS: 44

CHAPTER 3
    SOCIAL STUDIES AND INQUIRY 47
        INTRODUCTION 48
        DIALOGUE WITH THE TEACHER 50
        LIMERICKS 52
        A SAMPLE OF ATROCIOUS PUNS 53
        SOCIAL STUDIES PUNS 54
        THE PUN DICTIONARY 55
        BIOGRAFFITI 56
        WHY DO WE SAY THAT? 57
        FAMOUS LAST WORDS 58

NEWSPAPERS AND SOCIAL STUDIES	59
THE TELEPHONE AND SOCIAL STUDIES	60
MENUS IN HISTORY	61
LUDICROUS LAWS	62
SONGS AND INQUIRY	63
DIALOGUE WITH THE TEACHER	66
CONCRETE GEOGRAPHY	68
TEAM PUNS	69
ANIMALS AND GEOGRAPHY	70
FACING EAST	71
FACING WEST	73
DIALOGUE WITH THE TEACHER	74
LOGOS	76
HISTORIC FACES	77
VISUALIZATION OF PEOPLE	78
MISPLACED WORDS	79
DIALOGUE WITH THE TEACHER	80
WHAT IF?	82
CREATING NEW CIVILIZATION AND LIFE FORM	84
CRAZY PREDICTIONS IN HISTORY	85
NEWSPAPER STORIES IN THE FUTURE	86
ALTERNATIVE FUTURES	87
ADDITIONAL IDEAS	88
ADDITION INQUIRY IDEAS IN SOCIAL STUDIES	90

CHAPTER 4
INQUIRY AND STUDENT EXPERIENTIAL LEARNING 97

INTRODUCTION	98
DIALOGUE WITH THE TEACHER	100
VALUES GAME BOARD	103
VALUE SIMULATION: PUBLIC LAW 94-142	104
PRACTICE IN VALUE SIMULATIONS	105
DIALOGUE WITH THE TEACHER	108
MOCK TRIAL OF THREE PIGS AND THE WOLF	110
CHRISTOPHER COLUMBUS: A MOCK TRIAL	111
EARTH ON TRIAL	115
ADDITIONAL IDEAS FOR MOCK TRIALS	116
DIALOGUE WITH THE TEACHER	117
DIALOGUE WITH THE TEACHER	120
FRANK HARRIS CASE STUDY	121
DO NOT WEAR HATS IN SCHOOL	126
CRIME IN THE BRITISH COLONIES OF NORTH AMERICA	127
WHAT CAN WE LEARN	129
MUST THE TRUTH ALWAYS BE THE TRUTH?	131
A PROBLEM ABOUT PIGEONS	132
PROPERTY RIGHTS	133
THE CHEATING DOCUMENT	134

CALAMEC VS ORISCO (THIS IS BASED ON AN AZTEC LEGEND)	135
DIALOGUE WITH THE TEACHER	136
THE DOCTOR'S DILEMMA	138
UNCERTAINTY	141
DIALOGUE WITH THE TEACHER	146
CASE STUDY ON TEAPOT	147
DETAIL DETECTIVE	148
INSPIRATION OR PLAGIARISM IN ART?	149

CHAPTER 5
INQUIRY AND THE LANGUAGE ARTS ... 151

INTRODUCTION	152
DIALOGUE WITH THE TEACHER	154
METAPHORIC THINKING	157
METAPHORIC THINKING	158
PERSONIFICATION	159
SYNESTHETIC QUESTIONS	160
INVENTING A POEM	161
CONCRETE POETRY	163
EMBLEMATIC POETRY	164
PUZZLE POETRY	165
ACTIVITIES	167
NOTICING POEMS	168
SOUND POEMS	168
SMELL POEMS	169
OBITUARY POEMS	170
DIALOGUE WITH THE TEACHER	171
VISUAL WRITING	172
REBUS	173
AUTHOR LOGOS	174
DIALOGUE WITH THE TEACHER	175
PROVERBS	176
WORDS OF WISDOM	177
DIALOGUE WITH THE TEACHER	178
INTERACTING WITH FAIRY TALES AND STORIES	180
ENTERING THE MIND OF CHARACTERS IN STORIES	182
DIALOGUE WITH THE TEACHER	183
HANS MORGENTHAU: "THE FUTURE OF DIPLOMACY"	185
SNOW WHITE: A STUDY IN FOREIGN POLICY	186
A CONFLICT ANALYSIS MODEL	188
DIALOGUE WITH THE TEACHER	190
IDEAS TO STIMULATE WRITING	192
UPSIDE DOWN WRITING	193
OXYMORONS	194
WRITING AN ESSAY	196
COLLECTIVE WRITING	197
DIALOGUE WITH THE TEACHER	199

CRAZY LETTERS 201
DEAR ABBY 202
ADDITIONAL INQUIRY IDEAS IN LANGUAGE ARTS 205

CHAPTER 6
MULTICULTURALISM 209
INTRODUCTION 210
DIALOGUE WITH THE TEACHER 212
THE CHADOR 214
A MODERN AMERICAN CRIME 216
DIALOGUE WITH THE TEACHER 217
"WE WANT THEM BUT WE DON'T WANT THEM" 220
A DIALOGUE BETWEEN AN IRSIH WORKER
    AND AN AFRICAN AMERICAN WORKER – 1850S. 222
A CASE STUDY OF THE KILLING OF THE CHIEF OF POLICE 225
IN NEW ORLEANS 225
GERMAN AMERICANS AND TEMPERANCE
    IN NINETEENTH CENTURY AMERICA 227
SHOULD WE LET THEM IN? 230
AN INTERVIEW WITH FREDERICK DOUGLASS: 233
AFTER THE FACT 233
DIALOGUE WITH THE TEACHER 236
DIALOGUE WITH THE TEACHER 242
BREAKFAST AROUND THE WORLD 244
THE HORSE AND THE GIRAFFE 245
THE RABBIT, THE SQUIRREL AND THE FOX 246
ADDITIONAL IDEAS FOR TEACHING ABOUT MULTICULTURALISM 248

CHAPTER 7
CREATIVITY AND INQUIRY 251
DIALOGUE WITH THE TEACHER 257
BRAINSTORMING 259
FORCED RELATIONSHIPS 260
REDESIGN THE COAT HANGER 262
MORPHOLOGICAL FORCED CONNECTIONS 263
SYNECTICS 264
DEVELOPING ANALOGY SKILLS 265
ANALOGY EQUATION 266
LATERAL THINKING IDEAS 267
LASER THINKING 269
LASER THINKING PROBLEM 271
CROSS MATRIX THINKING 274
CROSS MATRIX IMPACT 277
LITERARY CHARACTER CROSS MATRIX 278
THE IDEA TREE 279
THE DIG 280
IDEAS FOR CREATIVITY 282

Chapter 8
Inquiry And Interacting With Textual Materials 295
- Restating Information 296
- Dialogue With the Teacher 298
- Dialoguing With Textual Materials 300
- Additional Tips for Interacting With Textual Materials 307

Chapter 9
Inquiry on the Internet 311
- An Innovative Educational Tool 312
- Dialogue With the Teacher 315
- Web Sites on Climate 317
- Dialogue With the Teacher 318
- Web Sites on the United States Supreme Court 320
- Additional Ideas for Inquiry on the Internet 321

Chapter 10
Fostering Inquiry Through Memory Power 325
- Enhancement of Memory Retention 326
- Dialogue With The Teacher 328
- The Planet Exercise 338
- Linking 340
- Memorizing Textual Material 344
- Recalling Data 347
- A Few Last Suggestions 354

Chapter 11
Inquiry And Science And Math 355
- 110 Ideas to Stimulate Science Inquiry and Math Inquiry 356

Postlude
A Few Last Chuckles 367
- The Animal School 368
- If Jesus Came To School 369
- Dear Teacher, Please Excuse... 370
- School Cheers 371
- Just a Minute Late 372
- How Long Have You Been A Teacher? 379
- Wacky Ways To Teach For The Brave At Heart 380

DEDICATION

To Elizabeth and David Stopsky
for keeping me young at heart.

Chapter 1

An Introduction To Inquiry

"The true test of intelligence is not how much we know how to do, but how do we behave when we don't know what to do."
John Holt

It is inherent in the human condition to quest for knowledge. From the moment of birth, humans, unlike other animals, are driven by a quest for new information. Babies instinctively grasp objects, place things in their mouth, touch, turn their heads at a strange sound, and observe people move. We humans are a curious creature. The process of inquiring begins with a gathering information and applying our senses of hearing, smell, touch, seeing, and taste to learn about our world.

Jerome Bruner suggests there are four dominant models of pedagogy practiced in schools. The first regards youth as learning through imitation and thus emphasizes learning skills through examples and demonstration. Talents, skills, and expertise are emphasized in this approach. A second view believes students learn from didactic exposure. Many classrooms are based on the principle that students should be given facts, principles, and rules that are to be learned, remembered and applied. A third view claims students are capable of thought and can be meaningfully engaged in discussions and collaborative learning. Bruner also believes there is a fourth perspective which holds that children can grasp the distinction between personal knowledge and what is taken to be known by any culture at a given moment.

Neither of these views in themselves can be the foundation upon which children learn. Inquiry is the process by which individuals seek information, knowledge and skills and thus are dependent upon all of the above. Perhaps, in a bygone era when people lived in isolated communities, memorization of basic skills and knowledge sufficed to participate in a productive life. However, we now inhabit a time in which information explodes at an exponential rate making it impossible to communicate even a fraction what is known in the world about the world. At this very moment, the Hubble space telescope is gathering information that changes our scientific knowledge and thus makes what is presently taught in science textbooks out of date. It becomes increasingly imperative for each student to understand the process by which knowledge is gained, and how one makes informed decisions.

Educators frequently become engaged in either/or arguments. One group argues students should memorize data while another group claims the process of learning is important, not what is learned. One cannot inquire without an information base. It is important to master data if one is to ever inquire about the data. Memorizing information without grasping the context of the data leads to short term memory rather than to understanding and comprehension. At the core of any theory of inquiry is the proposition that applying and using information best understanding underlying concepts.

Knowledge concerning content of a subject is vital if individuals are to engage in any form of inquiry. An important component of inquiry is discerning patterns and meanings which cannot be accomplished without knowledge. If one learns facts without grasping an over arching conceptual understanding, then use of these facts is limited. The essence of creative thinking is identifying new patterns within existing information. After all, the inventor of the hula hoop took his knowledge of round objects and applied it to placing the round object around a hip. An inquiring mind is able to transfer and apply knowledge to new settings.

Didactic centered education establishes a relationship between teacher and student in which teacher knows and the student does not know. A student is cast into the position of ignorance and must accept the teacher's data as presented. Inquiry education enables students to gain understanding because they are able to establish connections between disparate strands of information. There is a vast difference between blindly following directions versus understanding the principles underlying the direction. It is the difference between being a stranger in a city for the first time and receiving directions from a native as contrasted with someone living in the city who is attempting to get her bearings and simply needs some additional data to assist in clarification. Inquiry education allows learners to associate information within a context that has personal meaning.

It is unfortunate that discussions about inquiry education become entangled in expressions such as "teacher centered" and "student centered." Inquiry requires teachers to train students in the process of investigation. Inquiry necessitates continual experiments and failures. A teacher who supports failure assists students to become empowered learners.

The author recalls a conversation with the editor of The Sporting News which is the most famous publication about baseball. They were at lunch when the author asked the editor to explain the career of Dick Wakefield. Dick Wakefield was a young outfielder who came up to the Detroit Tigers in the late 1940s. He was Rookie of the Year in his first year in baseball and hit 340. The next year he hit about 290 and by the third year had left baseball. The editor responded with: "He wouldn't learn from his mistakes. Dick was a natural hitter who was successful in high school and college. He had little experience with failing. But, once you reach the major leagues people study you carefully and invariably they find a weakness. His coaches explained to Dick that he had to make changes to adjust to the pitchers. He refused because what he had done in the past had always been successful. His refusal to learn from his mistakes led to him being forced to quit baseball." This story illustrates the relationship between teacher and student. A teacher is a coach who aid students to work their way through experimental failures. "Educare" is from the Latin meaning "to lead forth." A teacher is an Educare who leads students forth into enlightenment.

The inquiry process focuses upon learning and using content as a means of information processing and problem-solving. There is less emphasis upon "what do you know" and more upon "do you understand?" There is less emphasis upon students responding to content-driven questions and more emphasis upon students posing questions. If students are free to pose questions and to pursue inquiry into those questions, there is greater likelihood teacher and student are functioning as a collaborative learning team.

In traditional classes "listening" necessitates students focusing upon what the teacher says in order to respond to test questions about what was stated. In an inquiry classroom, students listen to the sound of questions, to questions by other students and engage in dialogue with teachers. It is often claimed that inquiry learning is more concerned with process. Former President John F. Kennedy often said he preferred teaching someone how to fish than giving fish to someone because learning how to fish ensured the person could take care of himself.

Inquiry education is concerned with aiding students to develop habits of mind that aid them in problem solving. For example, in learning social studies students should learn the tools utilized by historians in delving into historical issues. The study of science requires understanding the scientific method of investigation in order to verify data and the study of literature necessitates grasping the complexity of examining textual understandings. Traditional classrooms assume all academic disciplines function according to agreed upon methods and principles, but inquiry centered classrooms recognize differences in approach. A goal of inquiry is empowering students to be able to function employing a variety of intellectual methods in their pursuit of knowledge.

Perhaps, the most fundamental difference between inquiry oriented classrooms and traditional education centers on the topic of "work." Inquiry requires students to be engaged in intellectual pursuits that continually demand difficult and complex thinking because the goal is "comprehension" and understanding. Traditional classrooms demands no more than being able to recall data stored in short term memory and if that information is forgotten after the test, so be it. The act of inquiry more readily results in storing data in the long term memory because one has gained knowledge rather than information. This is hard work. Inquiry classrooms repeatedly witness students working collaboratively in order to solve problems and ask questions. They are not passive receivers of information which is characteristic of memorization for short term memory storage. Students who inquire ask questions, experiment, wander into dead ends, go back to the original point of departure and try again. They have to work themselves through failure and discouragement because what they are learning has personal meaning.

David Hawkins, a scientist, coined the expression "messing around" to describe inquiry centered science education. He argued the quest for scientific understanding meant scientists investigated many roads knowing full well many did not lead to their desired goal. The act of creativity entails much "wasted time" because individuals explore alternative possibilities. Messing around usually results in students going much further intellectually than what textbooks seek. We ordinarily in life learn from our failures as much as from out success.

Traditional textbook driven education operates on the assumption that we "know" history or science or literature or what constitutes art. The most common form of questions posed in such settings are "how much" and "is this right?" The underlying assumption is that some expert "knows" and that all other experts in the field agree with that "knowing." As a result failure is a negative since the student is unable to inform the teacher of what he/she has learned. Inquiry education recognizes diversity of thinking within any academic discipline. It seeks to empower students to select from among opinions in an informed manner.

Nothing in the preceding paragraph obviates the need for students to learn information. The difference between how students gather information within traditional and inquiry classrooms centers much more on tone and methodology. The task of teachers in an inquiry classroom is educating students to learn how to learn. The goal is for students to become self directed learners and this can be achieved only if there is trust between teachers and students. Students must believe they can stumble and fall without being punished since the goal is ultimately to learn how to avoid serious injury to one's intellectual capabilities.

There are subtle variations to the process of inquiry which are frequently overlooked. In "Guided Inquiry" teachers identify a topic and direct the process so it results in students uncovering what the teacher wants them to find. A Guided Inquiry approach is an excellent beginning point for students who lack familiarity with the process of inquiry. For example, if my goal is having students understand contrasting viewpoints about the origin of the American Revolution I will provide them documents and materials reflecting supporters and opponents of the Revolution. They might read how the English government justified its behavior or views of Loyal Colonists or the attitudes of Native Americans and slaves during the time period. Students subjected to this variety of views are less apt to conclude that the American revolutionaries were correct. However, it does educate students to understand that any issue contains contrasting viewpoints. Guided Inquiry enables teachers to control the parameters of differences.

On the other hand, Student Initiated Inquiry allows students to identify a topic or questions for investigation. It is much more open ended and the teacher is certain regarding outcomes of the study. For example, a Student Initiated Inquiry into the Spanish American War might result in learning how people in the Philippines went from welcoming Americans to organizing a rebellion against American rule. The wider the parameters available for student initiated inquiry the more apt are students to investigate roads never conceived by teachers. We suggest practice with Guided Inquiry until students have gained confidence in their abilities to decide on a starting and concluding point for their investigations.

Inquiry is a complex process of gathering information and extrapolating from it major concepts. Elie Wiesel, Nobel Prize winner and survivor of the Holocaust has often said "it is the questions we ask rather than the answers we provide that separate the wise person from the fool." A classroom in which students are trained to regurgitate information are being educated to be mentally weak since they are unable to formulate their own questions and conclusions. Students engaged in inquiry are learning to pose questions and to live comfortably in the realm of uncertainty. One must inhabit uncertainty before gaining an insight. Inquiry centered classrooms also educate students to understand there are times when no clear result is available and we really don't at this moment know the "solution." After all, has anyone come up with "the solution" to urban traffic? Students in inquiry classrooms are comfortable with gray uncertainty which is most probably a state of mind they will frequently discover in their lives. The reality of modern life is that frequently there are no simple clear answers. To inhabit the post industrial world is to live simultaneously in the realms of certainty and ambiguity. This is a new psychological phenomenon in human existence.

CHAPTER 2

INQUIRY AND THE ART OF QUESTIONING

Chapter Outline:

1. Introduction
2. Recall, Analytic and Divergent Questions
3. Inquiry Training Activities
    a. Identifying a Central Idea
    b. Seeing But Not Seeing
    c. Assumptions
    d. Textual Questions for Critical Thinking
4. Questions for Preamble to the Constitution
5. Questions for the Declaration of Independence
6. Gettysburg Address
7. Questions for Fairy Tales
    a. Little Red Riding Hood
    b. Hansel and Gretel
8. Questions for Songs and Nursery Rhymes
    a. African Song of an Unlucky Man
    b. Nursery Rhymes
9. Questions for Textbooks
10. Student Initiated Questions
    a. Cherry Tree
    b. Activities to Stimulate Student Questioning

Questions are coded according to Bloom's Taxonomy:
    Knowledge   (K)
    Comprehension   ©
    Application   (A)
    Analysis   (A)
    Synthesis   (S)
    Evaluation   (E)

INTRODUCTION

Children are natural inquirers. They master language, learn how to walk, and solve daily problems. They befuddle parents with "why is the sky blue" questions and learn how to manipulate adults to satisfy their needs. The task of educators is not teaching children how to be an inquirer, but how to extend the range and breadth of their innate inquiry approach to life.

The ability to identify questions is critical in the quest to inquire. Shortly after President Franklin D. Roosevelt took office in 1933 he was meeting with his chief assistant, Harry Hopkins about how to cope with unemployment during the Depression. Harry Hopkins recalls in his autobiography that the meeting ended and as his hand touched the door knob, he turned and asked a question: "What about unemployed artists and writers and musicians, what do we do about them?" President Roosevelt threw his head back, thought a moment and said: "Oh, throw them into the WPA and give them jobs." As a result of that question, art and literature bloomed in America. Until the question was asked, no one thought about providing employment to intellectuals.

Questioning is vital to intellectual growth and problem solving. An important task of teachers is establishing an environment in which students are fee to initiate questions. During the early stages of the Mercury Space program a free wheeling atmosphere pervaded among its members who were attempting to solve problems never before encountered by humans. They pushed one another by continually asking probing questions. For example, Jack Herbelig was charged with developing a safe living area for astronauts on the space ship. He decided to use pigs for his experiments, but regardless of how the test was conducted, the pigs died. Herbelig was in a quandary since no one at the Space Center had any suggestions about solving the problem. Finally, one day, a fellow engineer asked a question: "Have you thought about asking a pig farmer if he had any explanation about the death of the pigs?" Herbelig went to a pig farm and explained what was happening to the pigs. The farmer calmly explained to him that pigs died if kept on their backs over an extended period of time. In questioning, one never knows who will emerge with an appropriate answer.

Questions suggest new directions or enable students to explore paths not previously considered. In this chapter, we shall examine alternative questioning strategies in dealing with materials ordinarily found in the curriculum. Ask a different question and it results in other than normal responses. Nothing dulls the senses more than regurgitating information that has been taught. Excellent teachers use the art of posing interesting questions in order to transform the ordinary into the extraordinary. They use questions for several purposes:

1. They enable teachers to learn what students know.
2. They encourage class participation in learning.
3. They stimulate creative thinking.
4. They maintain interest in class discussion.
5. They serve to review what has been taught.
6. They enable teachers to understand how students think.
7. They identify new areas for investigation.

Teachers should consider several factors in organizing the questioning process:

1. Questions should be clear and concise. Ambiguity leads to confusion. For example, asking "Compare Snow White and Cinderella is unclear," but "Compare the Stepmothers in Cinderella and Snow White" gives direction to students.

2. Avoid rambling questions. For example, "The homeless have many problems like finding a place to sleep and getting food or getting their children to school, how best can we aid the homeless?" A directed question is: "Give at least one way we can provide the homeless nightly sleeping arrangements."

3. Use vivid language when possible. For example, "Why do you think Theodore Roosevelt referred to Woodrow Wilson as having an eight guinea pig power brain?"

4. Avoid guessing games. "What am I trying to get across about DNA?"

5. Avoid fill in questions: "The man who discovered penicillin was.....?"

6. Avoid questions that ask one thing when you really want to say something else. For example, "Do you really mean that China is in Africa?" You could say, "You just said that China was in Africa, let's take down a map of Africa and check that out."

7. Avoid multiple questions: "Pablo Picasso changed his painting style several times and he became a radical in politics,. Why do you believe these actions made people angry at him?"

8. Avoid the "what else" type question. Instead of saying "what else" when a student responds, you could state: "You just gave one excellent point about why the house of the second pig was blown down. Could someone else tell me what happened to the house of the pig who used bricks to build the house?"

9. In the midst of asking questions about a topic, state: "I'll give an "A" to anyone who can ask me a question that helps us get a new idea about what we are learning."

10. Occasionally, ask yourself a question. "You know as we talk about the Spanish American War, it just dawned on me that I wish I knew more about how the people in Spain thought about the war. That would be an interesting question, "How did the people in Spain feel about the Spanish American War?"

Analyzing Classroom Questions

Following is a process to assist in analyzing questions posed in classrooms. Perhaps, you might tape yourself for an hour and then analyze the nature of questions being posed in your classroom.

Teacher Questions:

1. Recall of information. "What is the name of the inventor of the telephone?"
2. Clarifying: "Do you understand the meaning of…"
3. Analyzing information: "Do you understand what the author means when she says….."
4. Questions concerning behavior: "Why did you leave your seat?"
5. Questions about procedures: "Does everyone understand what to do when you get into the group?"
6. Personal Clarification: "Are you feeling sick?"
7. Socratic Dialogue.
8. Rhetorical questions posed to class: "Are you guys ready to learn today?…"
9. Hypothesizing questions: "What if…."
10. Summarizing questions: "Could someone summarize the…."

RECALL QUESTIONS

Recall questions are designed to elicit information regarding what students have learned regarding what was taught. Recall questions are best used in conjunction with other forms of questioning since they enable teachers to begin higher order thinking questions cognizant of the student knowledge base. Since in asking Recall questions, there is only one answer, students either know or don't know, but Analytic questions have the potential for an infinite number of responses, and thus students require more time for reflection.

For example, following are several recall questions about the War in Iraq.

1. What was the name of the dictator who ruled Iraq?
2. What was the name of the American President during the war?
3. Which two nations supplied most Coalition forces who fought?
4. Name at least one European country that opposed the war.
5. What was the name of the American general who led Coalition forces?
6. Which of the following numbers most closely approximates the number of Coalition troops who participated in the conflict?

    10,000   1,000,000   250,000

7. Match the name of the political party with the country in which it was found:

    Bath   England
    Republican   Iraq
    Labor   United States

8. Arrange the following in a correct sequence of events beginning with the first and concluding with the last.

    Invasion of Iraq   UN Inspections   Vote in Security Council

9. Rank order the countries which contributed most of the soldiers who were in the Coalition forces beginning with the most to the least:

    Australia   United States   England

Each of the above has only one answer. The only "discussion" about such questions is why the response is correct or incorrect. Recall questions are not designed for discussion.

ANALYTIC QUESTIONS

Analytic Questions are designed to engage students with the task of discerning patterns, making comparisons, and formulating conclusions. Obviously, students can not engage in such thinking without possessing a body of information. Since Analytic Questions require thought, students are entitled to more time in responding. An Analytic question is asked and since there is only one answer the student either knows or doesn't know, but Analytic questions have potentially an infinite number of responses and thus students need time to reflect and formulate their thinking. Analytic questions lend themselves more to collaborative interactions since students can aid one another in thinking through the problem. Following are some examples of Analytic Questions about the War in Iraq.

1. Compare and contrast military strategies used in the Gulf War of 1991 with those used in the War in Iraq.

2. Compare and contrast how Iraqi troops fought in the Gulf War with their fighting in 2003.

3. Identify an military criticism voiced in the War in Iraq by opponents of Secretary of Defense Rumsfeld's strategy. Present arguments for and against his strategy.

4. What evidence can you cite which most strongly supports the criticism voiced by France that Saddam Hussein was not in violation of the UN Resolution.

5. Compare and contrast American public opinion attitudes toward European nations in 1991 as contrasted with 2003.

6. Present a reasoned argument supporting or opposing the War in Iraq. Present evidence to support your views.

7. Compare and contrast attitudes among Arab nations during the Gulf War with those held in the War in Iraq.

8. Identify a trend in thinking about the Middle East among Americans from 1991 to 2003.

As the above questions clearly indicate, an intelligent response to any requires some thought and reflection on the part of students. Students need data in order to respond. All analytic questions should be formulated with realization of what students know about the topic.

DIVERGENT QUESTIONS

Divergent questions engage students in speculation and formulation of an hypothesis. It cannot be emphasized sufficiently that Divergent questions require students possessing a body of information in order to respond. It is doubtful if more than a handful of American students could respond to: "Imagine you are a woman in Bangladesh, what would be your major concerns?" If one is asked to speculate about what one does not know, it is an exercise in guessing. Divergent questions can be powerful because they require students delving into their feelings, emotions and value systems. Following are some divergent questions about the War in Iraq:

1. Assume Coalition forces encountered heavy resistance in Baghdad resulting in thousands of casualties, how might that have impacted American public opinion views about the war?

2. Assume Iraq forces rebelled and overthrew Saddam before the Coalition forces entered their country, which problems would that have created?

3. After reading arguments for and against invading Iraq in 2003, which viewpoint presents the stronger argument?

4. Assume you were President Bush in 2003, list one thing you would have done differently than what he did as President.

5. Identify any American President in history. Assume he was President in 2003. What might have been his policy toward Iraq? Provide an explanation for your views.

6. Assume there had never been a war in Iraq, how might that have altered events in the Middle East?

7. Present an argument to discuss: "If there had never been the September 11 attack, there never would have been a war in Iraq.

8. Assume you lived in Iraq and hated Saddam Hussein. Give one argument why you would have welcomed Coalition forces and one argument why you would have opposed their presence.

These Divergent Questions require a knowledge base and they require one to consider basic values and endeavor to view the world through a different lens.

Dialogue With the Teacher

It is our assumption that students require training in the essential tools of inquiry. Although humans are naturally curious and enjoy investigating the unknown, civilization has created sophisticated techniques of examining evidence, ascertaining meaning, and utilizing analytic tools of thought. It is necessary to acquaint students with the methodology of how one person pursues the course of inquiry.

The following lesson is designed to systematically train students in the process of inquiry. You may decide to add examples to the one presented that relate directly to materials currently being studied in your class.

Concept: Critical Thinking

Focus: Students will be able orally, in writing and visually to identify critical thinking questions and issues pertaining to textual materials.

Teacher	Student
1. Hand out material on "Focusing on Central Ideas." Ask students working in groups to review questions and to present to the class the group's view about central ideas.	1. Students in group examine material and share their views with the class.
2. Hand out material on "Rethinking Questions." The group task is examining Factors hindering critical thinking questions and then to add their own critical thinking questions.	2. Students in group carry out tasks pertaining to Critical Thinking questions.
3. Hand out material on "Seeing and Not Seeing."	3. Students in group do activities.
4. Hand out material on "Assumptions."	4. Students in groups do activities.

5. Hand out "Textual Questions for Critical Thinking."

   a. Ask students to perform similar tasks with textual material currently being studied in class. They are to write critical thinking questions in a group and present their ideas to the class.

   b. Hand out newspaper story or cartoon from a newspaper. Ask students to write critical thinking questions about it.

6. Select a piece of curriculum currently being taught and draw upon the strategies used in this lesson. Create your own critical thinking activities for the class. You could also assign students working in groups to use one of the critical thinking strategies on a particular part of the curriculum you are teaching.

5. Students in group do activities.

   a. Students in group do activities and present to the class.

   b. Students in group do activities and present to class.

Assessment: Ask individual students to write critical thinking questions based on material being studied.

Multiple Intelligences: Verbal Linguistic
Logical Mathematical
Visual Spatial
Interpersonal

Identifying a Central Idea

Examine the following paragraph and complete activities following the passage.

> Daniel Boone led his party across the Appalachian Mountains to the new area of Kentucky. Upon his arrival in the area, the Boone party was met by a group of Native Americans led by Chief Sundance. Daniel Boone noticed that Brown Bear, wife of Chief Sundance was teaching a young girl how to plant corn and gather berries. Boone and Sundance soon got into an argument because the Boone party claimed they had purchased the land in this area and therefore they had come to claim "ownership." Chief Sundance said he did not understand what they meant by "owning" since the land belonged to everyone. Boone told him the land had been bought from the American government. At this point, John Foster, turned to ask a member of the tribe how he built his wigwam. Mr. Foster's son and daughter asked him if they could go swimming because they were dirty from traveling. At this point, Chief Sundance told Boone the settlers could not claim ownership of what belonged to nature and to all humans. Boone answered they had bought the land and would soon divide it among themselves and Sundance and his tribe would have to leave the land. Chief Sundance said his people would not leave since no one owned the land and it belonged to all. Boone said he did not want to use force, but the land belonged to them.

Questions and Activities:

1. Which of the following is the main idea of the paragraph? (AN)
   a. The friendliness shown by Native Americans to settlers.
   b. Learning about Native Americans and their daily lives.
   c. The meaning of land ownership.

2. Write two Recall Questions about the paragraph. (K)

3. Write an Analytic and Divergent question about the main idea. (S)

4. Rewrite the paragraph to make something else the main idea. (AN)

5. Select a character in the paragraph and indicate what that person regards as the main idea. (AN)

Rethinking Questions

If one's goal is stimulating the spirit of inquiry, then questions should engage students in activities to support this concept. If one asks the "wrong" question one leads students away from focusing on critical thinking. Read the following paragraph and then complete Questions and Activities.

> One day Tashiba and Miguel were walking home from school. As they turned the corner they saw a man lying in the street. They noticed that next to his body was a brown paper bag. Tashiba and Miguel went to the man and asked if they could help him. He said: "leave me alone." However, they helped him to his feet and checked to see if he was hurt. The man mumbled something, shook his head and walked away. After he disappeared from their view, Tashiba and Miguel noticed he had forgotten the brown bag which was still in the street. Tashiba opened the bag and found some old photographs and a fifty dollar bill. She turned to see if the man was still in view but she could not see him. Tashiba and Miguel decided they should keep the fifty dollar bill and photos.

Following are questions which direct students away from critical thinking:

1. How many children are in the story? (K)
2. Where was the man lying? (K)
3. Who found the paper bag? (K)
4. What did the man do after the children helped him? (K)
5. What did the children find in the bag? (K)

Following are questions that stimulate critical thinking.

1. What would be a good title for this story? (AN)
2. What choices did the children have after the man left? (S)
3. Assume the children never helped the man, how would the story change? (E)
4. How might the parents react when the children came home and told them about the incident? (E)
5. (Write your own critical thinking question)_____

Seeing But Not Seeing

Examine the following list of words and answer the question that follows:

Voice	Low	Normal
Melody	Harmonious	Pleasant
Short	Breath	Snappy
Deep	Quick	Necessary
Raspy	Words	Important
Light	Ugly	High
Alto	Pull	Low

1. Identify at least one pattern in this list of words. (S)

Examine the following story:

> I recently took a trip to New York City. Upon my arrival in the town I immediately noticed the hustle and bustle of people in the street. Everyone seemed to move quickly. I became upset because people ignored me and were very discourteous. For example, I stopped a man carrying a brief case and asked him for directions. He never stopped by simply pointed in a direction. I asked three teenagers if they would mind taking a picture of my family and myself standing before the Empire State Building. They laughed and walked away claiming they had to go someplace. I do not think people in New York City help strangers.

1. What does the author "see" and what does he "not see?" (AN)
2. What else could he have seen in the behavior of the people? ©

ASSUMPTIONS

Read the following story and analyze how assumptions are made by characters in stories and unless we are aware of the assumptions we can be misled by the story.

> Mary was having a birthday party next week to celebrate being 13 years old. Her mother said she could invite no more than ten friends from school in addition to her other friends from their neighborhood. Mary asked Joan who sat next to her in language arts if she would come to the party. Joan told Mike who sat behind her about the invitation. Mike later told his friends that Mary did not like him and had refused to invite him to her party. Mary invited Peter who had worked with her on a report for social studies. Mary invited four girls who were on the cheerleader squad with her and she invited three boys who had worked with her on an art project. Mary decided to also invite Susan who already had invited her to a party as the Six Flags Amusement Park.

1. List one assumption you can make about Mary's decision making process of inviting people from school to her party. (AN)

2. List an assumption you can make about her choices, but this assumption is not directly supported by facts presented in this story. (S)

3. Make an assumption about why Mary invited boys to the party. (AN)

4. Write an assumption you can make about Mary's personality based on her decision to invite Susan to the party? (E)

5. (Identify an Assumption question you could pose) _____

TEXTUAL QUESTIONS FOR CRITICAL THINKING

Following are inquiry centered questions that can be posed about written or visual materials:

Assume you have just read the Snow White story.

1. Write a question whose answer is in the story, but can only be answered connecting at least two parts of the story. For example, "Compare and contrast Snow White's feelings about life after the woodman allowed her to live versus what she felt after Prince Charming kissed her." (S)

2. Write a question whose answer is not in the story, but which the reader can answer by drawing upon his/her life experience plus what the author says in the story. For example, "What are the advantages and disadvantages of being willing to take help from a stranger?" (AN)

3. Write a question whose answer is not in the story, but the reader can answer it drawing solely upon his/her life experience. For example, "Suppose Snow White had the personality of Brittany Spears, how might she have acted differently in this story?" (AN)

4. Write a question about illustrations in the story which requires the reader to compare those pictures will illustrations appearing in daily comic strips. For example, "Select a cartoon which has a female character in it. Compare how that female is visually presented with how Snow White is presented in her story." (A)

5. Pose a visual imagery question about the story. For example, "Inside your mind retell the story. As you do it change how at least one character is portrayed in the story. How does making this person physically different alter the story?" (A)

Dialogue With the Teacher

Document based questions increasingly are popular items on standardized tests. They require students to analyze a document and respond to analytic and divergent questions. The follow lesson is designed to provide students training in the analysis of documents.

Concept: Document based Questions

Focus: Students will orally and in writing analyze documents in order to respond to critical thinking questions.

Teacher	Student
1. Hand out Preamble to the Constitution. Ask students to respond to questions and activities following the Preamble.	1. Students in groups respond to questions and activities. Share these responses with class.
2. Hand out Declaration of Independence. Ask students to respond to questions and activities.	2. Students in group respond to questions and activities.
3. Hand out a document from something currently being studied. Ask students in group to identify 3 critical thinking questions about the document. They present these to class.	3. Students work in group on document and develop 3 critical thinking questions and present them to class.
4. Hand out Gettysburg Address and have students do questions and activities.	4. Students in group do activities.
5. Hand out document from a state or national assessment test. Have students practice working with the document.	5. Students in group analyze the document and respond to its questions.

Assessment: 1. Hand out document from a state assessment exam and require the student to respond to its questions.

Multiple Intelligences: Logical Mathematical
Interpersonal

PREAMBLE TO THE CONSTITUTION

We, the People of the United States to form a more perfect Union, establish justice, insure domestic Tranquility, provide for the common defense, promote the General Welfare, and secure the Blessings of Liberty to ourselves and our Posterity, do ordain and establish this Constitution for the United States of America.

Questions and Activities:

1. Who are the "People" referred to in this document? (AN)

2. If asked for your interpretation of what is meant by the "General Welfare of the People," how would you respond? Do you think your definition is similar to what was meant by the Founding Fathers? (S)

3. If you were charged with writing a Preamble to the United States Constitution, what would you write? (E)

4. Compare and contrast your State Constitution's Preamble with that of the federal Constitution's Preamble. (AN)

5. What is the purpose in writing a Preamble? (E)

6. (Add your own question) _____

7. (Add your own question) _____

Declaration of Independence

When in the course of human events, it becomes necessary for one people to dissolve the bonds which have connected them with another, and to assume among the powers of the earth, the separate and equal station to which the Laws of Nature and Nature's God entitle them, a decent respect to the opinion of mankind requires that they should declare the causes which impel them to the separation. We hold these truths to be self evident, that all men are created equal, and that they are endowed by their creator with certain unalienable Rights, that among them are Life, Liberty, and the pursuit of Happiness. That to secure these rights, Governments are instituted among Men, delivering their just powers from the consent of the governed. That whenever any form of Government becomes destructive of these ends it is the Right of the People to alter or to abolish it, and to institute new Government, laying its foundation on such principles and organizing its powers in such form, as to them shall deem most likely to effect their Safety and Happiness. Prudence, indeed, will dictate that Government long established should not be changed for light and transient causes and accordingly all experience hath shown, that mankind are more disposed to suffer while evils are sufferable, than to right themselves by abolishing the forms to which they are accustomed. But, when a long train of abuses and usurpations pursuing invariably the same Object evinces a design to reduce them under absolute Despotism, it is their right, it is their duty, to throw off such Government, and to provide new guards for their future Security.

Inquiry Centered Questions:

1. Rewrite the document from the perspective of George III. (S)

2. Based on this document, and not using other information, what can you deduce about the values, ideals, and beliefs of people who wrote this document? (AN)

3. Identify any argument in this document with which you agree? Identify an argument with which you disagree? (E)

4. Which expressions in this document would not be used today? Indicate how modern Americans would express these ideas. (S)

5. (Write your own inquiry question) _____

GETTYSBURG ADDRESS

Fourscore and seven years ago our fathers brought forth on this Continent a new nation, conceived in liberty and dedicated to the proposition that all men are created equal. Now, we are engaged in a great civil war, testing whether than nation, or any nation so conceived and so dedicated can long endure. We are met on a great battlefield of that war. We have come to dedicate a portion of that field as the final resting place for those who gave their lives that this nation might live. It is altogether fitting and proper that we should do this. But, in a larger sense, we cannot dedicate—we cannot consecrate—we cannot hallow – this ground. The brave men, living and dead, who struggled here, have consecrated it, far more than our poor power to add or detract. The world will little note nor long remember what we say here, but it can never forget what they did here. It is for us the living rather, to be dedicated here to the unfinished work which they who fought here have thus far so nobly advanced. It is rather for us to be here dedicated to the great task remaining before us – that from these honored dead we take increased devotion to that cause for which they gave the last full measure of devotion – that this nation, under God, shall have a new birth of freedom – and that government of the people, by the people, and for the people, shall not perish from the earth.

Questions and Activities:

1. Based solely on the words in this document, what do you learn about values of the society in which the author of these words lived? (AN)

2. Based solely on the words in this document, what do you learn about customs of the society in which the author of these words lived? (AN)

3. Based solely on the words in this document, what do you learn about the personality of the author of these words? (E)

4. (Add your own question) _____

5. (Add your own question) _____

Dialogue With the Teacher

Stories, poetry, and literature are excellent sources for developing questioning skills. Unfortunately, many teachers use these materials as a source of recall questions rather than building upon their inherent motivational qualities to foster higher order thinking skills. There is no need to change curriculum since the goals of inquiry can be accomplished with any curriculum provided teachers pose different questions.

Concept: Inquiry Thinking When Reading

Focus: Students will orally, in writing and visually demonstrate an ability to engage in analytic and divergent thinking.

Teacher	Student
1. Hand out material on Little Red Riding Hood and ask students to respond to questions and activities.	1. Students in groups respond to questions and activities. Share results with class.
2. Hand out material on Hansel and Gretel.	2. Students in group work on questions and activities.
3. Hand out poem entitled, "Song of an Unlucky Man."	3. Students in group work on questions and activities.
4. Hand out material on nursery rhymes.	4. Students in group work on questions and activities.
5. Hand out a story, poem, fairy tale, nursery rhyme, etc.. currently being studied in your curriculum.	5. Students in group identify analytic and divergent questions about material and pose them to class.

Assessment: 1. Provide students a story, poem, nursery rhyme, etc.. The student's task is to create analytic and divergent questions for the material.

Multiple Intelligences: Logical Mathematical
Verbal Linguistic
Interpersonal

Analytic and Divergent Questions About Fairy Tales

Most people know the story of Little Red Riding Hood who was sent by her mother to deliver food to a grandmother living in the forest. One the way she met a wolf who later rushed to grandmother's house, ate her, and put on her clothes to trick Little Red Riding Hood. During their conversation Little Red Riding Hood finally got suspicious and made some noise which alerted a woodsman in the forest who rushed in and killed the wolf.

Analytic and Divergent Questions and Activities:

1. Compare and contrast strategies used by the wolf in "The Three Little Pigs" with those used by this wolf. (S)

2. What do you believe is the moral of the story? (E)

3. Identify a person from your time period. How would that person tell this story and what moral would that person hope to get across? (AN)

4. How do you explain Little Red Riding Hood sitting on a bed talking with a wolf dressed like her grandmother who takes a long time to figure out it isn't grandmother. ©

5. (Add your analytic or divergent question) _____

6. (Add your analytic or divergent question) _____

ANALYTIC AND DIVERGENT QUESTIONS ABOUT FAIRY TALES

Hansel and Gretel is the story of two children who are dumped in the forest by their parents because of extreme poverty at home. The parents are unable to feed and clothe the children. The children wander around in what people of that era called the "enchanted woods" and eventually meet a witch who takes them to her house. The witch tries to kill the children, but they outwit her. They find precious stones and become reunited with their parents and live happily ever after.

Analytic and Divergent Questions:

1. What does the story reveal about parental attitudes toward children in this era?   (AN)

2. Why would people of this era refer to the woods as "enchanted?" (K)

3. Which places do children today regard as having "magical qualities." (A)

4. (Add your own analytic or divergent question) _____

5. (Add your own analytic or divergent question) _____

Song of an Unlucky Man

Following is a poem by an anonymous African poet:

> *Chaff in my eye*
> *A crocodile has me by the leg*
> *A goat is in my garden*
> *A porcupine is cooking in the pot*
> *Meat is drying on the pounding rock*
> *The King has summoned me to court*
> *And I must go to the funeral of my mother-in-law*
> *In short, I am busy*

Analytic and Divergent Questions:

1. What do you learn about the society in which the author of this poem lived based solely on what you are told in this poem? (AN)

2. Compare and contrast a busy day in your life with that of the author of this poem. (AN)

3. What does the poem teach you about the poet's daily diet? (AN)

4. (Write your own question) _____

5. (Write your own question) _____

Nursery Rhymes

What are little boys made of?
Frogs and snails
And puppy dog tails
That's what little boys are made of

What are little girls made of?
Sugar and spice
And all things nice
That's what little girls are made of

Questions and Activities:

1. Which images of boys come from this poem. Are those the images today we have of boys? (AN)

2. Which images of girls come from this poem? Are those the images today we have of girls? (AN)

3. (Add your own question) _____

_____

Nursery Rhymes

Sing a song of sixpence
A pocket full of rye
Four and twenty blackbirds
Baked in a pie
When the pie was opened
The birds began to sing
Wasn't that a dainty dish
To set before the king?
The King was in the counting house
Counting out his money
The Queen was in the parlor
Eating bread and honey
The maid was in the garden
Hanging out the clothes
When down came a blackbird
And picked off her nose.

Questions and Activities:

1. What do you learn about the society described in this poem? (AN)

2. Why do you think the poem was written? (E)

3. If the maid wrote the poem, what would she say in it? ©

4. (Add your own question _____

5. (Add your own question) _____

Dialogue With the Teacher

Students are trained to respond to teacher questions resulting in student questions that rarely go beyond expressions such as "how many words do I have to write?" or "do I have to turn this in?" or "when is it due?" Students rarely pose questions leading to intellectual discourse within the classroom. This lesson focuses upon Student Initiated Questions that result in higher order thinking. Students who learn to ask critical thinking questions are more prone to become engaged in the process of inquiry.

Concept: Student Initiated Questions

Focus: Students will orally and in writing demonstrate an ability to pose higher order thinking questions.

Teacher	Student
1. Hand out a copy of "The Cherry Tree." Pose to students: "Your task is to determine if this is an accurate document. You can ask me any question except whether or not this is an accurate document. Following is some background information for teachers to help respond to student questions. The excerpt is from the first biography published about George Washington. It was written by Mason "Parson" Weems who was an author, a printer, a minister, and a publisher during the course of his life. Students who previously did this task asked questions such as: a. "Do cherry trees grow in Virginia?" b. "Did they use guineas for money at this time?" c. "Who wrote this story? Did this Weems ever talk with Washington?" d. "Did Washington ever write down this story?" e. "Is there any letter or written account about this story other than the one given by Weems?" f. "Weems uses quotes. Can he use quotes if he wasn't present or if he didn't use a written source?"	1. Students working in groups identify questions to pose to the teacher in order to ascertain if this is an accurate document.

Following is a short summary of information about Weems and Washington. Washington is born in 1732 and the story appears to take place when Washngton is a young boy about the age of seven or eight which means Weems claims the story is occurring about 1740. Weems was born about 1748 in Massachusetts. Other than the account given by Weems there is no letter, no diary entry, nothing written by Washington or his wife or his father or mother or older brother which gives this account. Weems had a church in Virginia for a year but there is no record of Washington going to the church. Historians believe in the absence of a written account, Weems only could write, "There is a legend which Claims…" Even if someone told him the story he cannot use quotations. The goal of the lesson is training students to pose questions to teachers.

2. Pose the puzzle about "A Shot B and A Died." Tell students they can ask any question which has a "yes" or "no" response.
   a. Students get a bit frustrated after about ten minutes. At this point, I place on the blackboard all the information they have gained and pose: "OK, you now have this information, what other information are you lacking? For example, do you know where this event takes place or who is there? Now, ask me questions to get that data.

2. Individual student questions.

3. At the conclusion of the chapter are several suggestions on how to stimulate Student Initiated Questions. Try a few.

Assessment: 1. Students working in pairs create a puzzle to pose to the class which requires higher order thinking skills.

Multiple Intelligences: Logical Mathematical
Verbal Linguistic

THE CHERRY TREE STORY

One day in the garden where he often amused himself hacking his Mother's pea sticks, he unluckily tried the edge of his hatchet on the body of a beautiful young English cherry tree, which he barked so terribly that I don't believe the tree got the better of it. The next morning, the old gentleman, finding what had befallen his tree, which by the way was a great favorite, came into the house; and with much warmth asked for the mischievous author, declaring at the same time he would not have taken five guineas for his tree. Nobody would tell him about it. Presently, George and his hatchet made their appearance. "George," said his father, "do you know who killed that beautiful little cherry tree yonder in the garden?" This was a tough question and George staggered under it for a moment, but quickly recovered himself and looking at his father with the sweet face of youth brightened with the inexpressible charm of all conquering truth, he bravely cried out: "I can't tell a lie, pa, you know I can't tell a lie. I did cut it with my hatchet."

Questions and Activities:

1. As students formulate questions in their groups, ask them to identify a detective and ask what type of questions that detective would ask about this "crime." (AN)

2. Have students present an incident from their own lives. The task of other students is to pose questions to determine if the incident actually happened. (AN)

3. Have students examine accounts written by political leaders or famous entertainers to determine if what they claimed is accurate. (AN)

4. Have students examine accounts written in publications such as "The Star" to determine if they are publishing accurate stories. (AN)

5. Have students ask parents or grandparents for examples of stories they tell about their youth which they would have difficulty roving actually happened. (AN)

"A Shot B And A Died" – What Happened?

The actual story is as follows. Professor A who is a psychiatrist invites a colleague, Professor B and B's wife to a pleasant dinner at his home. B is also a psychiatrist who works with A. After dinner they retire to the den where A and B get into a lively dispute. A argues that it is possible to hypnotize an individual and have them commit a murder. B says it is impossible since people will not do things under hypnosis that goes against their basic beliefs. They finally agree that B's wife, we will call her C, is to go to the bedroom and wait. In the meantime, A hypnotizes B and tells him to go to the bedroom and kill his wife. B falls deeply under the hypnosis and begins walking to the door leading to the bedroom. As A watches him walk, A suddenly realizes he is having a serious heart attack. He reaches into his desk drawer, pulls out a revolver and shoots B in the leg to break the hypnotic spell. Then, A collapses and dies of the heart attack.

Students are allowed to ask any question which has a "yes" or "no" response. In my experience doing this activity students sometimes forget to even ask if A and B are humans. When they finally discover there is a "C" their questions usually center around love relations. Some sharp students ask if the "shot" is a needle. You usually receive many questions and some students become frustrated. If they get frustrated, direct them to ask questions about categories. For example, what do they know about occupations of the individuals or can they ask questions about the physical location of where this incident occurs.

An example of this type of puzzle I frequently ask younger children is as follows: "A is dead, there is broken glass on the floor and water. The room has bars on the window and the door is locked." The actual story is: A is a fish, a cat crawled through the bars and knocked over the fish bowl killing the fish.

Questions and Activities:

1. Have students working in pairs create their own puzzle story. It is a wonderful activity for students and can be used on a Friday afternoon to stimulate thinking before they depart for the weekend. (A)

ADDITIONAL IDEAS TO STIMULATE STUDENT INITIATED QUESTIONS:

1. Have students play "Twenty Questions" about a topic.
2. Have student identify which questions that Dorothy in *The Wizard of Oz* would have asked the Wizard in order to get home.
3. Have students develop questions the Dwarfs should have asked Snow White when she arrived at their door.
4. Invite a speaker. The day before the speaker arrives, have students develop questions they wish to pose the speaker.
5. Periodically, ask students working in groups to identify questions about the topic you are teaching they wish to pose you.
6. Have students identify questions they wish to ask about a profession.
7. Have students identify questions they wish posing a government official.
8. Have students identify questions they wish posing a policeman.
9. Prior to a test, ask students working in groups to identify an Analytic and a Divergent question they want on the test. The entire class should receive copies of these questions to study for the test.
10. Have students interview one another only asking Analytic Questions.
11. Have students interview one another only posing Divergent Questions.
12. Ask students to assume they are Martian anthropologists. Their task is to develop a questionnaire to ask humans in order to understand life on planet Earth.
13. Prior to beginning a new topic, ask students working in groups to identify questions about the topic they wish to ask you.
14. During teaching a topic, halt, and ask students: "What would a detective ask about this topic? What would a nurse? Etc...."
15. Periodically, ask students to create questions about a topic to which you do not know the answer.
16. After a test – for extra credit – ask students to indicate questions about the subject they wish you had included on the test.
17. Ask students to analyze textbook questions to determine which are recall, analytic or divergent in nature.

18. Ask students to analyze questions posed by TV hosts in order to determine which percent are recall, which are analytic, and which divergent.

19. The New York Times publishes transcripts of Presidential Press Conferences. Ask students to analyze questions posed by reporters to the President.

20. Create a file of interesting Student Initiated Questions.

21. Ask students to identify a famous person. Their task is developing questions they would wish to pose that individual.

22. Ask students to develop questions they would like to ask their parents about a topic they are currently studying.

23. Ask students to assume a famous person from the past suddenly arrive in our times. Which questions would they ask?

24. Ask students to assume a space ship crash lands on Earth. Which questions would the life forms immediately pose to Earthpeople?

25. Ask students which questions would they pose to life forms if they landed on another planet.

26. Have students collect interesting questions they hear posed around the school – no personal questions allowed.

27. Since most states have state developed examinations, have students develop questions they would like to pose to the State Education Commissioner about mandated state testing.

28. Have students interview their parents about questions they had about any aspect of life when they were younger.

29. Each week have students, anonymously, leave questions for you about what they are studying and which they find confusing.

30. Have students develop questions one should ask on a first date.

31. Have students compare and contrast questions asked them by doctors compared to questions asked by teachers?

Effective use of questions is among the most important skills of a teacher. Virtually any topic can be integrated within the curriculum by posing an interesting question. For example, the following was found in a newspaper advertisement. Students can be asked: "What is one alien saying to the other?" Or, "What is the response to the question?"

Chapter 3

Social Studies And Inquiry

Chapter Outline:

1. Introduction
2. Inquiry and Word Activities
    a. Limericks
    b. Puns
    c. Biograffiti
    d. Why Do We Say That?
    e. Famous Last Words
    f. Newspapers and Inquiry
    g. The Telephone and Critical Thinking
    h. Menus and Critical Thinking
    i. Ludicrous Laws
    j. Songs and Inquiry
3. Geography and Inquiry
    a. Concrete Geography
    b. Sports Geography
    c. Animals and Geography
    d. Geography and Society
4. Visual Activities and Inquiry
    a. Logos
    b. Historical Faces
    c. Visualization of People
    d. Misplaced Words
5. Future as History
6. Additional Ideas to Stimulate Inquiry in Social Studies

Questions are coded according to Bloom's Taxonomy:
Knowledge	(K)
Comprehension	©
Application	(A)
Analysis	(AN)
Synthesis	(S)
Evaluation	(E)

Introduction

Social Studies is the story of humanity. It is a drama filled with pathos and humor, triumph and tragedy. Social Studies opens entry points for youth to explore the multi faceted character of their own personalities as well as those of other people. Social Studies is not merely the history of great people, but it entails learning how I as a person came to be who I am. This chapter offers activities that engage students with a wide range of human behaviors.

Imagine being transported back to Europe in May, 1914, just a few months before the outbreak of World War I. According to textbook accounts, nations were preparing for war, but all you discover is people going through their daily activities with few thoughts concerning impending doom. Would you check out current fashions among youth? How about that new invention – motion pictures? If you could visit a home, what would you seek to gaze at?

Children should love social studies because it is a tale of mystery and intrigue that transports people to worlds filled with fabulous foods, interesting customs and hairstyles, and a variety of sports. History is not about a dead past, it is each person's past.

Textbooks present the past as a series or preordained events leading inexorably toward a specific outcome. Imagine meeting the following man in 1857. He has lost all but one election to public office and that was one term in the US Congress years ago. He just lost a race for the seat in the US Senate running as the candidate of a new political party. He is relatively unknown outside of his state and barely makes a living as a lawyer. He antagonizes many people with his crude sense of humor and his joy in telling risqué jokes. His main concern at the moment is building his law practice so he can take care of his family. Obviously, we are describing Abraham Lincoln three years before his entire life changed.

Leaders tell jokes, fall down stairs, make mistakes, argue with spouses, and usually don't know they eventually will become famous. They are simply members of a society going about their ordinary daily existence. In this chapter, we offer a variety of strategies to enable students to use their powers of inquiry to investigate the variety of ways in which humans live.

Unfortunately, social studies usually presents history from the top down by focusing on "important people." This is a necessary approach, but it should not dominate our study of humanity's past. It ignores average people who are the foundation of society. It ignores those on the bottom. Heck, what did Paul Revere's horse think on that famous ride? Leopold Von Ranke, the great German historian of the 19th century said it was the task of historians to describe, " wie es eigentlich gewesen" – life as it really was. We probably will never know life as it really was but we can offer youth a more extended voyage into the past than learning names, dates, and facts.

Dialogue With the Teacher

Reading and writing are vital to social studies. Inquiry is fostered when students have command over reading materials and being able to express their ideas. There is a different power in seeing one's words on a page than in speaking them; it is the power to focus in minute detail upon specific aspects of what one is expressing. Words are the life of the human mind.

This section offers students a variety of word activities to stimulate inquiry and creative thinking. Youth enjoys playing with words. Five year olds already are into silly jokes and play on words. In this section a variety of activities are offered which stimulate inquiry in a humorous manner. After all, humor is an important ingredient in every day life which enables us to cope with stress.

Concept: Inquiry Through Word Activities

Focus: Students will orally, visually, and in writing demonstrate understanding of the process of inquiry.

Social Studies Standards:
Standard 1: Culture – the study of culture and cultural diversity
Standard 4: Individual Development and Identity

Teacher	Student
1. Hand out examples of Limericks. Select something currently being studied and ask students to write a limerick about it.	1. Students in groups create limerick which are displayed on bulletin board. Extra credit for any student who wishes to add other limericks about what is being studied.
2. Hand out samples of "Atrocious Puns." Ask students for their own examples. a. Hand out examples from Puns, the Pun Dictionary, and Team Puns. The task of a group is to select one or more of these models to write puns about what is being studied.	2. Student responses. a. Students in groups create pun examples. These are displayed. Students can add to list as they proceed in studies.
3. Hand out examples of Biograffiti. a. Ask students to write a Biograffiti about someone being studied. Young children can write about an animal.	3. Students in group write Biograffiti of people or animals.

4. Hand out "Why Do We Say That?" and "Famous Last Words."
   a. Task is to identify an expression and trace its origins. Second task is to select a person being studied and write his/her last words.

4. Students in groups research origin of expressions. They also write last words of person or animal being studied. As individuals find new examples of expressions, they add to bulletin board collection. These should be displayed on Open School Night.

5. Hand out material on "Newspapers and Inquiry." Select one activity for students to do.

5. Students in group work on activity.

6. Hand out "Telephone and Critical Thinking." Have students develop at least one activity related to person, place, thing or animal being studied.

6. Students in group create example of "Telephone and Critical Thinking." Display.

7. Hand out "Menus and Critical Thinking." If appropriate, have students do example related to what is being studied.

7. If appropriate, students in groups develop menu.

8. Hand out "Ludicrous Laws" and have students do activities.

8. Students work in groups.

9. Hand out material on songs. Ask students to examine a current song to identify its relationship to study of society and human behavior.

9. Students in group examine song and report.

Assessment: 1. Students are asked to select either of the strategies in this lesson and create examples related to what is being studied.

2. On a test include two or more of these examples as test questions.

Multiple Intelligences: Verbal Linguistic
Logical Mathematical
Visual Spatial
Interpersonal

LIMERICKS

J is for jumping Andy Jackson
Who in a fight always gave the maximum
At New Orleans the British made a dent
But, in the end he became President
So, hurrah, for tough fighting Andy Jackson

There once was a prez named H. Hoover
Who in a Depression was not a mover
He tried hard to deny the crisis
Leading FDR to tear him to pieces
So, goodbye to forlon H. Hoover

There once was a gal named Cinderella
Whose heart throb was a price type fella
She ran away as the clock said midnight
Leaving behind a shoe in broad sight
Alas, shed a tear for three sisters who were not so bella

M is for marvelous Martin L. King
Who gave civil rights a wonderful zing
_____
_____
_____

There once was a traveler named Dan Boone
Over the Appalachians he went real soon
_____
_____
_____

Questions and Activities:

1. Remember, in writing a limerick, you wish to get across at least one central idea about the person, animal or place

2. Write a limerick about a person, animal or place

A Sample of Atrocious Puns

1. Why did the orange stop in the middle of the road?
   Answer: He ran out of juice.

2. A train just passed.
   How do you know?
   Answer: You can see its tracks

3. Hear about the accident at the army base?
   No.
   Answer: A jeep ran over a box of popcorn and killed two kernels.

4. An atomic scientist told me he was going on a vacation to do some fission.

5. Do you have cold winters in Arkansas?
   Answer: No, just Hot Springs.

6. Mary, can you spell the longest word in the English language?
   Sure, it is spelled S M I L E S
   But, "smiles" only has six letters.
   Yes, but there is a mile between the first and last letter.

7. Mike: Why was the mountain good at cards?
   Phil: Why?
   Mike: It was all in its bluff.

8. Why does the elephant wear purple sneakers?
   Answer: Because its red ones are at the shoe repair.

9. Pat: I just married a fine Irish lass.
   Oh really.
   No, _____ (identify the punch line)

10. Which animal played an important role in the Civil War?
    Answer: In the first battle, at _____ Run. (add the answer)

Social Studies Puns

1. Malcolm fought Xceptionally hard for black rights.
2. Richard wanted to put a nix on playing tapes.
3. Dolly Madison's favorite song was "we'll have a hot time in the old town tonight.
4. George Washington Carver made peanuts for his wonderful inventions.
5. Rosa parked her body on a seat and made history.
6. Jefferson declared his ideas to the world.
7. Al Gore was a bit sore about the election results.
8. The Little Mermaid made a _____ in life.
9. Sign on the astronaut's door: Out to _____
10. George Bush got ired about that _____ in his closet.

Reminders:

In writing a pun, it is supposed to be "bad." One is allowed to play with words, to alter their spelling, and to simply have fun in a gentle teasing manner. The key factor is identifying at least one idea you wish to get across. In number 10, the idea is linking George Bush with Iraq.

The Pun Dictionary

1. Anteater: A cannibal who doesn't like female relatives.
2. Beatnik: Santa Claus on the day after Christmas.
3. A French E: An eyeful of a tower.
4. KKK: Soiled white sheets meeting in the night.
5. Mt. Vernon: George Washington's Farewell Address.
6. Snake: An apple giver who got us all in trouble.
7. Ellis Island: A Repo Depo for the USA.
8. Walrus: Tusk luck animal.

Make Your Own

1. Hoover: A vacuum which got overloaded in the election of _____.

2. Wolf: He sure wished he kept his _____.

3. Pitcher: Molly brought a bucketful of water to douse the redcoat _____.

4. Truman: He awoke with _____ in his eyes but won the election.

5. Reagan: Ronald fired his _____ to win the election.

Reminders:

These samples indicate how one can assist students to remember a piece of history by transforming the material into a visual pun. Truman's opponent in 1948 was Thomas Dewey – get the point. Obviously, Ronald Reagan fired his "ray gun" to win the election. OK, make up a few of your own.

Biograffiti

1. Michael Jordan lives way up high.
2. Napoleon got caught in a snow storm.
3. John F. Kennedy sent people to the moon.
4. Marion Anderson sang over the heads of bigoted people.
5. Victoria had a majestic reign.
6. Jimmy Carter was a hostage to events.
7. Little Red Riding Hood needed X-ray vision.
8. Donald Rumsfeld likes to travel fast.
9. Shania likes to travel by twain. (I made this for my eight year old niece).
10. Trent did a Lot of apologizing for his remarks about past events.

Try Your Own:

1. Dwight D. Eisenhower led a Great _____.

2. The Pilgrims had a lot of _____ to _____ to the Native Americans for their help.

3. Snow White liked _____ men.

Reminders:

The key factor is identifying a single point to get across. General Dwight D. Eisenhower who led Allied troops in Europe termed the D-Day invasion, "The Great Crusade." Obviously, the Pilgrims had a lot of "thanks" to "give" and Snow White definitely liked "short" men. This is a fun activity for students but it also forces them to identify a single important idea they wish to get across about a person, place, or animal.

Why Do We Say That?

Have you ever wondered about the origin of a common expression? There was some reason this or that expression become part of our vocabulary. Even as I write, a new expression is being coined that people twenty years from now might say in their daily speech. Following are some explanations of expressions we still use.

Chew The Fat

Chew the Fat means to talk a long time, usually in a rambling manner about some topic of interest. In olden times, sailors preserved meat by packing it in barrels of brine. Salt was one of the few staples that could last through a long voyage because the salting process made the beef tough to eat. Seamen had to chew the beef in an endless pattern. This gave them periods of time to chew and talk.

A Ham Actor

A ham actor is one whose dreadful performance is shallow or over-played. The term arose when the slang for incompetence on stage was "hamfatter." Theater in 19th century America was very popular but money was in short supply for talented actors and actresses. The cheapest way for them to remove greasepaint or makeup was with ham fat. Thus, bad performers were called "ham actors."

Lick Into Shape

Early humans believed animals were born in a formless manner and were licked into shape by their mothers. The notion was particularly associated with bears who did not allow humans near their cubs. However, people could see bears licking a bundle of fur.

Activities and Questions:

1. Ask students to research the origin of common expressions. (AN)

2. Ask students to identify present day expressions they believe will still bepopular in the future. (AN)

3. Ask students to interview parents and grandparents about expressions that were popular in their youth, but are not common today. These could be made into a collage. (K)

4. Ask students to invent new expressions. They are to ask other students to hypothesize the meaning of their expressions. (A)

5. During a political campaign ask students to collect expressions that are used. (K)

Famous Last Words

Have you ever wondered what would be your last words before dying? The last words of people often reflect things they deem important. Following are the actual last words of some famous people.

1. Billy the Kid: "Who is there?"
2. Benedict Arnold: "Let me die in my old uniform. God forgive me for ever putting on another."
3. Alexander Graham Bell: "So little done, so much to do."
4. Anonymous Judge: "Gentlemen, case dismissed."
5. Alexander the Great: "To the strongest." (referring to who would get his throne).

Questions and Activities:

1. Ask students to hypothesize the last words of famous people. (E) Example: Richard Nixon, "You won't have me to kick around anymore. Did you get that on tape?"
2. What would be the last words of a teacher? A principal?
3. Young children could write the last words of a tiger, an elephant, mouse, etc.. (E)
4. Students could write the last words of famous people in the past. (E)
5. Students could write the epitaphs on tombstones for people (AN)
6. Ask young children to write epitaphs for animals or fairy tale figures. (AN)
7. What would be the last words of students? (E)
8. Have students examine graveyard tombstones. (K)
9. Have students write the last words of their current entertainment hero. (E)
10. Ask students to interview family members for examples of interesting last words. (K)

NEWSPAPERS AND SOCIAL STUDIES

Newspapers are sources of interesting information about human culture and behavior. An important task of newspaper reporters is capturing complex data in a succinct manner. Newspaper headlines exemplify this unique approach to critical thinking.

Following are some examples of headlines that actually appeared in daily newspapers. *The Columbia Journalism Review* monthly prints these examples:

1. "Reagan Goes for Juggler in the Midwest."
2. "Hospitals Offer Classes For Spanking New Grandparents"
3. "More Dogs Bring Complaints."
4. "Local Charity Helps Disable Man"
5. "Giant Roaches Set For Fall Practice"
6. "Navy Finds Dead Pilots Flying With Hangovers"

Questions and Activities:

1. Have students put out a daily newspaper for a past era in time. (S)
2. Ask students to hypothesize how an ancient Egyptian would describe modern sights or events. Ask they to write this description in a newspaper account. (E)
3. Ask students to write newspaper headlines for a topic being studied. (K)
4. Have students use Internet to examine how a current topic is reported in newspaper throughout the world with particular attention to the headlines. (S)
5. Have students identify the most interesting movie ad and explain why it is interesting. (AN)
6. Have students transform a current event into a comic strip. ©

THE TELEPHONE AND SOCIAL STUDIES

Even a simple old fashioned instrument such as the telephone can be used to stimulate inquiry and critical thinking on the part of students.

1. George Bush   843-7737   The Pres
2. Cleopatra   237-4226   African
3. Ida Tarbell   685-7253   Mukrake
4. James Baldwin   297-4837   A Writer
5. Attila the Hun   758-6337   Plunder
6. David Letterman 386-4678   Fun Host
7. Alex Rodriguez   466-3786   Home Run

Questions and Activities:

1. Ask students to write their own telephone number. It must state something that captures an important facet of their lives. (K)
2. Ask students to write a telephone number of an important person. (AN)
3. Ask students to write the telephone number of their favorite teacher. (AN)
4. Ask students to write the telephone number of a fairy tale or story figure. (AN)
5. Ask students to write the telephone number of an animal. (AN)

Menus in History

What we eat reflects our values, social mores, and desires. During World War II, food shortages created by having a large armed force compelled most Americans to alter their diets. Frontier people ate based on local animals or what could be grown in the soil. A study of foods enables students to get another perspective on human life.

Following is a menu describing what was served to the important people of Paris, France on December 4, 1870. They were at a dinner given at the largest hotel in Paris.

Consomme of horse, birdseed	Ragout of Rats by Robert
Skewered dog liver, maitre d'hotel	Dog leg flanked by ratlets
Minced cat's back, mayonnaise sauce	Escarole salad
Shoulder of dog, tomato sauce	Elephant's ear au jus
Stewed cat with mushrooms	Plum pudding with horse marrow
Dog cutlet with peas	Desserts and wine

OK, you are wondering about this wierd menu. Paris was besieged during the Franco-Prussian War of 1870 and the population ate everything in sight.

Questions and Activities:

1. Ask younger children to create a menu for a grand feast to be held for animals in the forest. (AN)

2. Students could create an "only in America" menu featuring foods native to the Western Hemisphere. (K)

3. Students could compare diets – including calorie intake – of people in varying parts of the world. (S)

4. Students could interview parents and grandparents about their diets and how they have changed their eating habits over time. (K)

5. Students could interview members of the armed forces as well as those who served in previous wars to compare wartime diets. (AN)

6. Ask students to identify a time in the past and study eating habits. (AN)

7. Students could hypothesize what diets will be in this century. (E)

8. Students could maintain a journal about relationships between their moods and eating habits. (E)

Ludicrous Laws

Laws are made by people and over time people change their minds. A law originates at a time and place when people decided a particular type of behavior would not be allowed. Two hundred years ago picking up horse manure was a major problem in urban areas, but the introduction of cars changed that concern as it also required a new definition of "fast." Following are some examples of laws still on the books:

1. In Brooklyn, New York it is illegal to allow an animal to sleep in your bathtub.
2. In Spades, Indiana, it is against the law to open a can of food by firing a revolver at it.
3. In Connecticut it is against the law to walk your pet bear along the highway.
4. In California, you need a hunting license to capture mice.
5. In Garfield County, Montana, people are forbidden to draw cartoons or funny faces on their window shades.

Questions and Activities:

1. Ask students to explain the origin of the above laws.
2. Divide students into two groups. Group one creates a Ludicrous Law, and group two has to figure out the rationale for the law.
3. Ask students which modern laws people in the past might consider ludicrous.
4. Ask students to assume they are living in 2080. Which contemporary laws will those people view as ludicrous?
5. Ask students to survey other students as to which modern laws they believe are ludicrous.
6. Ask students to survey parents and grandparents and ask them which laws that were in existence when they were young, they now consider outdated.
7. Have students research laws in another country and identify those which they consider ludicrous.
8. Ask students to identify a popular entertainer. Their task is to identify a law that person would want enacted.

Songs and Inquiry

Songs sung by people reflect their dreams, anxieties, hopes and desires. Civil rights advocates during the 1960s were inspired by "We hall Overcome" and sung the song even as they were being beaten. We learn about people through study of their songs. Future historians studying country music will learn about the everyday concerns of women and men in America just as rap music tells us about contemporary youth.

Following is a popular song from the nineteenth century which reflected a concern on the part of Irish Americans.

No Irish Need Apply

I started out to find the house
I got it mighty soon
There, I found the old chap seated
He was reading the Tribune.
I told him what I come for,
When he in rage did fly,
"No," he says, "You are a Paddy,
And no Irish need apply."

Then I gets m y dander rising
And I like to black his eye
To tell an Irish gentleman
No Irish need apply.

I couldn't stand it longer
So, a-hold of him I took,
And, gave him such a welting
As he'd get at Donnybrook.
He hollered "Milla Murther,"
And to get away did try,
And swore he'd never write again,
No Irish need apply.

Questions and Activities:

1. Ask students to compare and contrast images in this song with current attitudes toward Irish Americans. (AN)

2. Ask students to identify which people today are in the position of Nineteenth century Irish Americans. (AN)

3. Have students collect protest songs in American history. (K)

4. Have students identify a contemporary protest song and examine its imagery and desires. Which speak to student concerns? (AN)

5. Ask students in pairs or groups to write a contemporary protest song. (E)

6. Have students collect old folk songs which often contain protest imagery. (K)

7. Ask students to identify words in the song no longer used. (K)

Hallelujah, I'm a Bum

O, why don't you work
Like other men do?
How the hell can I work
When there's no work to do?

Chorus
Hallelujah, I'm a bum
Hallelujah bum again
Hallelujah, give me a handout
To revive us again.

An Original Version of *Casey Jones* which was called

Casey Jones, the Union Scab

The workers on the S.P. line sent out a call
But, Casey Jones, the engineer wouldn't strike at all;
His boiler it was leaking, and its drivers on the bum
And, his engine and its bearings, they were all out of plumb

Questions and Activities:

1. Ask students to identify a time period in American history in which "Hallelujah, I'm a Bum" was often sung.

2. Ask students to write a contemporary version of "Hallelujah, I'm a Bum" that reflects contemporary unemployment.

3. Older students might examine the original and the popular version of Casey Jones to consider how and why songs change.

Every genre of music faces the problem that frequent use leads to everyone knowing what will happen in the song. Following is an attempt by the author to write the perfect country song which contains every image ever found in country music (By the way, he loves country music).

The Perfect Country Song

I dreamed last night of meeting momma
At the gates of the State Prison
Where she's doing twenty to life
For killing my cheating pa

Alone, in the hobo hotel
Far from the green fields of Kentucky
Where a woman awaits my return
I grabbed a half drunk six pack
And stumbled down snowy streets
Where no hand reached to touch
And n woman's breast gave me rest

On, the outskirts of a northern town
A pick up truck slowed down
To take me in
A Southern man and family
Heading back to Dixie fields

We joined the trucker's convoy
Moving South with bootleg whiskey
Listening to sounds of Nashville music
Heading home to a woman's love.

We hit the road block on old Rt 66
Dodging bullets from angry cops
I shot one who killed little Sharon
And, now I await the gallow's greeting

Questions and Activities:

1. Have students identify a music genre and write a parody of it.
2. Ask students to identify all cliché's in this poem about Southern people and discuss if they have validity.

Dialogue With the Teacher

Critics of education frequently complain students lack knowledge of geography. Of course, one wonders if the critics themselves have that much knowledge of places and environments in the world. Geography is an abstraction since it entails attempting to visualize places and space that are not in the ordinary experience of most students. The author, who was born in New York City, recalls hitchhiking across America in 1951 and being overwhelmed by the distance between two points. A "thousand miles" on a page is vastly different from driving for a thousand miles. It is virtually impossible for most modern Americans to emotionally experience being in a wagon train going a thousand miles.

Geography has to be made visual for it to have any relevance to students. This lesson focuses mainly on strategies to create visual images for students about far away places. It is not designed as a complete geography lesson since that requires extensive work with students.

Concept: Visualizing Geography

Focus: Students will orally, in writing, and visually depict geographic locations.

Social Studies Standards:
Standard 3: People, Places and Environment

Teacher	Student
1. Hand out examples of "Concrete Geography." Ask students to develop examples of places currently being studied.	1. Students in groups develop examples of Concrete Geography.
2. Hand out "Team Puns." Each group is to create Team Puns for the teams in the league they selected.	2. Each group develops team puns.
3. Hand out "Animals and Geography."	3. Students work in groups. Each group selects a few of the activities to complete.

4. Hand out Facing East.

4. Students in groups complete Facing East. You could either have them develop their version of Facing West or give them this material.

Assessment: 1. Students are to transform a book or story being read into a geography activity based on examples furnished.

Multiple Intelligences: Verbal Linguistic
Visual Spatial

Concrete Geography

Questions and Activities:

1. Ask students to develop Concrete Geography examples.
2. Ask students to develop Concrete Geography examples from local sources – their neighborhood, immediate area around school, etc…

Team Puns

Have students build upon prior practice with writing puns to apply it to geography. Their task is to create a team pun which is linked to a geographical feature in the locale of the team. Or, they can develop a Pun which is linked to other characteristics of the area. For example, the Denver Rockies. Here are some other examples

1. Paris Wines
2. Moscow Blizzards
3. Buenos Aires Pampas
4. Oslo Fjords
5. Lagos Lions
6. Algiers Figs

Make Your Own:

1. Tokyo _____

2. Stockholm _____

3. Vienna _____

4. Cairo _____

5. Baghdad _____

ANIMALS AND GEOGRAPHY

It is common in many states to have a state bird or animal. Animals often conjure up images of particular countries. For example, most people associate kangaroos with Australia or the bear with Russia. Following are some suggestions of linking geography with animals.

New Mexico — Roadrunner **Indiana — Cardinal**

Questions and Activities:

1. Create a map of America which indicates state birds or animals.
2. Create a map of the world linking an animal with a nation.
3. Have students draw a map of the oceans of the world indicating which fish are most likely found in which ocean.
4. Have students draw a map of the world indicating a product with a nation.
5. A zoo space ship has crashed on planet Earth. It is carrying animals from many planets. Students working in groups can create an animal to go with a planet. For example, an animal from Venus would enjoy extreme heat. After developing their life forms, students must then place their animals in the geographic location on Earth which is most conducive to being able to live.

Facing East

Imagine you are living in the 1500s in the eastern portion of what is now the United States of America. You are a member of a tribe, the Iroquois or the Delaware, etc.. One day your hunting party comes across an area that obviously has been used by some people as a camp. You discover strange items lying on the ground and further search reveals what appears to be the body of a man. The man has much hair on his face and is dressed in garments you have not previously encountered. You have never seen such a creature before.

ITEMS: Make a list of the items that could be found in an area inhabited by English explorers. As you develop the list, consider what a typical European explorer would have taken with him on a voyage to the western hemisphere. Think in large as well as in small terms. For example, he undoubtedly had a sword or a musket. But, what about his clothes? Which items would the Native Americans have found?

_____

_____

_____

INTERPRETATION: Select a few items and hypothesize how an Iroquois would interpret the meaning or use of the item. For example, the sharp sword is used to cut.

1. _____

_____

2. _____

_____

3. _____

_____

4. _____

_____

IMPACT: Select any two items and hypothesize how the introduction of these items into cultures that had no prior knowledge of the items would impact the society. For example, suppose we found the wreckage of an alien ship and in it was a pill that proved to increase our life expectancy by 200 years. How would that impact our society?

1. _____

_____

2. _____

_____

Your task is to continue this exercise. Remember, you are attempting to enter the mind of a Delaware or Mohawk or Iroquois who lived in this eastern area.

1. Think of an issue finding these items would raise among the Native Americans who found the items. Create a question or activity.

_____

_____

2. Think of something visual they find and develop a question or activity around it.

_____

_____

3. Write a dialogue that might have taken place in the evening among the Native Americans.

_____

_____

_____

4. Identify a math or science issue arising from one of their discoveries.

_____

_____

5. Identify a food issue arising from one of their discoveries.

_____

_____

FACING WEST

Imagine you are with a group of English explorers in the late 1500s who are wandering along the east coast of America. You have yet to encounter any Indian tribes although you have heard rumors about them from Spanish sources. Late one afternoon your group comes across what appears to have been a camp. There are ashes from a fire, items are scattered on the ground and in the bushes you find the body of a man dressed in strange clothes.

ITEMS: Make a list of the items you might have found.

_____

_____

INTERPRETATION: Select three items and hypothesize how a European might have interpreted the meaning or use of the items.

1. _____

_____

2. _____

_____

3. _____

_____

IMPACT: Select two items and hypothesize how the introduction of these items into European civilization would have led to changes.

1. _____

_____

2. _____

_____

Your task is to continue this exercise. You can assume the European explorers continued their travels. Consider what they might have come across. What new sights would they have seen? Which activities might they see being done by the Native Americans? Can you create an activity linked to geography they encounter?

Folktales often arise from the experience of travelers in strange lands. You might wish to create a new folktale.

Dialogue With the Teacher

Teachers invariably discover that children enjoy visual components of the curriculum. Frequently, prior to having students read a history textbook, I would divide them into groups and have each group only examine the pictures in the chapter. Their task was to inform the class what they learned from this visual activity. This lesson presents several approaches to utilizing visual materials in teaching social studies. For example, historical faces offers an interesting opportunity to discuss the relationship between hair style and societal values. Ask anyone who was a teenager in the 1960s what hair meant to them. It was a symbol of protest. By the way, the last American President to have hair on his face was William Howard Taft who lost his re-election in 1912. Why? Some historians suggest the invention of the Gillette and Schick razor blade made shaving easier and won men and women away from having males with hair on their faces.

Concept: Visualization and History

Focus: Students will visually, orally, and in writing utilize visual materials to identify key ideas about life in America and be able pictorially to present ideas about prominent people.

Social Studies Standards:
Standard 1: Culture
Standard 2: time, Continuity and Change
Standard 3: People, Places and Environment

Teacher	Student
1. Hand out material on logos. Ask students to respond to the activities listed.	1. Students in groups respond to activities and share with class.
2. Hand out material on "Historical Faces" a. You could assign students to check yearbooks from high schools in their district, particularly those dating from the 1940s. Students could do research on percent of boys with short hair and examine hair styles of girls. This could be contrasted with hair styles in the 1960s.	2. Students in group do activities and as an option do research on hair styles among teenagers.

3. Hand out material on "Visualization of People."

3. Students in groups do activities.

4. Hand out material on "Misplaced Words."
   a. You could organize a contest for the most imaginative example of a misplaced word.

4. Students do activities.

5. Ask students before reading the next chapter to examine pictures in the chapter and present to class: (a) "Which questions are raised about this chapter simply by viewing its pictures?" (b) "Which important ideas did you get about this chapter just by examining its pictures?"

5. Students working in groups respond to questions and tasks.

Assessment: 1. Assign students working in pairs the task of presenting an idea in visual terms about something currently being learned.

Multiple Intelligences: Visual Spatial
Logical Mathematical
Interpersonal

Logos

Children learn at an early age to identify products with a logo. Advertising is based on the concept of association since by linking a name with an image, it makes it easier to sell items. Using logos to teach sharpens the ability of students to form linkages.

Questions and Activities:

1. Divide students into groups. One group uses a story or a chapter in a textbook and creates logos for various ideas within the textual material. The task of the other group is identifying the logo with the person, place or thing.

2. Have students create logos for events or products of the past.

3. Have young children create logos for characters in fairy tales.

5. Have students create a logo for other students in the class.

HISTORIC FACES

Throughout history, famous people have been identified by hair styles or moustaches or some aspect of the face. Below are examples of moustaches from famous people.

Mark Twain   Adolf Hitler   Josef Stalin

Martin Luther King   Charlie Chaplin   Salvador Dali

Questions and Activities:

1. Make a picture puzzle of one's face and then cut out the pieces. Other students select a bundle of pieces and recreate the face and guess who it was.

2. Make picture puzzles of people or animals currently being studied. Transform the activity into a competition.

3. Have students select any aspect of a face that is prominent in an important person and transform it into a puzzle for others to solve.

VISUALIZATION OF PEOPLE

Questions and Activities:

1. Ask students to make a visualization of their own name.
2. Ask students working in pairs to select a person or animal being studied and transform it into a visual activity.
3. Ask students to make visualizations of famous people.
4. Ask students to make a visualization of the teacher.

Misplaced Words

We frequently giggle when someone mispronounces a word. It is just as common for all of us to "see" something incorrectly. A teacher I know in St. Louis carried a camera with her in the car and takes pictures of misplaced words on signs. Her work is exhibited on this page. The other day while driving I gazed at a bumper sticker and continued to read it as: "God's Work is Shoplifting" when it actually said: "God's Work is Uplifting." I recently transformed "Buy a Whopper" into "Spy on a Shopper."

Questions and Activities:

1. Have students collect evidence of misplaced words and have a chart where these can be placed.

2. Have students change a letter or two to create a new concept. For example, "Pharmacy" becomes "Harmacy" when one removes the "P."

DIALOGUE WITH THE TEACHER

Much of what is taught in social studies concerns the past or present, but much less emphasis is given to the future. Young people live intently in the present and their major concerns are about the future, not the past. No one can predict the future with exactitude, but there are strategies to use systems of planning in order to get heightened awareness of possible problems or successes awaiting in the future. Future thinking is more than thinking about possible changes in human life in the future, it is also about how one thinks in daily life about tomorrow. This lesson explores the many dimensions of future think. Elementary age children have a different conception of "the future" than do middle school or high school students. Teachers should be cognizant of what "the future" means to students in their classroom. Teachers can ask high school juniors to consider where they will be in four years, but in dealing with second graders one can, at best, have them think about next week or their birthday.

Concept: Thinking About the Future

Focus: Students will visually, orally, and in writing make predictions concerning their personal futures as well as the future of various aspects of human society.

Social Studies Standards:
Standard 1: Culture
Standard 2: Time, Continuity and Change
Standard 5: Individuals, Groups and Institutions
Standard 8: Science, Technology and Society
Standard 9: Global Connections
Standard 10: Civic Ideals and Practices

Teacher	Student
1. Ask students: "Select one thing in the past week in which you thought about 'What if' about a decision you made." (E) a. Collate responses, categorize them, and develop a chart. b. Assign each group at least three of the What ifs on the sheet.	1. Students in group make a list of 'What if' incidents. Share with class. a. Listen and respond b. Each group does 3 What ifs and share with class.

2. Hand out Robert Heinlein ideas about basic rules of science fiction. Discuss with them its implications for how to think.
   a. Younger children might use a cartoon science fiction show and make changes in it.

3. Hand out "Crazy Predictions"
   b. Younger children can be asked to make a crazy prediction about what will happen on the day of their birthday or an upcoming holiday.

4. Hand out "Newspaper Stories in the Future."
   a. Younger children can write a newspaper headline about a story or fairy tale. Their task is to tell what happened to at least one of the characters in the story in their future life.

5. Hand out "Alternative Future" material. The task of students is to select a topic and write an alternative future. Emphasize it must have internal logic. In other words, Adolf Hitler can not suddenly turn out to be a peace loving man.
   a. Class discussion about the alternative futures that were created.

6. Select from among the other ideas for things you might wish to do with the class.

2. Students in group review Heinlein ideas. They create a future Situation using these concepts.

3. Students in group make three "Crazy Predictions." At least two should do with some aspect of society and one should pertain to their own lives. Share with class.

4. Students in group review material and select at least three of the ideas listed to pursue. Share with class.

5. Students in group create an alternative future. Share with class.

Assessment: 1. Each student is to select from among the ideas listed and respond in writing or visually.

Multiple Intelligences: Logical Mathematical
Visual Spatial
Interpersonal

What If?

Everyone has used this expression in their daily lives. What if I didn't bring my bike to school today, it never would have been damaged. What if I had invited Mandy to my party, I would be going to her party today. In November, 1981, Time magazine posed a "What if the British had won at Yorktown?" How would our lives today be different? Consider the following possibilities to that alternative history:

1. What would be the geographical features of America?
2. Would slavery have ended in 1830 when it did in British colonies?
3. What would be the structure of our modern government? Would it resemble that of Canada?
4. Would our population differ in terms of which immigrants came?
5. Would our food tastes and dress be different? For example, would we prefer tea to coffee?
6. What would be our popular sports?
7. How would textbooks describe Washington and Franklin?   Etc......

Questions and Activities:
1. Ask students to do a "What if?" For example, what if the South won the Civil War?
2. Ask students to do a "What if" about an historical figure. "What if John F. Kennedy had not been killed in Dallas?"
3. What if Native Americans had a rapid firing bow and arrow machine?
4. What if Dorothy had remained in the land of Oz?
5. What if historical figures from different time periods met one another? For example, what would be the conversation between Thomas Jefferson, Martin Luther King, and Abraham Lincoln?
6. What if rules of a sport were changed? For example, suppose the baseball "diamond" was designed as a triangle?
7. What if students designed school rules and regulations?
8. What if a character on a TV program had a different personality?
9. What if girls were bigger and stronger than boys?
10. What if dogs could speak?

CREATING NEW CIVILIZATION AND LIFE FORM

Robert Heinlein, noted science fiction writer believes that all science fiction should adhere to five basic rules in order to truly be science fiction.

1. The conditions must, in some respect, be different from the here-and-now situation.
2. The new condition must be an essential part of the story.
3. The problem itself – the plot – must be a human issue.
4. The human issue must be created by the new condition.
5. No fact shall be violated, and furthermore, when the story requires that a theory contrary to existing theory shall be used, the new theory shall be rendered plausible, and it must include and explain established facts as satisfactorily as the one the author saw fit to junk. It may be far fetched and seem fantastic, but it cannot contradict established facts. For example, if you believe humans are descended from Martians, then you have to explain our resemblance to terresterial anthropoid apes.

Practice:

1. Identify a situation. For example, humans are dying of a new disease.
2. Identify the problem. For example, there is no known cure for the disease.
3. Identify the plot. For example, a scientist believes aliens are the ones who have introduced the disease to planet Earth.
4. Identify at least one main character in the story. For example, one of the aliens wants to build friendship with humans and wants to help halt the disease.
5. Describe the outcome of the story. For example, events unroll and it turns out that aliens have no resistance to the common cold and therefore need human help in order to deal with this disease. In return, they share information about the disease they introduced onto Earth.

Crazy Predictions in History

Not a day goes by without some prediction concerning the future. We are assured the stock market is now going up or our favorite NFL team will win next Sunday. Despite spending billions of dollars on spying, no American spy agency predicted the fall of the Berlin Wall or the Gulf War of 1991 or the changes that have taken place in Communist China.

Crazy Predictions serve a purpose. They indicate how people at a particular time and place were thinking about their futures. We learn from mistakes as well as from success. Following are a few predictions from the past:

1. "Who the heck wants to hear actors talk?" Harry Warner, head of Warner Brothers pictures in 1927.
2. "Everything that can be invented has been invented." Charles Duell, Director of US Patent Office in 1899.
3. "Heavier than air flying machines are impossible." Lord Kelvin, President of the Royal Society of England in 1895.
4. "There is no likelihood that man can ever tap the power of the atom." Robert Miliken, Nobel Prize winner in physics in 1923.
5. "Babe Ruth made a big mistake when he gave up pitching." Tris Speaker, future Hall of Fame outfielder in 1921.

Questions and Activities:

1. Ask one group to make predictions. The task of another group is to provide logical reasons why the predictions will not occur.
2. Ask students to survey parents and grandparents about predictions made when they were young that turned out accurate or inaccurate.
3. In September, have students follow a columnist writing in sports or politics or entertainment and keep track of their predictions.
4. Each student is to make a prediction about what will happen in their personal life in the next twenty-four hours, three days, a week, a month. They are to analyze what happened to their predictions.
5. During a presidential election students can keep track of predictions made by candidates.

NEWSPAPER STORIES IN THE FUTURE

Following are several examples of what this author thinks will be newspaper stories in the future:

1. "Youth Products Announces Lowering Mandatory Retirement Age from 35 to 32"
2. "Riots Break Out in Wichita, Kansas When Dress Shop Hires Another Robot Sales Clerk"
3. "New York Giants Androids Win NFL Title"
4. "Mexican Government Bans Swimming Due to Rifts in Ozone Level"

Questions and Activities:

1. Ask students to create their own newspaper headlines of the future.
2. Ask students to select a fairy tale or story and write a headline about the future activities of a character in the story.
3. Ask students to write a headline of the future about their own life.
4. Ask students to write a headline of the future about something related to their school.
5. Ask students to write a headline of the future about one of their parents and share it with them. If possible, share with class parental reaction.

ALTERNATIVE FUTURES

Humans are interested in the future because it discusses their own lives at some future point in time. Following are several ideas about alternative futures.

Robots have been created which can perform most human tasks. Ask students to do the following:

1. Create laws that govern robot thinking and behavior. (Isaac Asimov, the famous science fiction writer has developed his laws to govern robot behavior)
2. Identify new issues arising from advanced intelligence of robots.
3. Create an alternative future centered around these robots.

Questions and Activities:

1. You are a group of alien psychologists, anthropologists, and political leaders who have been picking up human radio and TV communications for the past 100 years. All you know about planet Earth is what you hear or see. Write a dialogue in which these people discuss planet Earth.
2. Your task is to create an alternative future. For example, Nazi Germany won World War II or the Japanese won. The film, "Fatherland" is based on an alternative future in which World War II ended in a truce. Philip Dick's book, "The Man in the High Castle" deals with a Japanese victory.
3. Rewrite America's past. For example, the Chinese landed in California in the 1420s. There is a new book, "1421" which explores this possibility.
4. TV never got invented. How would your life be different?
5. Franklin D. Roosevelt was assassinated in 1933 – actually, the gunman aimed at FDR but killed someone else.
6. Create a different life form that emerged. For example, Neanderthals defeated the Cro-Magnons.
7. Select a topic. Change one factor in the story and hypothesize how that alters the ending.
8. Invent a monster who can not be killed by existing weapons.
9. Consider a present in which we still listen to music that was popular in the 1940s and most modern music never got invented.
10. Alter a fairy tale or story to create a different future.

Additional Ideas

1. Have students identify a new invention and analyze its impact on society. For example, cars that can fly.

2. Assume pills are available to raise intelligence. Ask students to discuss impact on society.

3. Have students put out a newspaper for the year 2020.

4. Have students create a civilization in which everyone is mentally linked.

5. Have students create a civilization with totally different technology than what we possess.

6. Create a new life form that emerges on Earth.

7. Write a dialogue that happens when humans make the first contact with an alien life form.

8. Create a time chart for your future life.

9. Select an individual and predict their future. Send them your predictions.

10. Have students identify a trend and track it into the future two ways. For example, hair styles. They can be predicted to evolve in weird ways or a law can be passed mandating baldness.

11. Have students predict what will be the nature of schooling in the year 2040.

12. Have students interview people in various occupations about their predictions for what will happen in their occupation in the future. For example, a car mechanic, hair stylist, lawyer, doctor, artist, musician, garbage collector, etc.. These can be shared in class. In fact, the class can produce a newspaper containing future occupational predictions.

13, Bring a boy and girl from Colonial America to the present. Students are to write a story about their reaction to modern life.

14. An American, a Chinese person, someone from India, someone from Iraq, a Russian and a Brazilian crash land on a distant planet and are stranded. Write a story about the issues they will confront.

15. An old TV series, "Mork and Mindy" depicts an alien who is visiting Earth and reporting back what he finds to his home planet. Have students create their own version of "Mork and Mindy."

16. Describe America today is slavery had never been abolished.

17. Have students investigate how different cultures view the future. For example, how did the Aztecs or Egyptians view the future? Are there differences among cultures represented in your school about how that culture views the future?

18. Jump eight hundred years into the future. Describe how a particular life form now in existence evolved over that time period.

19. Identify any aspect of life and describe how it will change over a 100 year time span.

20. Write your own life story until your death.

21. Change details of the "Robinson Crusoe" story. For example, introduce Mrs. Crusoe.

22. Create a situation in which a nuclear war threatens. Have students develop the dialogue that takes place in the President's Cabinet. Actually, you can obtain the dialogue that ensued in President Kennedy's discussion during the Cuba Missile Crisis of 1962 when there was talk of nuclear war.

23. Have students compare daily life in a particular area of the world in A.D.1, A.D. 1000 and today.

24. Have students create music from an alien culture.

25. Have students draw pictures of what they think aliens on Mars or Venus look like.

26. Ask students to design the car of the future.

27. An alien ship had landed on Earth. Have students describe reactions.

28. Have students identify a movie picture which deals with the future. Ask students to change the picture and its story line.

29. Ask students to identify a favorite TV personality. Place that person in a future situation.

30. Have students trace the evolution of something like "speed" over the past 5000 years.

Addition Inquiry Ideas in Social Studies

1. You have just been appointed fashion designer for Wyatt Earp, Harriet Tubman, George Bush, Ghengis Kah, etc... Draw them wearing clothes you design.

2. Review a book from an unusual perspective. For example, Denzel Washington reviewing, "Memoirs of a KKK Leader."

3. Create authors of improbable books: For example, Halle Berry: "I was a Spy in Nazi Germany."

4. Invent a new custom. For example, "wearing hats to bed."

5. Write misquotes in history. For example, "54/30 or Fight."

6. Create examples of "facts that lie." For example, many people believe oranges originated in the western hemisphere. Actually, Columbus spread orange seeds as he traveled.

7. Make a list of crazy Guiness Book of World Records. For example, "Bobby, the Mouse ate the most cheese in one day."

8. Create a weird test to evaluate what is being studied in social studies.

9. Make a list of incorrect facts in history.

10. Create a new social organization. For example, "Friends of Pollution" who are dedicated to encouraging pollution.

11. Place famous people in improbable situations. For example, Jennifer Lopez as Secretary of State.

12. Have students collect political cartoons.

13. Using Internet, have students collect political cartoons from the past.

14. Present "History from the Bottom up." For example, Paul Revere's ride as described by his horse.

15. Select a little known president like Millard Fillmore and create activities to celebrate his birthday.

16. Read a textbook from another country which describes something being studied in social studies. For example, a Mexican textbook on the War with Mexico.

17. Have students collect material about politics and world affairs written by humorists like Mark Twain, Will Rogers, Mr. Dooley, etc..

18. Have students draw cartoons about current events.

19. Invite a humorist to class and have that person discuss world events.

20. Ask students to redesign a chapter in the social studies textbook into a cartoon model.

21. Have students identify jokes from younger brothers and sisters in order to analyze patterns of humor development.

22. Have students interview parents about a political leader from their youth. Compare and contrast their view of the person with how that individual is presented in textbooks.

23. Have students design "Wanted Posters" for people in the past who did evil things.

24. Have students create a dictionary for topics being studied in social studies.

25. Have students compare and contrast old radio comedy with current comedy.

26. Have students create a "Humor Crest" which depicts what they view as funny in life.

27. Have students draw "Recruiting Posters" from the past. For example, "Join the Revolutionary Army."

28. Have students identify turning points in history. For example, the battle of Gettysburg.

29. Have students design bumper stickers about what they are currently studying.

30. Have students identify nicknames for past famous people. For example, "Davy, the Rocket Crockett."

31. Have students develop a history of slang after interviewing parents and grandparents about slang used in their own early lives.

32. Have students identify school customs as a prelude to studying customs in the past.

33. Ask students to assume their favorite entertainment star is principal of the school. How would the school be run and what would be the curriculum?

34. Have students create "Presidential Trading Cards" containing significant\information about the person.

35. Have students study the history of an occupation. For example, doctors or car mechanics.
36. Have students build models of ancient cities like Tenochtitlan in Mexico.
37. Have students study the history of war and weapons.
38. Have students study the history of children and how they were treated over time.
39. Have students get the UN Declarations of the Rights of Children and compare and contrast their present rights with what is stated in that document.
40. Have students study an important African civilization from the past. Their task is to hypothesize how the present would have changed if that civilization had remained powerful.
41. Have students study the use of airplanes over time. In other words, how did people initially conceive which uses would be made of airplanes?
42. Have students identify laws that emerged after the invention of the car.
43. Ask students to identify new laws that will emerge if space travel becomes common.
44. Ask students to assume they are an Earth colony on Mars. They are to assume the problems that will arise between their colony and mother Earth.
45. Have students study the history of bridges focusing on civilizations such as the Incas or Chinese. Have them build replicas of those ancient bridges.
46. Have students study the impact of an animal in history.
47. Have students create a newspaper story about the initial contact between the Tainos and Columbus.
48. Have students develop a chart depicting how leaders are selected in various societies.
49. Have students interview parents and grandparents about toys and develop a history of toys.
50. Have students interview parents and grandparents about childhood games. They are to then play those games.
51. Have students collect ancient maps and analyze how and why they conceived what they conceived to be true.

52. Have students study the history of punishments and compare and contrast old punishments with modern ones.

53. Have students study the history of education in America and develop a chart comparing and contrasting education in the past with the present.

54. Have students examine the history of female rights in American history and debate: "Resolved: Women Still Do Not Have Equal Rights."

55. Have students study the history of love and compare and contrast ancient love with modern love ideas.

56. Have students identify a Native American tribe and how it responded to its contacts with Europeans. For example, the Cherokee reacted very differently than the Sioux.

57. Rearrange maps. For example, draw the Mississippi River going east-west rather than north-south. How would it have changed American history?

58. Do a "What If." For example, Columbus remained on course and reached the shores of Virginia.

59. Have students compare instructions given commanders on Star Trek with what we give astronauts.

60. Have students make a list of "What we Know Less About." For example, our ancestors had better smell senses.

61. Ask students to analyze how murder was handled in an ancient society as contrasted with modern ways of handling murder. For example, in many societies like Native American or Polish the murderer paid the families of the victim.

62. Have students develop a bar graph depicting changes in composition of American society in the 20th century.

63. Have students identify a place they want to visit. Their task is developing an AAA Trip Ticket packet.

64. Hide an object in the room. Students are to find the item based on your instructions which are given in geographic terms. For example, "Latitude 20 or go north."

65. Have students investigate the origin of comic strips. They can compare and contrast old comic strips with modern ones.

66. Have students develop a guide book to their community for someone coming from Japan.
67. Have students identify names of cities in states that are similar to ones in Europe. For example, New Madrid in Missouri.
68. Have students identify a local problem land develop an action plan to solve it. For example, the need for a traffic light near school. Their plan is to be presented to the local city council.
69. Have students develop an Action Research project about an issue in their school. For example, they can study how many students are actually late to school.
70. Have students develop historical post cards.
71. Have students make a list of crimes today that were not crimes in the past.
71. Following are causes as death as listed in an English Register in 1809:

Colick and Gripes	15
Jaw Locked	4
Palsy	123
Water in the head	252
Overjoy	1
Grief	5

After students analyze this list have them identify causes of death in their own community.
72. Have students research causes of death at various times in American history.
73. Have students create a country and draw its map including geographical features.
74. Have students analyze a current movie which depicts events in the past. Arecent Mel Gibson film, "The Patriot" has been denounced in England as a false representation of events in the American Revolution. Students could analyze the film in term of its historical accuracy.
75. Have students study the wives of American Presidents.
76. Have students identify an animal and analyze how many jobs were created due to that animal's presence.

77. Have students write "Personal Ads" for another time in history. For example, here are a few:

Kentucky, 1785 Seek bearded m an who is good shot, owns farm and can read and write. Must be gentle to women and does not want to move.

Athens, Greece, 323 B.C.   Seek wife who can bear children. Must be obedient, and able to direct servants and run household. Prefer woman who enjoys music and oratory.

CHAPTER 4

INQUIRY AND STUDENT EXPERIENTIAL LEARNING

Chapter Outline:

1. Introduction
2. Simulations
   a. Value Simulations
   b. Training in Creating Value Simulations
3. Mock Trials
   a. Goldilocks and the Three Bears
   b. Christopher Columbus: A Mock Trial
   c. Earth on Trial
4. Negotiating Simulations
5. Case Studies
   a. Frank Harris and the American Revolution
   b. Sesame Street Character Case Study
   c. School Rule: Do Not Wear Hats in School
   d. Crime in the American Colonies
   e. What We Can Learn About Societies
   f. Must the Truth Always Be The Truth?
   g. A Problem About Pigeons
   h. Property Rights
   i. Is This An Accurate Document?
   j. Calamec Vs. Orisco
6. Dialogues As Case Studies
   a. The Doctor's Dilemma
   b. Uncertainty
7. Visual Materials as Case Studies
a. The Teapot Case Study
b. The Detail Detective
c. Plagiarism in Art?

Chapter Questions are coded by Bloom's Taxonomy:
Knowledge   (K)   Analysis   (AN)
Comprehension: ©   Synthesis   (S)
Application   (A)   Evaluation   (E)

INTRODUCTION

The dream of child centered educators has always been to engage young people with real situations rather than be confined to written documents. Unfortunately, it is difficult within classroom settings to allow children to directly experience events such as violence or poverty. Obviously, many children bring to the class these daily occurrences, but teachers shy away from compelling other children to have these experiences. On one hand, class discussions or projects teach "about" certain life situations, but it is impossible to provide children direct experiences.

Simulations and case studies are attempts to replicate a reality within a classroom setting. There are many places in society in which simulations and case studies are utilized when it becomes impossible to replicate the actual situation. For example, engineers build models of bridges or buildings to anticipate problems. Astronauts have been trained in regions such as deserts or in the wasteland of Greenland in order to replicate the moon's environment.

The famous D-Day invasion of June 6, 1944 required extensive simulations and examining case studies. Military leaders could not practice an invasion so they had to create situations that were analogous to the actual invasion or they created case studies of potential problems in order that experts could anticipate behavior and solutions. In the business world, most corporations engage in simulations or develop case studies when they are introducing a new product because they want to anticipate success as well as prepare for failure.

Harvard's MBA program has long been noted for its reliance upon case studies and simulations. Students are required to simulate creating a company or they examine case studies of successful and unsuccessful corporations. The goal of using case studies and simulations is anticipating and preparing for what might happen. One can never replicate with exactitude what will occur, but it is possible to become sensitive to potentialities.

Simulations and case studies foster collaborative learning experiences. They invariably benefit when two or more students work at solving problems and many simulations require several students to participate in its implementation. Role playing is an important component of simulations. There are several characteristics of role playing:

1. Students become aware of values, impulses, anxieties, and pressures influencing human behavior.
2. Students practice "walking in the shoes" of another person.
3. Students become more empathetic.
4. Role playing enhances interpersonal skills and awareness of other people.
5. Knowledge gained in role playing can be transferred to other situations.

There are several key rules to follow in role playing:

1. The issue or situation must be clearly defined.
2. Participants are allowed sufficient time to research their role.
3. The physical environment should be conducive to role playing.
4. Participants are allowed leeway in playing a role, but they are not allowed to violate the essential characteristics of the role.
5. Observors cannot critique during the role play. There should be a debriefing.
6. Participants should be referred to by their role name, not their real name.

Dialogue With the Teacher

The initial lesson focuses upon use of a Value Simulation approach to studying human behavior. Value Simulations are designed to make students aware that in any value conflict situation, there is a continuum of possible attitudes. Value Simulations are not designed to "teach a lesson" or "teach a moral value." The goal is confronting students with moral conflicts and allowing them to decide how they would react. There is no "right" or "wrong" answer, the goal is providing opportunities for students to express their views.

The structure of the Value Simulation consists of posing a situation in which an individual made a choice. The room is divided into six strips with headings of:

Absolutely Agree   **Absolutely Disagree**
Agree With Some Reservations   **Disagree With Some Reservations**
Agree With Many Reservations   **Disagree with Many Reservations**

The teacher reads the situation and tells how the individual in the situation decided on his/her action. Students are then asked to move to the strip which reflects their feeling about the decision. After students move to the appropriate spot, the teacher selects several students and asks: "Please explain why you are standing there." No one is allowed to challenge what a student says; individuals can only express their reasons for standing in a particular spot. It would be dangerous for a student to be the only one who Absolutely Disagrees with a decision and then have to confront hostile questions by other class members.

Each situation adds to the complexity of the original decision, and each time new information is provided, students are asked if they agree with the decision. For example,

Situation 1: John entered a classroom and saw a twenty dollar bill on the floor. He picked it up since no one was around. Do you agree or disagree with his decision?

Situation 2: Later, John looked at the dollar and noted that it had the name of a classmate on it. He decided it was probably a coincidence and kept the twenty dollar bill. Do you agree or disagree with his decision?

Situation 3: Later that day, Mary, a classmate told the class she had lost a twenty dollar bill and asked if anyone had found it. John decided that if he now told, he would get into trouble so he decided to remain silent. Do you agree or disagree with his decision?

Ordinarily, many students might Absolutely Agree with the decision in Situation 1, but change to Agree With Many Reservations by Situation 3. At that point, the teacher asks, "Jose, please tell me why you moved from Absolutely Agree to Agree With Many Reservations."

The key to construction of a Value Simulation is making each new situation slightly more complex. There is no "fun" if the situations are so clear cut that everyone in the room goes to the same spot on the Value Simulation Board. A hidden agenda of this process is fostering good listening skills since each student must listen to what others say without agreeing or disagreeing.

Concept: Value Simulations

Focus: Students will physically and orally express their reaction to a problem situation.

Social Studies Standards:
Standard 4: Individual Development and Identity
Standard 10: Civic Ideals and Practices

Teacher	**Student**
1. Teacher lays out room with strips of paper indicating choices.	1. Students stand.
2. Teacher reads first situation in the Simulation entitled: Public Law 94-142. a. Ask several students why they moved to a particular spot. If a student declines to answer tell them it is OK, since by moving their body they have already indicated their decision. b. Students are read other situations. c. After all situations are read, class returns to seat. Teacher can pose: "Could anyone explain what led them to change their viewpoint about the actions?" "What did you find to be most difficult about making a decision in these situations?	2. Each student moves to the spot coinciding with their agreement or disagreement with the decision. a. Students move and explain their decision for moving. b. Students move and explain. c. Student responses.

3. Pass out Practice Simulations and have students work on them in groups.	3. Students in groups work on Practice Value Simulations.
4. Ask students if they wish to design a Value Situation about something currently being studied.	4. Students in Triad design Value Simulation and present to class.

Assessment: 1. Ask students to write an essay explaining what led them to change in any of the situations posed in class during the simulation.

2. Student designed Value Simulation

Multiple Intelligences: Verbal Linguistic
Logical Mathematical
Intrapersonal

Values Game Board

What do you think?

Absolutely wrong	Wrong with some reservations	Wrong with many reservations	Right with many reservations	Right with some reservations	Absolutely right
(White)	(Yellow)	(Blue)	(Green)	(Red)	(Black)

VALUE SIMULATION: PUBLIC LAW 94-142

Teacher lays out room with appropriate six positions. Students are asked to stand. Inform students: "Move to the spot which best reflects your attitude about the decision. There is no right of wrong answer."

Situation 1: John is a twelve year old boy who has been in constant trouble at school. He fights with children and disrupts classes. Today, John got angry at Ms. Jones and gave her a bloody nose. The principal talked with John and told him he was suspended. The principal called John's parents and told them he was suspending John. Do you agree or disagree with the decision of the principal?

Situation 2: The parents came to school and met with the principal. They said it was the school's responsibility to handle John while he was in school. They said they handled John at home but the school has to deal with him when he was at school. The principal said he could not return John to his class with Ms. Jones until the parents agreed to cooperate with the school in working out punishments for John if he did not behave correctly in the future. The parents refused saying it was the school's job, not their job to handle John in school. The principal told the parents that John would not be allowed back in school until the parents agreed to cooperate. Do you agree or disagree with the principal's decision?

Situation 3: The parents met with the Superintendent of Schools and demanded that John be allowed back in school. The Superintendent suggested that John be placed in a special class run by a teacher with training in handling children with emotional problems. The parents refused this suggestion and demanded John be returned to his original class. The Superintendent assigned John to a special class for children with emotional problems. Do you agree or disagree with the Superintendent of School's decision?

Situation 4: The parents took the case to court. The court case eventually came to the United States Supreme Court. The Supreme Court ruled that John had a right to be returned to his original class and that the school should work out a special program to help John deal with his emotional problems. Do you agree or disagree with the decision of the US Supreme Court?

At this point, have the class return to their seats and open discussion with questions suggested in the Dialogue With the Teacher. Students can also pose any questions they desire at this point.

Practice in Value Simulations

The following Value Simulations are designed to provide training for teachers in constructing their own Value Simulations.

Shanna and the House

Situation 1: Shanna, an eleven year old girl, got lost walking home from school. She found herself in a strange neighborhood and didn't know anyone. Shanna went to a house and knocked on the door. No one answered. She knocked harder and the door suddenly pushed open. She walked in. Do you agree or disagree with Shanna's decision to enter the house?

Situation 2: There was no one in the house. Shanna walked into the kitchen and noticed someone had left a box of doughnuts on the counter. She was very tired, hungry and thirsty. She took a doughnut, then opened the refrigerator and took a bottle of soda. Do you agree or disagree with her decision to eat the doughnut and drink the soda?

Situation 3: Shanna suddenly felt very tired. She saw a nice comfortable sofa. She decided to rest for a while before trying to find her way back home. She soon fell sound asleep. Do you agree or disagree with her decision to sleep on the sofa?

Situation 4: An hour later the husband and wife returned to their home to find the front door wide open. They entered and noticed someone had eaten doughnuts and taken a soda from the refrigerator. They went into the living room and found a girl sound asleep. They called the police and had the girl arrested for breaking and entering. Do you agree with the decision of the husband and wife?

Obviously, the above is taken from Goldilocks.

Bill and the Watch

Situation 1: Bill is playing outside with his friends at recess. His teacher, Ms. Lopez asked him to go back to the room and get her sweater. As he enters the room, Bill finds his best friend Sam taking a watch from a desk. Sam asks Bill not to tell anyone since it will result in his suspension from school. Bill feels loyal to his friend and decides not to say anything. Do you agree or disagree with Bill's decision?

Situation 2: Later Bill talks with Sam. He tells Sam that the watch must be returned. Sam says he took the watch from Norman because he knows

Norman stole his baseball glove. He refuses to return the watch and reminds Bill that Norman was the one who gave him a bloody nose last month. Bill agrees not to tell about the watch. Do you agree or disagree with Bill's decision?

Situation 3: (At this point, it is your turn to add a new twist to the situation. You can create new information that again results in Bill not telling or you can introduce new information which leads Bill to turn in his friend. Remember, try to make the situation complex and open to question)

_____

_____

Jill and the Cheerleaders

Situation 1: Jill is from a poor family and decides to try out for the cheerleaders in hope of winning a cheerleader scholarship to college. There are three openings on the cheerleaders. Jill is told by the Sponsor of the Cheerleaders that she came in fourth and if one person drops out she will get the spot. Jill's locker is next to Brenda who beat her out for the last position on the cheerleaders. Jill notices that when Brenda opened her locker, there were three marijuana cigarettes lying on a shelf. Jill tells the Sponsor of the Cheerleaders that Brenda has marijuana in her locker. Do you agree or disagree with Jill's decision?

Situation 2: (Create some additional complexity to the situation. The possibilities are endless. For example, Brenda is dating Jill's brother or Brenda has a sick mother, etc... Make it complex and open to differing viewpoints)

_____

_____

Situation 3: (Create still another piece of complexity)

_____

_____

Additional Ideas About Value Simulations:

1. Develop a Value Simulation about a current issue in school or a school rule.

2. Create a Value Simulation about a topic being studied in class. For example, in explaining why some people did not flee Nazi Germany create value situations in which someone is buying a home on a hillside outside of Los Angeles that has been the scene of several earthquakes.
3. Create a Value Simulation about a current or past conflict.
4. Create a Value Simulation about a current issue facing teachers in the district.
5. Conduct a mini-version of a Value Simulation for parents on Open School Night.
6. Encourage students to create a Value Simulation about a topic being studied.
7. Create a Value Simulation in relation to a conflict in a book being read.
8. The war against Iraq fits perfectly into a Value Simulation activity.

Remember:

1. There are no "right" or "wrong" answers in Value Simulations.
2. Value Simulations are designed to help student understand that in any conflict situation there are varying ways in which people can think or behave.

DIALOGUE WITH THE TEACHER

Among the most popular TV shows is Law and Order which depicts investigation of crime and the ensuing court trial. On any night, TV has several shows dealing with trials and there is even a Court Cable network which deals with issues related to crime and punishment. Americans are addicted to courts and trials. There is a built in interest in law and order that can be used to stimulate interest in learning. This lesson focuses upon the use of Mock Trials in the curriculum.

The use of Mock Trials benefits education in several ways. It brings to life many literary works. For example, "To Kill a Mockingbird" is widely read in schools. The book contains a powerful courtroom scene which can be translated into a mock trial within any classroom. At the heart of education in a democracy is awareness of rights and responsibilities. Mock Trials enable students to directly experience the complexity surrounding issues of rights in a free society. After all, the Supreme Court frequently has 5-4 decisions which indicate division of thinking among justices about rights.

Mock Trials require role playing which previously has been discussed. Role playing is an invaluable tool in helping many students learn about other perspectives and values. Most fairy tales contain conflict over rights and responsibilities so use of Mock Trials enables young children to gain additional skills in thinking and listening. Students can also learn more about our legal system through utilization of Mock Trials.

You are provided three examples of Mock Trials with sufficient information for students to conduct the trials. You might decide to use one or all three. Or, you might decide to use these examples as models for construction of your own mock trial.

Concept: Our Legal System

Focus: Students will physically, orally, and in writing take a stand about a legal issue and be able to explain the American legal system.

Social Studies Standards:
  Standard 5: Individuals, Groups, and Institutions
  Standard 6: Power, Authority and Governance
  Standard 10: Civic Ideals and Practices

Teacher	Student

1. Introduce the Three Pigs and the Wolf Mock Trial. Assign roles to conduct the Mock Trial
   a. Debrief after Mock Trial. "Do you agree that everyone remained within their role?" "Would the trial be different if people role playing altered their roles?"
	1. Students conduct Mock Trial
	   a. Student responses.

2. Introduce the Mock Trial of Cristoforo Colon.	2. Students conduct Mock Trial.
3. Introduce "Earth on Trial."	3. Students conduct Mock Trial.

Assessment:
1. Students can write an essay regarding any aspect of the Mock Trial.
2. Younger children can draw a picture about any aspect of the Mock Trial they found interesting.

Multiple Intelligences: Verbal Linguistic
Logical Mathematical
Interpersonal

MOCK TRIAL OF THREE PIGS AND THE WOLF

Charges: Mr. Wolf sues Three Pigs for attempted murder, burning him and causing serious physical and emotional damage.

Three Pigs: We plead Not Guilty.

Mr. Wolf: He argues that he was simply trying to develop a spirit of sharing and cooperation in the neighborhood until he was viciously attacked by John Pig and nearly burned to death. He, Mr. Wolf, never meant any harm to anyone and was simply being a good neighbor.

John Pig: He lives in a stone house and was the one who tried to burn to death Mr. Wolf. He believes Mr. Wolf tried to kill his brothers and in the process destroyed their houses. John Pig is a careful and hard working individual who makes certain to examine every detail of a situation. He rarely takes time to relax and is always working.

Harry Pig: He lived in a wood house until it was destroyed by Mr. Wolf when he refused to allow Mr. Wolf to enter his house. Harry Pig is a relaxed individual who works hard in spurts, but then likes to relax and enjoy life. However, he really doesn't like Mr. Wolf or anyone from thatfamily.

Bob Pig: He is the youngest brother and admits to often acting lazy. Life is too short and he wants to enjoy every moment. He is not friendly with the Wolf family but doesn't particularly like them hanging around the neighborhood. He thinks they should move and quit pestering pigs.

Prosecutor: Mable Dog. She dislikes wolfs and wants to set an example to the other wolfs to quit bothering other animals. She is known as a tough prosecutor who usually demands the highest penalty for those who break the law.

Defense Attorney: Jose Owl is known for his quiet attitude and his desire to help everyone in the forest. He is always finding loopholes in the law to justify behavior that others consider criminal.

Debrief:

1. At conclusion of the Mock Trial have students identify strongest arguments posed by each side in the trial. (AN)
2. Ask students if they can identify a way of defense or prosecution they thought about during the trial that was not done in the trial. (AN)
3. Ask students to identify a prominent person whose presence as defense attorney or prosecutor would have resulted in a different type of trial. (A)

CHRISTOPHER COLUMBUS: A MOCK TRIAL

Charges: Cristoforo Colon, known to the world as Christopher Columbus, is charged with crimes against humanity. He is charged with invading peaceful nations, attacking and killing innocent civilians, using germ warfare, and physically destroying large areas of the Western Hemisphere. He is further charged with Genocide which involves the systematic and deliberate murder of an entire group of people.

"How do you plead, Cristoforo Colon?"

Response: "I, Cristoforo Colon plead Not Guilty to all charges. This entire trial is illegal since I obeyed the laws of Spain. Since I obeyed my country's laws I cannot be charged with crimes."

Christopher Columbus: He is a man in his late fifties, reddish hair, face tired and worn by years of physical exhaustion. He is a proud man who sometimes comes across as not caring about other people or their feelings. He is loyal to friends. He firmly believes that he knows the truth and points out that throughout his life others ridiculed his ideas, but he eventually was proven correct. He is very religious and considers it his duty to spread Christianity throughout the world. He believes the Indian people of the New World are simple, primitive creatures and that he has helped them by introducing them to modern ideas and ways of life. He regards himself as a friend of Indians and only wants to do good by them. He wants to live on in history as a great man.

King Guacanagari: He is in his forties and for many years has ruled this island which is located in the West Indies. He is proud of his Taino people whom he regards as peace loving, sharing, kind, and possessing high standards of civilization. He feels hurt that despite the aid he gave Columbus, this supposed friend treated Tainos in cruel ways. The King personally likes Columbus, but is disappointed in how things turned out. King Guacanagari deeply resents the Spanish for destroying his people and society.

Bartolome de las Casas: Bartolome de las Casas has great affection for the Columbus family which helped him come to the New World. His uncle sailed with Columbus on the first trip and Columbus has been generous to the las Casas family. During his first decade in the New World, las Casas backed Spanish policies toward Indians. He had a revelation from God, became a priest and has devoted his life to protecting Indians, defending their civilizations, and trying to get them legal rights. He wants Indians to have equal rights, he wants the Spanish to respect other civilizations and cultures and ways of thinking. He opposes forcible conversion of people and on a trip to Spain he even argued for the right of Jews to pray in freedom. He wants Spain to recognize that people in the New World have great civilizations. Personally, he likes Columbus and considers him a great man.

Taina: Taina is a young Taino woman. She welcomed Columbus and the Spanish when they first arrived on her island. She brought them food and drink. She was brutally attacked by Spanish soldiers who then killed her husband. All her children died of diseases brought to her land by the Spanish. She is confused about the Spanish desire for gold. She believes Columbus is a murderer.

Rodrigo Bermajo: He was a crewman on the Santa Maria and was on watch the night before land was sighted. Rodrigo was first to see the land, but Columbus ignored what he did and then claimed the King's reward for the person who first sighted land. Rodrigo believes Columbus is a deceitful man who lies and seeks credit for the work of other people. He believes Columbus lied to his crew and has taken all the riches of the New World for himself. Rodrigo believes Indians are savages and that Columbus is too gentle with them because he uses Indians to get their wealth.

Amerigo Vespucci: He is a man in his fifties who has a peaceful look on his face and is always calm. Vespucci is well educated and spent time with Michaelangelo when he was young. He was a successful banker for the Medici family until he decided to become an explorer. Vespucci dislikes slavery and disagrees with Spanish policies to enslave or treat Indians with brutality. He considers Columbus a good friend, but disagrees with his friend's desire for gold and glory and spreading religion. Vespucci does not want to impose Christianity upon anyone, and was even asked by the Jews of Lisbon to find them a place of refuge in the New World which he tried to accomplish. Vespucci believes Indian societies should be studied and Europeans can learn from the Indian practice of democracy. He believes Columbus is a brilliant man who has made major discoveries, but thinks his friend sometimes gets carried away with spreading religion upon people who don't want it.

Francisco Bobadilla: He is a proud member of the Spanish aristocracy and a close friend of King Ferdinand. The King, who dislikes Columbus, sent Francisco to the New World to keep check on Columbus. Bobadilla believes Columbus is simply an incompetent leader who continually makes mistakes. He is particularly upset at the failure of Columbus to be tough on Indians and force them to reveal where their gold is kept. Bobadilla regards himself as a tough minded individual who intends to crack down on Indians and halt the lax practices of Columbus.

Queen Isabella: She is a proud and deeply religious person who believes her religion is the only true one in the world and everyone must accept it. She wants Indians forcibly converted because she believes that is what God desires. Although, personally she doesn't like to enslave people, she is willing to accept it as a temporary measure to ensure that Indians become Christians. She believes Columbus is an honorable man and that Spain has a right to use these new lands in any way she desires.

Defense Attorney:

Diego Columbus: He is the son of Columbus and backs the ideas of his father. He has sailed with his father and knows first hand what his father has done for Spain. He believes Indians are backward and lack civilization and his father was right to force Christianity upon them. Diego dislikes King Ferdinand who he believes has tried to cheat his father.

Prosecutor:

Enriquillo: He is an Indian born in Cuba who converted to Christianity. He was treated as an inferior by the Spanish and his wife was attacked by soldiers. After the authorities refused to punish these soldiers, he took to the hills and began a rebellion. He always treated captured soldiers with dignity. He finally agreed to end the rebellion upon the pleas of Bartolome de las Casas who promised to take the fight for Indian rights to Spain. Enriquillo is a proud man and defender of his people and culture.

Judge:

Students can identify a person from the past or present to be the judge.

Jury:

Several students should act as the jury. They should be instructed that as a jury they must lay aside personal feelings and only judge the evidence.

Guidelines:

1. Assign at least two people to research and present the ideas of an individual. Remember, some time should be allocated to research roles.
2. Review with members of the jury and judge normal rules of evidence.
3. Review with students normal rules for examination and cross examination.
4. Do not allow members of the audience to interrupt with comments or questions.
5. You may wish to video tape the trial.

Debriefing:

1. Ask students to list strongest arguments for or against Columbus. (AN)
2. Ask students which issue raised in the trial caused them the most personal difficulty to resolve. (E)
3. Ask members of the jury to explain their rationale for the final conclusion they reached in the trial. (AN)
4. Ask members of the audience if they wish to express how they would have voted if they were on the jury. (E)

EARTH ON TRIAL

Unknown to humanity, representatives from planets throughout the universe have been observing planet Earth. This group is charged with responsibility of deciding which planets are qualified to enter the Galaxy Confederation. The Galaxy Confederation is based on the idea that all life forms life in peace and harmony with one another. In their observations of Earth people, members of the Galaxy Confederation have obtained serious questions as to whether or not Earth should be allowed to enter their Confederation. A trial is to be held to determine if Earth can enter. Representatives from planet Earth are invited to attend the trial and present their reasons for admittance.

Following are descriptions of the members of the jury which will rule if Earth can be accepted into the Galaxy Confederation.

Tumor: Tumor is from the planet of Tumor where all life forms are linked with one another via telepathic means. They think, act, and feel with full understanding of how other life forms on their planet feel. They have no understanding of the meaning of "conflict" since that does not exist on their planet. All life forms are in harmony with one another.

Zadek: Zadek is from the planet Cruxx. On Cruxx there is only one gender. Zadek has been raised to believe in the right of each life form to be completely individual in its thoughts. On Cruxx all life forms have the right to be different in thinking and behavior.

Flom: Flom is from the planet Bestar. Bestar went through thousands of years of warfare and conflict before all life forms agreed to cease the violence. On Bestar, life forms only consume vegetables and there is no concept that one should eat meat.

Triar: Triar is from the planet Cotr which is highly mechanized and computerized. Androids handle most physical tasks and recently were granted full citizenship rights. All disputes and conflicts are resolved by a central computer.

Students are to identify who they wish to represent Earth at this trial. The task of human representatives is to offer reasons why Earth can be trusted to enter the galaxy Confederation. The class should have the option of adding other life forms to the jury.

Additional Ideas for Mock Trials

1. Individuals from the past or present can be put on trial.
2. A Mock Trial can be conducted about an issue pertaining to the school.
3. A Mock Trial can be conducted related to a book being studied.
4. A Mock Trial can be conducted about a national or international event.
5. Invite a lawyer to observe and comment on your Mock Trial.
6. Follow a current trial and comment on what you think should be the verdict.
7. In medieval France, animals were put on trial if they helped kill a person.

Dialogue With the Teacher

Negotiating simulations were quite popular in the 1960s and continue to be used in many schools. The essential characteristic of Negotiating Simulations is engaging students into the art of negotiation and compromise. An important object is education students about the art of compromise and the necessity of giving something in order to receive what you deem to be important.

Negotiating Simulations ordinarily are divided into rounds. A topic is selected and at least two sides are present in the topic who oppose one another's ideas. The goal of each group is to persuade the other side to accept a significant portion of their ideas or programs. In a sense Negotiating Simulations are akin to negotiation between labor and management over a contract and working conditions. Each of these sides needs the other in order to survive. Neither side can give the other everything it desires, but it can offer some components in order to persuade them to accept a compromise solution.

Concept: Negotiation

Focus: Students will orally, in writing, and physically present evidence they are able to persuade another group to engage in compromise concerning an issue to which both sides differ on.

Social Studies Standards:
Standard 4: Individual Development and Identity
Standard 6: Power, Authority and Governance

Teacher	**Student**
1. Divide students into three groups and review tasks. Each group is provided information about their goals in terms of what type of foods they wish in the school cafeteria. Each group can make modifications in their goals. Their task is negotiating to achieve their food cafeteria goals. a. Group 1: They wish healthy foods in the cafeteria. They want to eliminate fatty foods which lead to	1. Students work in group to identify their goals. A primary task is deciding how they will approach either of the two other groups in order to get them to agree to what they wish in the cafeteria. Each group has to determine their minimal goals and what are they willing to surrender.

high cholesterol. Their particular targets are French Fries, pizza, and hamburgers. The group has the leeway of identifying healthy foods they wish to be introduced into cafeteria.
b. Group 2: The enjoy current menu. They believe students are old enough to decide which foods best suit their desires. They are not opposed to introduction of new foods, but simply want to maintain the current menu offerings.
c. Group 3: They represent the cafeteria staff. They understand the need for healthy foods, but also feel a need to provide foods that students will actually eat. They fear healthy foods will be so unattractive that students will not eat in the cafeteria.
d. Group 4: This is a coalition of Moslem, Asian, and Jewish students who want foods from their ethnic background. The Moslem and Jewish students want all pork foods banned from the cafeteria.

2. Announce start of Round 1. Determine length of the Round. Then, conclude Round 1 and ask students to return to Group and rethink their strategy.

3. Announce start of Round 2. Determine how many Rounds you wish to have in the Simulation.

2. Each group approaches as many other groups as possible to begin negotiation. After conclusion of Round one, rethink their strategies.

3. Begin Round 2.

4. After end of Rounds, bring students together for a debriefing. You might pose during the debriefing:
a. "Identify which strategies were most successful." (S)
b. "Identify which strategies ran into trouble." (S)
c. "Give any examples of when you were able to get an agreement to your goals." (K)
d. "What frustrated you about attitude of people with whom you negotiated?" (AN)

4. Students sitting in groups respond.

Assessment:

1. Students write an essay on their reflections about this experience.

2. If time permits, meet with individual students and have them verbally review their reflections.

Multiple Intelligences: Verbal Linguistic
Interpersonal

Dialogue With The Teacher

Case Studies are somewhat different from Simulations in that they do not require physical activities. Case Studies can be written, oral, visual, a movie or TV program, a poem, a story, an incident. Virtually, anything can be transformed into a case study. Case studies are extensively utilized in management training programs because they assist students to analyze a situation in a systematic manner.

This lesson present a wide variety of case studies in order to broaden your awareness of the endless possibilities in using this instructional strategy. We do not mean to suggest that you use all of these case studies, but suspect several will capture your attention and can be included within your existing curriculum. Our more important goal is making you aware of possibilities so that you can create your own case studies.

The case studies presented in this lesson cut across a spectrum of grade levels ranging from primary grades to high school. Ironically, secondary teachers might find they could use the Sesame Street case study to help teach how characters think and behave. The initial case study entitled: Frank Harris is actually a metaphor for the causes of the American Revolution as seen by the English government and the revolutionaries in America. Two students who teach in poverty area high schools in Brooklyn recently told me they used Frank Harris with their students and provoked discussions about the topic of the American Revolution which ordinarily does not arouse passion or interest among contemporary students. We hope as you examine these case studies it sparks interest on your part to create your own for particular components of your curriculum.

Ad added benefit of case studies is they are best done with students working in collaborative groups. They foster discussion between students about a common issue. Case studies can also be transformed into simulations. For example, in the Frank Harris case study previously cited, teachers have asked students to role play both sides of the conflict.

Concept: Case Studies and Conflict

Focus: Students will orally and in writing analyze situations entailing conflict and differing viewpoints.

Social Studies Standards:
Standard 1: Culture
Standard 4: Individual Development and Identity
Standard 6: Power, Authority and Governance
Standard 9: Global Connections
Standard 10: Civic Ideals and Practices

FRANK HARRIS CASE STUDY

The subject was born in Baltimore, Maryland, and lived there during his childhood. At the age of fifteen, he decided to leave home. His father, the only parent, agreed to this on condition that if the boy found a job, he would contribute a minimum of $15 a week to his father who was deeply in debt due to his son's early illnesses. Frank found employment and gave money to his father.

The father frequently visited his son. The visits were friendly and the father often brought groceries or left a $5 bill. The father often gave advice to his son about how to behave. For example, he told the subject not to smoke or drink or associate with people on drugs and to get a good night's sleep. The father told the subject his debts were increasing due to the interest he paid on his son's hospital bills and he needed an increase in payment to $25 per week.

The subject did not agree to all advice given by his father. He found some suggestions made sense, but other suggestions were totally ignored. He also told his father that his own expenses prevented him from paying the increase and refused to pay the $25 a week. The father was not happy, but did nothing when the son refused to pay the increase.

After three years had passed, the subject encountered some problems. Two boys in the boarding house where he lived began to bully and harass him. They demanded money and when the subject refused to pay they beat him up. The boy told his father about his problems. The next week the father arrived and confronted the two bullies. They had a violent argument. The father was a strong man and he physically attacked and beat up the two bullies. They wound up in a hospital with severe injuries. During the fight, the father received a broken nose, a broken arm, and a gash in his head. He was hospitalized for two weeks.

The two bullies moved away so the son no longer had a problem. The father upon release from the hospital was given a bill for $350. He brought the bill to his son and asked for help in paying it. He also wanted the increase in weekly payment from $15 to $25 a week. The son refused to pay for the hospital bill or increase weekly payments.

The father then decided to move in with the son and also to enforce new rules of behavior. He also went to the son's employer and asked that $10 a week be deducted from his pay until the hospital bill was paid off. The employer was sympathetic to the father's arguments and made the deductions.

The subject then quit his job. He used his savings to handle daily expenses and refused to give any money to his father. One night during a discussion the father agreed to stop taking money from the son, but he insisted he had a right to supervise the son's behavior since he was still a minor. The youth said nothing.

The son got a new job. The father began to make new financial demands on the son. The two had argument after argument. The son particularly disliked the father telling him how to behave. After six months the two had a serious argument about the son's refusal to halt smoking. The father hit the son and the son hit the father. They had a bad fight with both receiving many blows. The son then moved out and got a job in another city. The father told the son he intended to take action against the son for his behavior.

Activities:

1. Ask students working in groups to identify arguments in support of each side in this conflict. (AN)

2. Ask students to make a list of the strongest and weakest arguments by either side of the conflict. (E)

3. Organize a debate between the father and son. (AN)

4. Organize a role play between the two parties. Feel free to introduce a third party to this role play. (E)

5. Ask students which arguments in this dispute they have encountered in their daily lives. (A)

6. Have students examine an American history book and review the chapter on the American Revolution to identify what in the case study fits historical events. (K)

7. Rewrite the Case Study into a Value Simulation.

CHARACTERS:

ERNIE

Ernie is short and plump. He is always optimistic in his outlook on life. He finds the good in every situation and everyone. He is happy-go-lucky and has a wonderful sense of humor. He loves his rubber ducky. His best friendis Bert.

BERT

Bert is the average person. He is average in size, in looks, and in his sense of humor. He is a pessimist who expects things to always go wrong. He likes to collect ordinary things such as paper clips or bottle tops. He loves pigeons. He and Ernie are roommates.

BIG BIRD

Big Bird is big. He is taller than just about everyone who lives on Sesame Street. He always looks at all side in an argument and tries to figure out how he can make everyone happy before making a decision. He wants everyone to be happy. He is a friend to all who live on Sesame Street.

OSCAR

Oscar is not very tidy. He is sloppy and dresses very poorly. He is a grouch who is always complaining about everything. He enjoys it when things go wrong. He lives in a garbage can. He does not enjoy it when others act friendly to him.

RESPONSIBILITY: On a recent visit to Sesame Street a glass jar which had a paper clip collection was knocked off a shelf. Paper clips and glass were found all over the floor. This happened when the owner of the paper clips and glass was out of the room. Several characters entered the room. These are their comments. Match the comment with the character:

* WOW! What a mess, what a mess. The whole thing is ruined. Can I have it? (Oscar)

* I am really sorry this happened, but you should have put the paper clip collection in a container and set it in a safe place. I will help you organize it. (Big Bird)

* Don't worry. I'll help you buddy. This will give me a chance to polish them as I pick them up. Then, they will really shine. (Ernie)

* Oh great! The whole thing is ruined. All my hard work was for nothing. I might as well throw them away. There is no way they can now be saved. (Bert)

HONESTY: Some candy was missing from Mr. Hooper's Corner Drugstore. The police were called in to help find the missing candy. They began to question some of the characters who live on Sesame Street. Match the character to the correct response.

* I do not know anything about the missing candy, but I am sure that whoever took it will pay for it later. (Ernie)

* Yuk! Candy is sweet. I don't even like sweets, but I like what it does to your teeth. (Oscar)

* It wasn't me, but I'll probably be blamed for it anyway. I always get blamed for thing that I didn't do. (Bert)

* I'm sure there is an explanation for the missing candy. I will be glad to help you find the answer to this mystery. (Big Bird)

EFFORT: The local bakery on Sesame Street caught fire and had great damage to the kitchen. The neighbors got together to decide what to do. Match the character with the response:

* I guess we just won't be able to have any bakery on Sesame Street. The job is just too big for us. What do we know about fixing kitchens? (Bert)

* This looks like a big job, but if we all pull together, I'm sure we can make it as good as new. Maybe, even better. (Ernie)

* I'm sure most of this is covered by insurance. I bet Mr. Cooper had fire insurance on his store. All we have to do is to file an insurance claim. I'll be glad to help do the paperwork.   (Big Bird)

* What needs fixing? The soot, the ashes, the smell of melted plastic smells wonderful. This place looks better than before. Let's leave it as it is. I don't like fresh-baked stuff anyway.   (Oscar)

COURAGE: A new character has moved in on Sesame Street. He scowls a lot and threatens those who live on Sesame Street. The neighbors get together to talk about how to handle this bully. Match the character with the response:

* I know it is hard being the new kid on the block. He is probably scared of us as we are of him. I think he needs special friends. I will help him fit in. (Big Bird)

* I like his style. He seems like the kind of person I could get along with. We need more friends like him on Sesame Street.   (Oscar)

* I don't know about you guys, but I don't like getting hurt. I know that is what will happen if we try to approach him and act friendly.   (Bert)

* The best way to make a friend is to be a friend. If we are all nice to him, I'm sure he will act nice to us. What's not to like?   (Ernie)

Additional Ideas:

1. Select a fairy tale and create similar situations and comments to fit the characters in the fairy tale. (S)

2. Identify a story or novel being read. Create situations and comments and have students match the comment to the character. (S)

3. Identify situations. Then, have students working in groups create the comment they think a particular character would make about the situation. (AN)

4. Present an incorrect identification of the comments in the situation. The task of the group is to identify which are correct and which are incorrect identifications. (AN)

5. Ask students to transform these comments and situations into a cartoon format with dialogue in the boxes within the cartoon strip. (A)

Do Not Wear Hats In School

A school policy handbook contained the following rule: "No student is allowed to wear a hat in the school building." The policy statement was posted around the school. You are a new teacher in the school. One day, you encounter several students wearing hats. Which of these students is violating school policy about wearing hats?

1. Samuel is an Orthodox Jew who must wear a Yamulka.
2. Joan had a plate put in her head after a fall. She wears a pull over hat to cover up the plate.
3. Ibrahim is on the football team and is wearing his helmet for the pep rally.
4. Michael, an African American, is wearing a red cap. He says it is needed because of his hair.
5. Phyllis forgot she had rollers in her hair and her hair still is not dry. She has a plastic cap to cover it and will comb her hair when it gets dry.
6. Douglas got lice in his hair after his younger brother got lice. The doctor had to shave his head and put an ointment on it. He then wrapped the hair turban like.
7. Sarah has recently arrived from Russia where it is the custom for girls to wear a babushka to cover their hair.
8. Terry is wearing his baseball team's hat because they have not lost a game since he began wearing it. He wants to wear it until they lose.
9. Elena takes pride in her hair ribbons. Today, she is wearing ribbons she made.
10. Shamia is a devout Moslem who wears a Chador to cover her head.
11. Doad is a Sikh and his religion requires boys to wear a turban.

Activities:

1. Present arguments which, if any, of the above do not violate the school rule. (AN)
2. Identify any of the above which you believe clearly violate the school rule. (AN)
3. Write a new school rule about wearing hats. (A)
4. Identify another school rule and write a case study about it. (A)

CRIME IN THE BRITISH COLONIES OF NORTH AMERICA

Following is a list of crimes committed in American colonies during the time period 1620-1776. These were all crimes identified by local authorities, not the British government. After the list of crimes, you are provided with a list of punishments. Match the punishment to the crime.

1. _____Grain is stolen by a man after his neighbor harvested the wheat.
2. _____Two men get drunk on a Sunday morning.
3. _____Two men get into a fight and one breaks the arm of the other.
4. _____A single girl becomes pregnant by a local boy.
5. _____ A visiting gambler is caught cheating at cards.
6. _____A husband hits his wife during an argument and accidentally kills her.
7. _____A stranger is caught attempting to rob a local innkeeper.
8. _____A slave is caught stealing lace from her mistress.
9. _____A thirty year old local man is found begging at a fair.
10. _____A woman poisons her husband, the church deacon. He is known as a wife beater.
11. _____A wife is caught by her husband having an affair with a local man.
12. _____Three children are caught stealing pies from a neighbor.
13. _____A man is caught milking a neighbor's cow without permission.
14. _____An indentured servant runs away and is caught.
15. _____A man is unable to pay his debts at the local store.
16. _____Two women are charged with spreading gossip about the local minister.
17. _____A man tells the Minister that he does not believe in God.

Punishments:
A. Branding
B. Whipping
C. Place in Stocks
D. Place in ducking stool.

E. Hanging
F. Fine
G. Repay cost
H. Banishment
I. Sewing first letter of crime on a garment
J. Wearing a rope or halter around the neck
K. Cutting off an ear.
L. Put tongue in cleft stick.

Answers:

1. C and G. Stealing from local people is serious because they are neighbors.
2. D It is a minor crime and making them look foolish is enough punishment.
3. G Repaying the cost solves the problem. No harm was meant.
4. No punishment if the boy and she marry. If not, it could be H—banishment. Puritans are very pragmatic. About 30% of girls were pregnant on wedding day.
5. K A stranger is an enemy. Cutting off the ear marks him for others to know.
6. B if he is not liked. E, hanging is a possibility but probably not if he has friends.
7. K Strangers who damage the community must be marked for life.
8. A to serve as a lesson to other slaves. B is another possibility.
9. C. They will embarrass him, but not hurt him.
10. This is an actual case. They took her out to be hung, placed the rope around her neck and made her stand there all day. She soiled herself. Then, they let her go home since her husband was not well liked.
11. I This is the famous Scarlet Letter.
12. G, if they repay cost it is sufficient punishment.
13. G and possibly D to add to his embarrassment.
14. A or K to make the servant stand out as evil.
15. J is a possibility. Colonial Americans were lenient with debtors.
16. L. The cleft stick is for people who gossip.
17. E or H depending on the person's connections in the community.

What Can We Learn

Following are several crime situations. your task is to identify the society in which the crime happened. The aim is learning about the thought process of the society since what we deem a crime reflects our values and goals.

1. _____ In this society, over weight people are considered to have committed a crime. They are ordinarily fined for this crime.
2. _____ In this ancient society, if a criminal died while in jail, the guards were punished.
3. _____ In this society if a member of the clergy committed a crime, he was excused if he could read from the Bible.
4. _____ In this European society if the criminal came to church, knelt in a "Black Box" and confessed his crime, the priest was expected to forgive him.
5. _____ In this society if a criminal reached a church and entered, the authorities could not enter to get him.
6. _____ In this Asian society if a man broke his marital vows, he was not subject to punishment. If his wife broke her vows the husband had a right to kill her as well as the man with which she had an affair.
7. _____ In this European society if an animal was responsible for a person's death, the animal could be put on trial.
8. _____ In this society it is legal to kill a new born female baby.

Societies: Following are answers to the above questions.
A. Sparta
B. China
C. England
D. Russia
E. Many medieval European societies
F. India
G. France
H. Many societies in the world.

Additional Activities:

1. Ask students to select a current crime and offer an explanation as to why this crime is a crime. (AN)

2. Have students research what used to be a crime but is no longer a crime. (K)

3. Ask students what they learned about the values of the societies listed above. (AN)

4. Ask students to identify a crime that will emerge later in this century. (AN)

Must the Truth Always Be The Truth?

The President of the United States is informed by the Chairman of the Joint Chiefs of Staff that photographs reveal a foreign power is constructing plants to produce new forms of chemical warfare. American secret agents have uncovered definite evidence there is no antidote to this new chemical weapon. The Chairman believes there is need to launch a secret research program to develop an antidote, and fears leakage about the research program might provoke the foreign power to use the weapon.

After discussing the situation with a few close advisors the President decides she must secretly put money in the upcoming budget for the research program. She fears revealing the program to key members of Congress increases the possibility of leakage.

Questions:

1. Is the President's decision to lie to Congress an ethical one? (E)
2. Is there a rationale which allows the President to lie to Congress or the American people? (E)
3. Can you identify an example in American history when a President deliberately misled Congress about a secret research program? (K)
4. Make a list of other ways a President can handle such a situation without deceiving Congress. (AN)

A Problem About Pigeons

In the mid-1800s, the passenger pigeons were so abundant in America that flocks measuring 200 miles were commonly reported. These flocks would sometimes darken the skies for five hours at a time. The nesting area of a single flock could take up to 1,000 square miles of forest. Sometimes, so many of these nine-ounce birds would occupy trees in the forests that full grown oak trees would topple over from the weight.

Yet, by the late 1880s, finding a small flock of passenger pigeons was exceedingly difficult. By the turn of the century there were only a few hundred passenger pigeons left in America. Then, in 1914, the last passenger pigeon died in an Ohio zoo.

Questions:

1. Offer a logical explanation as to the disappearance of the passenger pigeons. (AN)

2. Research the disappearance of passenger pigeons. (K)

3. Create a scenario which explains why a current animal becomes extinct in fifty years. (A)

Property Rights

A very popular story for elementary school students is "The Little House" which depicts the tale of a house in the country which used to be in the city. As urbanization proceeds, the Little House is eventually swallowed up and becomes part of the city. Finally, years later, the daughter of the original owner of the Little House finds the House in the city and brings it back to the country.

Following are examples related to property rights.

1. Susan lives in a suburban area. The county decides there is need to expand a road which runs next to her house. Her parents are told they must sell the house to the county and move.
2. Billy's family has owned a restaurant in a neighborhood for thirty years. During the past few years the restaurant has become surrounded by several large office buildings. The owner of one such building has petitioned the city to condemn the building which houses the restaurant so he can build another large office building. Such a new building would bring in new taxes to the city.
3. Angela's aunt is coming to visit her parents next week and will stay at her house. Her mother tells Angela she must give up her room to the aunt for one week and sleep on the couch.
4. Alphonso wants a dog for a pet. His parents agree he can have a dog. However, the owner of the apartment building where they live says he will not allow pets in his apartment building.
5. Lisa usually parks her bike in front of the drugstore when she goes in to buy some merchandise. The new store owner has posted a sign which forbids people from parking their bikes in front of his store. He claims bikes prevent customers from entering the store.

Questions:
1. List reasons why Susan's parents should not have to sell their house. List reasons why they should be forced to sell the house. (AN)
2. Do Billy's parents have a right to keep their restaurant? Or, does the city have a right to make them sell the restaurant? (E)
3. Present the arguments Angela can offer her parents as to why it is unfair for her to surrender her room to her aunt. (AN)
4. Develop a list of reasons why pets should be forbidden in apartment buildings. Develop a list why tenants have a right to keep pets. (AN)
5. Present Lisa's reasons why she has a right to park her bike in front of the store and in so doing, she is acting like any customer. (E)

THE CHEATING DOCUMENT

The following document was found in the basement of a house that was built in 1480. Is this an accurate document? Your task is to analyze the speech, references, and words used by people in this document in order to prove whether or not this document is false or accurate.

Snow White: Look, you guys. I'm tired of always doing the housework and cooking the meals. I mean, if we had a microwave, then it would be a lot easier doing the cooking.

Happy: Babe, I know you are upset. I mean like you have to wear those old jeans and those Gap sweatshirts. But, you know, like President Ronald Reagan says, look on the bright side.

Sleepy: I'm really bushed and I don't mean George Bush. Snow White, I know you're under the weather and feeling the blues. Maybe, if you turned off that CD with all that music, you might be able to relax.

Snow White: Wow! Your words hurt me like someone shot me in the heart. I think I'll go shopping in the mall to take it easy. It's been a bad day. The radiator in my car over heated, I got a flat tire, and the cop gave me a speeding ticket.

Grumpy: I promise on my favorite baseball cards to help you out. You are making me act real nice. What if I bought you some chocolate and your favorite chewing gum? If you want, I'll even take you to Starbucks for a cup of coffee.

Snow White: Gee whiz and odds bodkins, you guys are real nice. I'll make you a plate of spaghetti and get some pizza. Then, we can have ice cream and popcorn for dessert. Or, would you rather have some strawberries?

Bashful: Gee, you are nice. I'm going to buy you some nice roses and get you that wristwatch.

Activities:

1. Have students make a list of words in this dialogue that would not be used in 1480. (K)
2. Have students make a list of products mentioned in this dialogue which were not present in England in 1480. (K)
3. Have students make a list of all foods mentioned in this document which were not available in England in 1480. (K)
4. Ask students to write an inaccurate document based on a fairy tale or a story. (A)

CALAMEC VS ORISCO (THIS IS BASED ON AN AZTEC LEGEND)

Once upon a time in the kingdom of the Aztecs two hunters appeared before their ruler, Montezuma with the following dispute. Calamec said he had been out hunting for deer. He spotted one and began to chase the deer. He threw a sling shot which hit the deer on the side of the head and slowed it down. Just then, Orisco appeared with a bow and arrow. He shot an arrow into the deer which led to its final death. Calamec argued that he had (a) initially spotted the deer; (b) chased the deer into exhaustion, and (c) slowed it down with his sling shot. Therefore, he claimed the right to the deer. Orisco argued that the rock had only done minor damage, and it was his arrow which really killed the deer.

How should Montezuma decide this case?

1. This case could be role played. (E)
2. The class could be divided into teams charged with coming up with a solution. (AN)
3. Or, one team could be charged with explaining why Calamec was entitled to the deer, one team could present the arguments of Orisco, and the third team could come up with another explanation for the death of the deer. (AN)
4. The class could be divided into teams to come up with the most imaginative solution to this problem. (A)

DIALOGUE WITH THE TEACHER

In this book, the author has utilized the methodology of "dialogue" in order to convey information. The "Dialogue" is essentially a process of imparting ideas in an informal manner. People engage in dialogues during their daily lives. We might chat with a neighbor about a problem with the lawn mower and in the interacting dialogue, information is provided.

This lesson utilizes a dialogue format in order to raise inquiry issues. Dialogues frequently are easy for students to read and understand. They are also fairly simple to write since we often contain information about the topic within our own minds. The central element of a dialogue is identifying an issue to be raised, then identifying who will be the main characters in the dialogue who will discuss the issue. A dialogue can be between two or more people, between animals or even inanimate objects.

Several years ago the author was asked to write a chapter dealing with behavior of Nazi doctors in death camps for a book about the Holocaust. After reflecting on the topic for many weeks he was watching a TV program when a solution to the problem of this topic became apparent. He was watching the TV series, MASH when it became apparent that at least one character in the series – Frank Burns – had the mental attitude toward orders that frequently were found among Nazi doctors. In the following dialogue, the author endeavored to raise issues concerning human behavior during the Holocaust by employing the words of MASH characters.

In the second dialogue, the author used a dialogue to deal with issues raised in a play he saw dealing with ethical behavior on the part of scientists during World War II.

Concept: Ethical Behavior

Focus: Students will orally and in writing state their views regarding ethical Behavior.

Social Studies Standards:
   Standard 4: Individual Development and Identity
   Standard 10: Civic Ideals and Practices

Teacher	**Student**
1. Hand out "The Doctor's Dilemma." a. Ask students in groups to respond to questions at the end of the dialogue.	1. Students in group review the dialogue and respond to questions. Share their responses with the class.

2. Hand out the dialogue on "Uncertainty."
   a. Pose to students:
   "Are there any conditions under which a scientist should refuse to work on a weapon?" (E)
   "What is your reaction to the argument of Heisenberg that Bohr had a moral responsibility to share information on the atomic bomb because if both sides had the a-bomb neither would use it?" (E)
	2. Students work in group to read the dialogue and respond to the questions.
	   a. Students discuss in group and present their views to the class.

Assessment: 1. Students write essay on either of the moral issues presented in these dialogues.

Multiple Intelligences: Verbal Lingistic
Logical Mathematical
Intrapersonal
interpersonal

THE DOCTOR'S DILEMMA

General Herker: Gentlemen, please come in. How are conditions at MASH?

Major Burns: Very bad, sir. The new type of typhus germ is killing many men. My staff is close to exhaustion since we lack a good vaccine. However, I am certain we will solve the problem.

Captain Pierce: Major Burns is correct as usual. We are confident as hell, but I think we are confident of failure. We don't have a clue how to cure the new illness.

General Herker: Unless you find a cure, the illness could force a halt to our attack.

Major Burns: Sir, we are working as hard as possible. But, we lack the time and staff to do the necessary work.

Captain Pierce: What the good major is saying is that we could find a solution if we could isolate infected men as soon as they got the disease. Then, we could observe the course of the disease. Unfortunately, MASH units don't lend themselves to Research.

General Herker: What if I could establish a proper research environment? Could you come up with a vaccine?

Major Burns: Oh, yes sir, I am certain we could. I have training in research.

Captain Pierce: Hold on Frank. We are being offered the right solution to solve the problem. What's the catch, General Herker?

General Herker: There is no catch. I am proposing we assign a team of your officers to a POW camp. You will select several POWs for use as subjects in the research we need to find a vaccine.

Major Burns: I don't understand General. Has the typhus epidemic hit the POW camp?

Captain Pierce: I don't think that's what the General is saying, is it?

General Herker: Captain, we are not at some medical convention or in some ivory towered university. This is war. Our goal is to win. That means we must save American lives, not those of the enemy. Our men are dying and our responsibility is to save American lives regardless of the cost.

Major Burns:	Sir, you know I am loyal to America. I think we should do what is necessary even if it means infecting people. After all, when we find the cure, we can take care of those who were infected so no harm is being done.
General Herker:	Exactly right, Major.
Major Burns:	But, I have one qualm. Isn't what we are doing a violation of my oath as a doctor?
General Herker:	Which comes first, Major, some words on a piece of paper or our soldiers?
Captain Pierce:	It's more than words on a paper we are being asked to forget. You want us to commit a criminal act. You want us to be like the loyal Nazi doctors who killed Jews. You want to turn POWs into guinea pigs. After all, we kill guinea pigs all the time so what's the big deal about killing a bunch of enemy soldiers?
General Herker:	I'll ignore your flippancy. The purpose of war is to win because if you lose then your people get hurt. We are fighting to protect our nation from a ruthless enemy. The enemy fights with many weapons – guns, planes, tanks, and propaganda. Suppose the enemy introduced a new strain of typhus as part of chemical warfare. Would you then be willing to conduct research on those POWS?
Major Burns:	If they started this chemical warfare, we have a right to defend Ourselves. Sometimes, you can't be perfect.
General Herker:	Well stated, Major. If a plague was raging, wouldn't you isolate those who have been infected , and wouldn't that increase the possibility they would die sooner?
Captain Pierce:	Hold on, General. A doctor has a moral obligation to cure, not to make people sick.. Those POWs are humans. They surrendered and are entitled to be treated according to provisions of the Geneva Convention. I don't recall anything in that document which permits us to infect people. I am not a Nazi doctor.
General Herker:	No, you would rather see thousands of decent American soldiers die than violate your precious principles. In war, we sometimes have to put aside our moral beliefs. American lives come first.

Major Burns: The general has a point. After all, prisoners in jail often volunteer to be guinea pigs for medical experiments. What's the difference in this case?

Captain Pierce: The difference, Frank, is that we are not asking for volunteers. We are deliberately killing innocent people.

General Herker: You can try to make me a monster. I am not. In war,, as in medicine, you sometimes sacrifice a few to save many. I am asking you to infect a few of the enemy to save thousands of American lives. What's your decision, gentlemen, do we infect POWs or not?

Activities:

1. Ask students working in groups to complete the dialogue. (E)

2. During World War II, German doctors conducted experiments on people in death camps. They argued that since these people would die anyway, in the long run the experiments would save lives. What is your response? (E)

3. If an American army was fighting in jungles – as they did in Vietnam – is it morally justifiable to defoliate areas of the jungle to force the enemy to come out into the open? (E)

4. Is it permissible for a doctor to train special forces to go behind enemy lines and poison enemy drinking facilities? (E)

5. Ask students to create an ethical dialogue about a topic being studied. (E)

UNCERTAINTY

The year is 1942. After launching World War II in 1939, Nazi Germany swept over most of Europe. She controlled Denmark, Poland, Belgium, Holland, Yugoslavia, France, Hungary, Rumania and Czechoslovakia and her army was deep inside Russia. Niels Bohr was a famous Danish physicist. One of his students was a young German named Werner Heisenberg who studied with Bohr and then returned to Germany in the 1930s where he became a leading scientist under the Nazi government. One day in 1942 Heisenberg visited Bohr and his wife, Margrethe in Copenhagen, Denmark. Following is a dialogue concerning what they discussed.

Neils Bohr   My dear friend, Werner, please come in. What brings you to Copenhagen? We have not seen one another for such a long time.

Heisenberg   Too long, too long. And is Margrethe here? Oh, how I miss the two of you.

Margrethe   Werner, so glad to see you. What brings you here? Is the Fuehrer planning another surprise for we Danes? After all, how many nations are fortunate enough to be under the supervision of Nazi Germany?

Neils Bohr   Dear, this is our friend, not one of those Nazis. The Nazis do enough evil without we Danes attacking innocent Germans.

Margrethe   Oh, Werner, are you innocent?

Heisenberg   Innocent.... Such an interesting word. Guilt or innocence. In the old days it was quite clear what we meant about guilt and innocence. Today, ... life is different, conditions are different.

Neils Bohr   My dear, Werner, you are a friend and always will be one. We spent too many years arguing and discussing issues about science and life, oh, how I remember those walks in the forest sharing ideas with one another. Those were wonderful times.

Heisenberg   I think back to those days. But, also to the times before them when my nation was defeated in World War I. People forget what we Germans went through after the defeat. We suffered in poverty. It is not pleasant to lose.

Margrethe   Yes, we know all about losing. Somehow, I think losing to Germans is the worse type of losing.

Heisenberg	Please Margrethe, you are not going to tell me another one of those stories about Jews being killed in the East. I remember as a teenager in 1916 hearing the Allied propaganda about Germans killing nuns and smashing the heads of babies.
Neils Bohr	Enough, so what brings you to Copenhagen? Official business or pleasure?
Heisenberg	Official business. Well, not exactly.
Margrethe	Ah, the mystery thickens. Why are you here, Werner?
Heisenberg	My friends you have my word of honor that what we talk about tonight will remain in this house. No one else shall ever know about this talk.
Margrethe	So, it is partially official, isn't it?
Heisenberg	Yes and no. My superiors do not know that I am here.
Neils Bohr	So, there is something you wish to talk to me about. Well, get on with it.
Heisenberg	Before I ask my question, I want you to recall the poor young man who came to study with you in 1924. My family had lost everything in World War I. All around me were people in poverty and feeling hopeless. I shudder at those days. Defeat plays a melancholy tune.
Margrethe	My husband awaits your question.
Heisenberg	Bohr, years ago we discussed the possibility of a bomb being made from atomic energy. Are the Allies building one? Are the British and Americans building such a weapon?
Neils Bohr	Werner, our talk in those days was about a theory, not about a weapon. But, let me be perfectly frank with you. If the Allies were building such a weapon I would not tell you anything about it.
Margrethe	Have your masters in Germany told you to build such a weapon?
Heisenberg	No, No. Albert Speer talked to me about atomic fission, but we did not pursue the topic. After all, our Fuehrer believes atomic physics is a "Jewish science" and does not want Germany pursuing such a direction. I suspect my leaders prefer building rockets since there are few Jewish scientists in that field.
Neils Bohr	As you know, I am half Jewish. And, you want to know if the Jewish science of physics is building an atomic bomb. How ironic!

Heisenberg	Yes, I must know.
Margrethe	Why?
Heisenberg	If the Allies are building such a destructive weapon like an atomic bomb, they will use it on Germany. It would lead to utter devastation of my homeland. Therefore....
Margrethe	Therefore, what, build your own Nazi atomic bomb?
Heisenberg	No, I didn't say that. Who could conceive of the horrors that would ensue if a nation found the means to use atomic energy for the purpose of destruction.
Neils Bohr	But, you must know if the Allies are working on it. Why?
Margrethe	Husband, our dear Werner is the famous inventor of the Theory of Uncertainty. There is something uncertain in his request.
Heisenberg	Bohr, you and I agreed years ago that the idea of atomic fission had the potential to aid humanity. But, we also made a passing glance at the prospect of this wonderful potential being used to destroy humanity. Are the Allies working to transform beauty into evil?
Neils Bohr	I cannot answer. I live in a conquered nation. Your homeland has spread evil, hate and destruction throughout Europe. Millions of people are dead because of the Nazi government and millions live in agony. I cannot help such an evil nation.
Heisenberg	Yes, the Nazis commit evil. But, remember, Germany is the land of Beethoven and Bach and Wagner as well as great scientists and thinkers. Should innocent Germans be made to suffer because they live under an evil government?
Margrethe	Back to innocence and guilt. Can the innocent also be guilty? Or, are the guilty innocent?
Neils Bohr	Werner, is this the only question you wish to ask of me? Or, is there something else you wish to ask?
Margrethe	Perhaps, Werner, you want to return to the old days when you encountered a problem and came to ask Bohr for help?
Heisenberg	Problem?
Neils Bohr	Werner, are you working on an atomic bomb?

Margrethe	And, you dare asking help from a half Jewish scientist?
Heisenberg	Life is terrible today. Life is confusing. If Germany came to posses an atomic bomb then no one would dare to use such a weapon. The world would be saved. There is a possibility under such conditions neither side would use the weapon.
Neils Bohr	So, you want my help in building this atomic bomb?
Heisenberg	I would not make such a request if the Allies were not working on an atomic bomb. And, I give you my word that Germany would never use such a weapon.
Margrethe	There is something ironic in this discussion. Nazi Germany drove out of its nation the great Jewish scientists, including many in the field of atomic energy. Now, Nazi Germany wants the help of a Jew.
Heisenberg	Don't you think I'm opposed to those stupid attacks on Jews? I did my best to protect Jewish scientists. But, the Himmlers and the uncouth fools who run Germany ignored my pleas. They are driving our nation to destruction.
Neils Bohr	But, if you could find a way to build an atomic bomb, then....
Margrethe	Our friend Werner would become a national hero.
Heisenberg	I do not seek personal glory. Never.
Neils Bohr	But, Werner, if you found a way to build an atomic bomb....
Margrethe	You would become a hero and even receive a medal from the Fuehrer.
Neils Bohr	Remember, your science success helps Nazi Germany.
Heisenberg	I hate the Nazis. I detest their foolish ideas. I want to help Germany.
Neils Bohr	But, don't you see? Nazis and Germany are as one.
Heisenberg	But, what about humanity? If the Allies create an atomic bomb then people in Germany and elsewhere will suffer. Atomic bombs do not distinguish between the innocent and the guilty. All die.
Neils Bohr	I cannot answer any questions about atomic bombs. Many of my friends have fled Germany or were driven out. Now they work...
Heisenberg	Is Bohr helping them to build an atomic bomb to wipe out the world?

Margrethe	It is Germany, not the world that concerns you.
Heisenberg	I take it by your silence that the Allies are working on atomic weapons.
Neils Bohr	Uncertainty, your famous uncertainty theory. My silence reveals nothing. It is mere silence. Take it as you wish. I will never help Germany.
Heisenberg	But, you would hurt Germany, wouldn't you?
Neils Bohr	Yes, I would. In hurting Germany I save millions of innocent people. You can tell the people in Berlin that Bohr seeks the end of Nazi rule.
Heisenberg	I came on my own.
Margrethe	Werner, you work for the Nazi government. You are not on your own.
Heisenberg	But, I would never do anything to hurt either of you. You are my friends.
Neils Bohr	You hurt me by helping Nazi Germany. You hurt me and yourself.
Heisenberg	This is hopeless. I came as a friend, as a colleague, as a scientist. I believe science should help, not hurt humanity. I must go back, and…
Margrethe	And? Uncertainty. Everything is uncertain isn't it?

(A few months after the conversation Bohr and his wife fled to England)

Activities:

1. List the arguments advanced by each participant in this dialogue. ©
2. Heisenberg, raises the issue that if a nation has a horrible weapon, then scientists in that nation should ensure that other nations know about the weapon in order to prevent its use. What is your reaction to this idea? (E)
3. Are there any conditions under which you would do something to hurt your own nation if you thought it would benefit humanity? (E)

DIALOGUE WITH THE TEACHER

Case studies come in many forms. In this lesson, the use of case studies in art is explored. Two visual case studies depict how an ordinary object can be transformed into a subject of inquiry. There is also an example of using an issue in art to present an inquiry style lesson to students.

Hopefully, the models presented in this lesson plan will stimulate your endeavors to foster visual formatted inquiry lessons for students.

Concept: Inquiry in the Visual Arts

Focus: Students will visually, orally, and in writing analyze visual materials in order to identify key issues.

Teacher	Student
1. Present the "Tea Pot" visual and ask students in groups to respond to questions.	1. Students in group respond to questions and share with class.
2. Hand out "Detail Detective."	2. Students in groups respond to questions.
3. Hand out "Plagiarism in Art."	3. Students in group respond to questions.

Assessment: 1. Students identify a visual piece and transform it into an inquiry experience.

Multiple Intelligences: Visual Spatial
Verbal Linguistic

Case Study on Teapot

The English are famous for their love of tea. Tea was first imported to Europe from Asia about 1600. It initially was very expensive so only wealthy people could afford it. Tea was believed to be beneficial in curing headaches, giddiness, colds, fever, and scurvy. As tea spread through the population it became a national drink. Fascination with tea led to design of elaborate tea pots.

American colonists also enjoyed tea. During the Revolutionary War, tea became scarce and most Americans chose to sip raspberry leaf tea or coffee. Americans also took pride in their teapots. The dainty cauliflower teapot shown below came from the late 1760s and was made at the Wedgewood factory in Staffordshire, England. Cauliflowers, pineapples, melons, etc.. were popular designs for teapots.

Questions:

1. How do teapots and coffee pots differ in shape? (AN)
2. Compare and contrast this teapot with modern designs. (AN)
3. What does this teapot design tell about the society that produced it? (A)
4. Design a teapot which combines elements of the past and present. (S)

148 ✧ A Teacher's Handbook to Inquiry Learning

Detail Detective

After viewing the Detail Detective, identify an object and transform it into an inquiry experience.   (A)

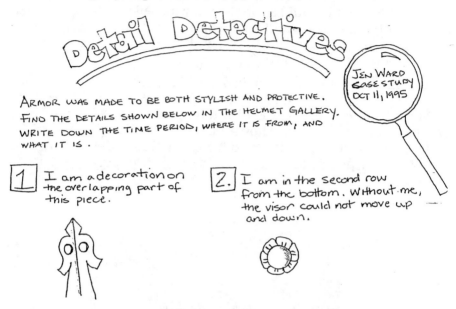

Detail Detectives

Jen Ward
Case Study
Oct 11, 1995

Armor was made to be both stylish and protective. Find the details shown below in the Helmet Gallery. Write down the time period, where it is from, and what it is.

1. I am a decoration on the overlapping part of this piece.

2. I am in the second row from the bottom. Without me, the visor could not move up and down.

3. I am in the same row as #2. I help my knight hear better.

4. Almost every inch of this fancy suit is covered with heros, crowns, initials, and fantasy creatures like me

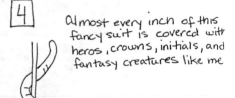

5. Edges can be attractive too. I am on something used during a joust.

6. I protect something that helps a knight hold things in his hand.

Inspiration or Plagiarism in Art?

1. Ann creates a silver bracelet to sell at a craft sale. While setting up the booth she notices Mike has a bracelet displayed which is identical in all respects to her design. She complains to Mr. Hernandez, chairman of the art fair. Mr Hernandez tells Ann that she does not have exclusive rights to a design. Mike is allowed to sell his bracelets.

2. Carlos is hired to design a poster for a local hairstylist. He uses a portrait created by a famous artist in 1980, but Carlos alters the hair style in the portrait. Carlos tells the client he can use the portrait of the artist because the artist died two years ago. He also points out that he made changes in the portrait.

3. Martha created a belt buckle. Bob's Belt Company offered to pay Martha to mass produce her buckle. Martha agreed with the proviso that she would receive $1 for every belt sold with her design. Another company called Betty's Belt Company began making copies of Martha's buckle design. Martha contacted Betty's Belt Company and asked them to pay her the same $1 fee for each belt sold. Betty's Belt Company refused to pay.

4. Mark is working on a painting in art class. Instead of a paintbrush, he is using a toothbrush to splatter paint on his canvas. It took Mark weeks to perfect his technique. Ava brought a toothbrush to class and imitated Mark's method. Mark complained to Ms. Abbas about Ava. Ms. Abbas informed Ava that she was not allowed to copy Mark's ideas.

5. Jenny decided to make a collage depicting city life which she intended to sell at a school fundraiser. She took books out of the library which had photos of city landscapes. Jenny made photocopies of the photographs. She then cut out shots of people and scenes from the photos to form her collage. Mr. Henson, the art teacher, warned Jenny that she cannot use scenes from the photographs because she is stealing from the original photographer.

6. Terry copied a contemporary painting from his local art museum. The museum guard asked Terry what he was doing and Terry said he was practicing how to use the style of the artist. The guard allowed Terry to continue. As Terry was working, a visitor asked Terry if he would sell him the painting. Terry made it clear that he was not the original artist. He sold the replica of the original painting which hung in the museum.

Questions:

1. Which, if any, of the above are examples of plagiarism? (AN) (K)

2. Can you cite an example in your life in which you engaged in plagiarism? (AN)

3. What would be your ethical feelings in regard to copying work from an artist? (E)

For further information, contact: Copywright Office, Information Section LM-401, Library of Congress, Washington D.C. 20559

CHAPTER 5

INQUIRY AND THE LANGUAGE ARTS

Chapter Outline:

1. Introduction
2. Metaphoric Thinking
3. Inventing a poem
    a. Aztec Poems
    b. Concrete Poems
    c. Puzzle Poetry
    d. Noticing Poems
    e. Sound Poems
    f. Obituary Poems
4. Visual Writing
5. The Rebus
6. Author Logos
7. Proverbs
8. Words of Wisdom
9. Fairy Tales
10. Using Fairy Tales and Stories to Teach Foreign Policy and Conflict
11. Ideas to Stimulate Writing
    a. Opening and Closing Lines
    b. Upside Down Writing
    c. Oxymorons
    d. Writing An Essay
    e. Collective Writing
12. Writing Letters
    a. Crazy Letters
    b. Dear Abby Style Letters
13. Additional Ideas to Stimulate Inquiry in Language Arts

Chapter Questions are coded by Bloom's Taxonomy:
Knowledge   (K)   Analysis   (AN)
Comprehension: ©   Synthesis   (S)
Application   (A)   Evaluation   (E)

INTRODUCTION

Humans ordinarily write for either of two reasons – to express emotions or thoughts and to convey information to other people. In a sense, writing is analogous to conducting an inner dialogue only the words are being spoken for public knowledge. Writing for children should be an opportunity to learn about their individual personalities and to assist them in communicating ideas and feelings.

In this chapter, numerous ideas are offered to assist young people in finding joy in their writing. Writers undoubtedly work very hard at their profession, but it is also a source of joy. The same should true for student writers. If writing is an "onerous task" then it is doubtful if quality writing will emerge from their endeavors. Writing has to be fund but writing requires diligent work at writing. The more we write the more probable writing will become part of our lives.

An educational program which is centered in writing will not only meet the needs of society, but will empower children to gain control of their own thoughts and feelings. The author believes in the importance of creative thinking, but prior to that goal, students must master the essentials of writing and reading. Ironically, technology has been touted as supplanting books, but it has resulted in an enormous increase in writing – emails! Technology writing should be a springboard in helping teachers to stimulate writing.

It is unfortunate we lack information how people reacted to the original writers. What did people think as they gazed as the scratchings on a stone? What were the initial emotions and thoughts regarding the task of reading? Primary age children love to read. Reading extends our understanding of the human condition, but for many youngsters reading whets curiosity, provides enjoyment, and is still another tool in the quest to understand one's behavior and the antics of others.

A wise dean once told the author, "Ladies and gentlemen, one must read junk in order to understand quality." The goal of every teacher is to witness students exploring the rich resources of literature and poetry, but one must not ignore that pursuing the road to wisdom also entails many detours. The more students read and write, the more they gain confidence in their reading and writing abilities, the higher is the probability that these skills will become embedded in their personalities and desirable qualities.

We must not forget that in the contemporary world, many youngsters are inundated with commercials both written and visual. They learn a new form of communication which derives from the entertainment and public relations world. It is the responsibility of educators to assist youth in becoming more aware of the importance of visual literacy which represents a revolutionary shift in human history. Teachers can not change the dynamics of world civilization, but we can assist students to control these forces and make use of them in their individual quests for self understanding.

On the following pages are dozens of ideas designed to stimulate reading and writing. They are designed so that students will enjoy reading and writing experiences. After all, the greatest gift any teacher can convey to a student is the love of reading and writing.

Dialogue With the Teacher

The essence of good writing is the capacity to create visual images in the minds of readers that convey important ideas. Metaphoric thinking is the capacity to formulate images connections between a problem at hand and some other aspect of life or nature. Humans have been delving into nature for thousands of years in order to solve their daily problems. The initial part of the introductory lesson focuses upon stimulating metaphoric thinking skills of students. In the second half of the lesson, students engage in writing poetry. The goal of this lesson is stimulating students to express their feelings, emotions, and ideas through poetry. There is no need to complete this unit in one time frame. You may decide to do parts of the unit in an initial time frame and do other parts scattered throughout a term or the academic year.

Concept: Metaphoric Thinking and Poetry.

Focus: Students will demonstrate in writing understanding of metaphoric Thinking and writing poetry.

English Language Arts Standards:
Standard 4: Students adjust their use of spoken, written and visual language to communicate effectively with a variety of audiences.
Standard 11: Students participate as knowledgeable, reflective, creative, and critical members of a variety of literacy communities.
Standard 12: Students use spoken, written, and visual language to accomplish their own purposes.

Teacher	**Student**
1. Ask each student to complete exercise on Metaphoric Thinking. Instructions are to write whatever first enters the mind. If they do not wish to write a response to a particular question, they are allowed to pass.	1. Students complete exercise.
2. Divide students into groups to share responses. A student has a right to pass on sharing a particular response.	2. Students share.
3. Ask students individually to complete Teabag exercise.	3. Students complete exercise.

4. In groups, students share what they wrote.	4. Students share.
5. Ask students to complete Synesthetic Question exercise.	5. Students complete exercise.
6. In groups, students share.	6. Students share.
7. Students are asked to take out paper, and sit by themselves to complete the Creative Invention activity.	7. Students work individually.
8. Ask students to identify an object or animal. They are to draw an outline of the object or animal. Inside the outline they are to place descriptive words in order to write a Concrete Poem.	8. Students in pairs do exercise.
9. Students in groups, do Aztec Poem activities.	9. Students in groups do Aztec Poem activities.
10. Students do Puzzle Poem activity.	10. Students in triad do Puzzle Poem activity. Each group of three is write a Puzzle Poem to present class. Class must guess what is being described.
11. Students in groups do Noticing Poem activities. Each group then Writes a Noticing Poem.	11. Students in groups write poem.
12. Students in group do Sound Poem activities.	12. Students in groups write poem.
13. Students in group do Obituary Poem activities.	13. Students in group write poem.

Assessment: 1. Poetry written by individual students.

2. Poetry written by students working in pair or group situations.

3. Ask students for homework to write a poem about any aspect of their life by employing any of the genres of poetry they have studied.

Multiple Intelligences: Verbal Linguistic
Intrapersonal
Naturalist
Interpersonal
Visual Spatial

METAPHORIC THINKING

(For secondary students) (E)

1. Eating pizza is like taking a vacation because _____

2. A parachute is like summer because _____

3. Rainfall reminds you of which animal? _____
4. Winter is like taking an exam because _____

5. Being in love is like which experience in nature _____

6. Hitting a homer in baseball reminds you of which animal? _____
7. A sunset is like falling to sleep because _____

8. A school dance is like a thunderstorm because _____

9. Going to the principal's office is like meeting which animal in the forest?

10. Which animal comes to mind when the doorbell rings? _____
11. Lying on grass on a warm day makes you feel like _____

12. A tiger pursuing its prey is like what in life _____

Metaphoric Thinking
(For elementary students) (E)

1. Which animal would have given humans the idea for a water hose? _____

2. A monkey swinging from a tree reminds you of what in life? _____

3. Which animal would have given humans the idea for a zipper? _____

4. Kicking a soccer ball makes you feel like _____

5. A swordfish would have given humans the idea for which invention? _____

6. A tiger growling reminds you of which sound? _____

7. A rainy day makes you feel like _____

8. A dark night makes you think of which animal? _____

9. Saturday morning is like a vacation because _____

PERSONIFICATION

(AN)

1. You have now become a Teabag and are to think like a Teabag. Your Teabag body is now being put into a cup of boiling hot water. How do you feel as you enter the cup? _____
   _____
   _____

2. You have been in the boiling hot water for about a minute. Now, how do you feel? _____
   _____
   _____

3. A big hand takes you out of the cup and places you on a counter in the kitchen. Now, how do you feel? _____
   _____
   _____

4. Oops, you have been placed back into the hot boiling water. How do you feel? _____
   _____
   _____

5. What advice would you give a new Teabag who has never been placed in a hot cup of boiling water? _____
   _____
   _____

6. What in nature is most like being put in a cup of hot boiling water? _____
   _____

7. (If you wish add your own question to the Teabag) _____
   _____

(Thanks to William Gordon who gave me the idea for this activity)

SYNESTHETIC QUESTIONS

(E)

1. What would the taste of eating a marshmallow sound like? _____

2. What would the sound of breaking glass smell like? _____

3. What would be the smell of hitting a baseball? _____

4. What does the taste of paper sound like? _____

5. What is the sound of walking in a park like? _____

6. What is the smell of school like? _____

7. What is the sound of a raindrop? _____

8. What is the smell of fire? _____

9. (Add your own) _____

10. (Add your own) _____

INVENTING A POEM

(E)

Step 1: When you hear the following word — THUNDER— write the name of the first animal who enters your mind. There are no right or wrong answers.

For example, I will write "Gorilla."

Step 2: Write ten complete sentences in which you describe that animal. Describe how the animal feels, thinks, moves, its fears, its hopes, its dreams, etc… Use as many descriptive adjectives as possible.

For example, following are my ten sentences.

1. I am furry, strong, and powerful.
2. Animal fear me when I am angry.
3. I jump up and down when angry.
4. My sharp teeth tear into my enemies causing them pain.
5. I am silver, black, with shiny gray streaks on my body.
6. I sleep under wet, soggy, greenish brown leaves.
7. I pound on my black hairy stomach when angry.
8. My feet trample on the green grassy forest floor.
9. I am afraid of humans with their black shiny sticks.
10. My piercing black eyes shine in the moonlight.

Step 3: At this stage of the process, the subject will be changed back to THUNDER. I will now take either any of my complete sentences or a fragment of a sentence or a word from a sentence in order to write a poem.

For example: THUNDER
　　　　I am silver, black with shiny gray streaks
　　　　　　Jumping up and down when angry
　　　　My piercing black eyes shine in the moonlight,
　　　　　　Animals fear me when I am angry.

　　　　I am strong
　　　　　　　　Powerful

　　　　　　I pound
　　　　　　　　　Trample green grass
　　　　　　Then
　　　　　　　　　Sleep

Students could also extract three descriptive words for their own version of a Haiku poem:
　　　　　　　　Piercing
　　　　　　　　Powerful
　　　　　　　　sleep

CONCRETE POETRY

Any object, person animal or aspect of life has the potential of being transformed into poetry. Concrete Poetry is a strategy of transforming a person, animal, object, etc.. into a poetic form. The process is rather simple.

Step 1: Draw an outline of the person, animal, object, etc… (K)

Step 2: Place descriptive words inside the outline about the person, animal, object, etc… (K)

Step 3: Give a title to what you have created. (E)

For example: A Concrete Poem of a Dog.

```
     ...
     it                                          h    .t
     stay                                      tay .  eak
     com                                       .tch speak
     l fetc.                                   lay down l
      r heel                                   play dead hee.
       me sit                                  .r jump fetch stay u
        'h come .
         .'t play dead sit come ..., down beg stay roll over sit'.
          d down fetch stay beg speak jump play dead fetch hee'
          s roll over jump play dead beg speak fetch heel s'
          l sit beg lay down speak roll over stay d
          n stay come jump sit heel fetch lay de
          .it roll over speak lay down stay beg
          ped play dead come jump speak roll ov
          .ed fetch jump heel play dead speak fe
          cch sit stay speak jump roll over stay
     ,peak fetch            .d b play dead co
     heels cor                      beg lay
     stay sta                       roll o
     downs                          me lay
     'etch roll u.                  ip down sp.
      umped play                    'el play dea
       tch roll ov                   'ay sit 'hee
```

Anonymous

Emblematic Poetry

Concrete Poetry was termed Emblematic Poetry in the nineteenth century. Following are two examples which appeared in *Harper's Weekly* on May 8, 1868:

Students could write Emblematic/Concrete Poems about animals, objects, their clothes, something in school, etc...

Emblematic Poetry

Although specimens of emblemnatic poetry of the seventeenth centure may be familiar to the reader, yet we venture to subjoin a modern imitation in the present vernacular, which will please at least patrons of the curious. The following is form the Musical World, and is entitled

The Poor Fiddler's ode to his fiddle.

```
                    Torn
                    Worn
              Oppressed I mourn
                    Bad
              Three-quarters mad
                 Money gone
                 Credit none
                 Duns at door
                 Half a score
                 Wife in lain
                 Twins again
                 Others ailing
                Nurse a railing
                 Billy hooping
                 Betsy crouping
                Besides poor Joe
                With fester'd toe.
           Come, then, my Fiddle,
           Come, my time-worn friend,
         With gay and brilliant sounds
       Some sweet tho' transient solace lend.
       Thy polished neck in close embrace
       I clasp, while joy illumes my face.
       When o'er thy strings I draw my bow,
       My drooping spirit pants to rise;
       A lively strain I touch — and, lo!
       I seem to mount above the skies.
         There on Fancy's wing I soar,
           Heedless of the duns at door;
       Oblivious all I feel my woes no more,
           But skip o'er the strings,
            As my old fiddle sings,
             "Cheerily oh! merrily go!
               Presto! good master,
              You very well know
             I    will    find    Music
           If   you   will   find   bow,
         From E, up in alto, to G, down below."
        Fatigued, I pause to change the time
        For some Adagio, solemn and sublime.
        With graceful action moves the sinuous arm,
        My heart, responsive to the soothing charm,
        Throbs equably; while every health-corroding care
        Lies prostrate, vanquished by the soft mellifluous air.
      More and more plaintive grown, my eyes with tears o'erflow,
        And resignation mild soon soothes my wrinkled brow.
        Reedy Hautboy may squeak, wailing Flauto may squall,
        The Serpent may grunt, and the Trombone may bawl;
        But, by Poll my old Fiddle's the prince of them all.
        Could e'en Dryden return, thy praise to rehearse,
        His Ode to Cecilia would seem rugged verse.
        Now to thy case, in flannel warm to lie,
        Till called again to pipe thy master's eye.
```

The following is a second example of torturing verse into the form of

The Wine-Glass.

```
                THE WINE-GLASS.

         Who hath woe?  Who hath sorrow?
             Who hath contentions?  Who
             hath wounds without cause?
              Who hath redness of eyes?
              They that tarry long at the
               wine!  They that go to
              seek mixed wine!  Look
                not thou upon the
                wine when it is red,
                 when it giveth its
                  color in the
                     CUP;
                    when it
                   moveth itself
                     aright.
                       At
                    the last
                 it biteth like a
        serpent, and stingeth like an adder.
```

PUZZLE POETRY

(AN)

Jewish and Moslem cultures in Medieval Spain were known for their artistic creativity. The "rage" of the 12th and 13th centuries among Moslem and Jewish poets was Puzzle Poetry. Following are some examples – answers are spelled backwards:

> Who is the sun's sister
> but serves thee at night,
> as he reaches up to heaven
> it shines like a golden spear
> but tears run down its cheeks,
> because fire gnaws at its body.
> When it is ready to die, we behead it,
> and put new life into it.
> I never saw anything else which
> laughs and cries at the same time.
>   Answer: (eldnac)   Moses ibn Ezra

> What is it that is blind but has one eye
> which men cannot live without,
> because it devotes its life to clothing others
> but itself is always naked and bare?
>   Answer: (eldeen)   Jehuda Halevi

> Lucky loves, learn our law,
> be as united as one, like us,
> even if separated a time
> we will always become one again.
>   Answer: (srossics)   Jehuda Halevi

Puzzle poems eventually drifted into other societies in medieval Europe. Following is an example from France:

> At once I am in Spain and France
> and likewise many nations more,
> While I am in my gloomy reign
> I give the world a mighty store
>   Answer: (The Nus)

Q. As I walked thro' the streets,
It was near twelve o'clock at night;
Two all in black I chanc'd to meet,
Their eyes like flaming fire bright
They passed by, nothing said,
Therefore I was not much afraid.

A. Two long lighted Links carried along the Street.

Q. Promotion lately was bestow'd
Upon a person mean and small;
Then many persons to him flow'd,
Yet he return'd no thanks at all;
But yet their hands were ready still,
To help him with their kind good-will.

A. It is a Man pelted in the Pillory.

Q. A visage fair,
And voice is rare,
Affording pleasant charms;
Which is with us
Most ominous,
Presaging future harms.

A. A Mermaid, which betokens destructi to Mariners.

Q. At once I am in France and Spain,
And likewise many nations more,
While I am in my gloomy reign,
I give the world a mighty store.

A. The SUN.

Q. Tho' it be cold I wear no cloaths,
The frost and snow I never fear,
I value neither shoes nor hose,
And yet I wander far and near:
Both meat and drink are always free,
I drink no cyder, mum, nor beer,

What Providence doth send to me,
I neither buy, nor sell, nor lack.

A. A Herring swimming in the Sea.

Q. I saw five birds all in a cage,
Each bird had but one single wing,
They were an hundred years of age:
And yet fly and sweetly sing,
The wonder did my mind possess,
When I beheld her age and strength:
Besides, as near as I can guess,
Their tails were thirty feet in length.

A. A Peel of Bells in a Steeple.

ACTIVITIES

1. Ask students to write a puzzle poem about an object or place. (S)
2. Ask students to write a puzzle poem about something they are studying in school. (S)
3. Ask students to write a puzzle poem about a famous person. It could be someone in the entertainment field or a prominent political leader. (AN)
4. Ask students to write a puzzle poem about themselves. Place all the poems in a hat and mix them up. Read the puzzle poems and the class has to guess who is the person in the puzzle poem. (AN)
5. After reading the puzzle poems in this chapter, ask students what they learn about the societies that produced the poems. (AN)
6. Ask students to write a puzzle poem about their favorite teacher. (AN)
7. Ask students to write a puzzle poem about their parents. The poem is to be shared with their parents. (AN)
8. Invite students to ask their parents to write a puzzle poem. The poem is to be brought to school. (AN)
9. Ask students to write puzzle poems about physical objects around school. (AN)
10. Ask students to write a puzzle poem about something in nature. (AN)

Noticing Poems

A good writer notices even the smallest objects within his or her environment. Improving writing skills can be linked to writing poetry by training students to focus on small details.

Ask students working in pairs to divide a piece of paper into three columns – Sights, Sounds, and Smells. Have students walk around the outside of the school and each team fills in the three columns based on what they saw, heard, or smelled when on the walk. The team is then asked to write a poem based on the theme of: "I Noticed." (K)

For example:

> I noticed the custodian
>
> Picking up crumpled pieces of white paper
>
> To place in the brown trash can
>
> What does he think about
>
> Pushing the broom
>
> Or arranging seats
>
> In empty classrooms?

Sound Poems

After the pair has completed the Sight component of the I Noticed poem, the team is asked to write a poem based on: "I Heard"   (K)

> I heard rain on the window
>
> Teeth chattering
>
> The sound of a typewriter
>
> A door closing.

Smell Poems

After the pair has completed the I Heard aspect of the assignment, they are asked to write a poem about: "I Smelled" (K)

> I smelled dirty socks
> While the aroma of lunch
> Drifted down the corridor
> And perfume entered my nose

Activities:

1. Ask students for homework to write a poem about sight, sound or smell around their home. (K)
2. Have students lie on grass and write a poem using either of the three styles. (K)
3. In pairs, have students describe the classroom in specific detail (K)
4. Ask students to use either genre to write a poem about going to a concert. (K)
5. Ask students to write a poem about taking a shower. (K)
6. Ask students to write a poem about sounds or smells of school. (AN)
7. Ask students to create a sound out of something they have and write a poem. (K)
8. Ask students to write a poem about "Silence." (AN)

Obituary Poems

An Obituary poem is a way of playing with the idea of death through a different lens. Ordinarily, we associate death with the death of a person. A creative teacher transformed the ordinary into something different by creating an Obituary Poem. Following is her example:

> Harry Toaster
>
> Died at age 6 of lung disease
>
> An overload of bread crusts did him in.
>
> A fine father
>
> Who tanned the hides of his children—Whole Wheat
>
> And Sourdough
>
> Survived by lovely wife Mabel Microwave Toaster
>
> Harry will be cremated.
>
> (Thanks to Linda Brakemeyer for this idea)

Activities:

1. Take students on a trip to a graveyard and work with etchings on tombstones. (E)

2. At the graveyard find examples of poetry. (K)

3. Ask students to take a physical object and write an Obituary Poem about it. (AN)

4. Ask students to write an Obituary Poem about an animal. (AN)

5. Ask students to write the poem they want on their tombstone. (AN)

6. Ask students to write an Obituary Poem about a famous person. (AN)

7. Ask students to write an Obituary Poem about failing a test – this can be used to help raise their grade if they did fail a test. (AN)

8. Ask students to write an Obituary Poem about losing an athletic event. (AN)

Dialogue With the Teacher

The initial lesson plan emphasized drawing upon one's senses in order to express ideas and feelings. Our concerns about test scores and accountability are important ones and can never be ignored. However, we tend to forget that the most important component of success in school is liking to be in school and engaging in activities that stimulate interest. The next lesson builds upon the prior by focusing upon visual elements in education. Howard Gardner has written extensively about Multiple Intelligences. This lesson focuses primarily on Visual Spatial aspects of the Language Arts.

Concept: Visualizing Learning

Focus: Students will visually, orally and in writing engage in critical thinking.

Standards for the English Language Arts

Standard 4: Students adjust their spoken, written and visual language to communicate effectively.

Standard 12: Students use spoken, written and visual language to accomplish their own purposes.

Teacher	Student
1. Ask students to write a paragraph in which they describe an animal or event. a. Hand out examples of Visual Writing.	1. Students write paragraph. a. Students review examples and rewrite their paragraph in a visual manner. Share with class.
2. Hand out Rebus. a. Assign students to groups. Each group is to identify an expression and transform it into a Rebus.	2. Students examine Rebus. a. Students write Rebus and present it to class to guess its meaning.
3. Hand out examples of author logos. a. Student is to select his or her favorite author and create an author logo.	3. Students examine logos. a. Students write author logo. Present to class and allow students to guess the author.

Assessment: 1. Ask students to write a visual essay employing visual writing strategies.

Multiple Intelligences: Visual Spatial
Verbal Linguistic

Visual Writing

Rebus

Activities:

1. Ask students to translate a saying into a Rebus. (K)
2. Ask students to write a letter using a Rebus as the form of communication. (K)
3. Each day begin the lesson by posing a Rebus. (K)
4. Assign a group of students to convey a current events incident via means of a Rebus. (K)
5. Ask students to write a Rebus backwards. Class must then guess its meaning. (K)
6. Create a "Stump the Class Rebus Contest." Each week a pair of students presents their Rebus to the class which must guess its meaning. (K)
7. Write a Rebus about a song. ©
8. Include a Rebus on a test for extra credit. (K)
9. Allow students for extra credit to write a Rebus on a test. (K)

Author Logos

RUDYARD KIPLING.

THOMAS HARDY.

A. CONAN DOYLE.

BERNARD SHAW.

H. G. WELLS.

Activities:

1. Identify an author and write a logo for the author. (S)
2. Create your own logo for yourself as a writer. (S)
3. Create a logo for a famous person in history. (S)
4. Create a logo for a fictional character. (S)

DIALOGUE WITH THE TEACHER

Students frequently fail to realize their everyday speech contains rich sources for creative writing. In the verbal interactions between young people are modern manifestations of ancient ways of speech. Throughout human history, people have expressed themselves in various forms of proverbs or words of wisdom. This lesson enables students to play with language as a prelude to more extensive writing.

Concept: Words and Sayings

Focus: Students will verbally and in writing express ideas utilizing theform of proverbs.

Standards for English Language Arts
- Standard 5: Students employ a wide range of strategies as they write and use different writing process elements.
- Standard 9: Students develop an understanding of and respect for diversity in language use, patterns, and dialects across cultures.

Teacher	Student
1. Ask students if anyone knows a proverb.	1. Student responses.
2. Read examples of Proverbs from around the world. a. "Which of these proverbs are familiar to you?" (AN) b. "Do you find that any of these proverbs go against your values or beliefs?" (AN) c. "In triad, write a proverb that you wish passed on to future generations." (K)	2. Students listen and comment. a. Students respond. b. Students respond. c. Students write proverb and share with class.
3. Read "Words of Wisdom." a. "Your task in a group is to create words of wisdom that you wish to give younger children." (K)	3. Students listen and comment. a. Students in group create words of wisdom.

Assessment:
1. Students obtain from parents their favorite proverb.

2. Students obtain from parents or grandparents their favorite words of wisdom.

Multiple Intelligences: Verbal Linguistic

PROVERBS

Bulgarian   God does not shave, why should I?

Japanese   Haste makes waste, but too slow is also a mistake.

Nigerian   There is no medicine against old age

Hebrew   An eye for an eye, a tooth for a tooth

Swahili   The grumbler is given more

American   Early to bed, early to rise, makes the man healthy wealthy and wise

Nupe   Force will never be without a place to sit down

Activities:

1. Ask students to offer their explanation why these proverbs were written. (AN)
2. Ask students to collect proverbs from family members. (K)
3. Ask students to write proverbs related to life in school. (E)
4. Ask students to use Internet to obtain proverbs from other societies. (K)

Words of Wisdom

The elders of society usually pass on to future generations the wisdom of their experience. Youth is forever being exposed to these words which they ordinarily regard as attempts to teach them lessons of life. Following are some examples:

All that glitters is not gold

You can't judge a book by its cover

Truth wins in the end

Beauty is only skin deep

All is well which ends well

Still water runs deep

A rolling stone gathers no moss

A friend in need is a friend indeed

If you try to please everyone, you will soon not please anyone

Activities:

1. Ask students to reverse the meaning of a wise saying. For example, "You can judge a book by its cover." ©
2. Have students create a list of words of wisdom they wish to share with adults. (K)
3. Have students collect words of wisdom from other students. (K)
4. Have students keep a diary containing words of wisdom from adults. (K)
6. Ask students to identify a list of words of wisdom they wish to place in a time capsule to leave for the future. (AN)
7. Each week assign one student to conclude the lesson with a wise saying. (K)

DIALOGUE WITH THE TEACHER

Reading and writing remain central to language arts education. This lesson focuses upon strategies of stimulating inquiry in the course of interacting with textual materials. The lesson begins with inquiry activities related to fairy tales and moves on to exploring how characters behave in stories. The object of this approach is enabling students to become aware of many ways in which one can read stories and respond to their emotional impact.

Concept: Inquiry in Reading

Focus: Students will verbally and in writing analyze behavior of characters in textual materials.

Standards for English Language Arts
Standard 2: Students read a wide range of literature from many periods and genres to build an understanding of the many dimensions of the human experience.
Standard 3: Students apply a wide range of strategies to comprehend, Interpret, evaluate, and appreciate texts.

Teacher	Student
1. Hand out 19th century version of "Goldilocks and Three Bears."	1. Students in groups read and respond to questions.
a. "How does this version compare with the one you know?" (AN)	a. Group response
b. What does the fairy tale teach you about life in 19th century America that you didn't know?" (AN)	b. Group response.
c. "How does having an old woman rather than a young girl be the center of action change the story?" (AN)	c. Group response
d. "In the story, the expression 'House of Correction' is used. Today, we say 'prison.' Is our use of 'prison' the same as their use of 'House of Correction'?" (E)	d. Group response
e. Ask students in group to write a modern version of this story. (A)	e. Students in group write a modern version and share with class.

2. Ask students in groups to identify a list of three modern characters they know very well.
   a. "In your group, brainstorm what are the ways in which your characters think about life." (K)
   b. "Select at least seven of the possible situations listed on the worksheet and apply them to your characters." (E)

3. Ask students working in groups to identify a story currently being read. "Complete the worksheet tasks using your story as the focus for the assignment."

2. Students in group compile list of characters.
   a. Students brainstorm list.
   b. Group does worksheet task.

3. Group does task.

Assessment:

1. Ask students to analyze a story being read according to either of the worksheets.

2. Ask students to analyze a character on TV on in the movies according to at least five of the questions on the worksheet.

Multiple Intelligences: Verbal Linguistic
Interpersonal
Intrapersonal

INTERACTING WITH FAIRY TALES AND STORIES

Fairy tales reflect the concerns of people at a particular time and place in the past. They originally were written for old and young and endeavored to capture interesting events and tales. Characters in fairy tales may or may not be based on real people, but they all reflect the thoughts, hopes, and fears of individuals living at a particular time. Following is the last paragraph of "The Three Bears" which appeared in Harper's New Monthly Magazine in 1875. Note that instead of Goldilocks, her character is portrayed by an old woman.

"The Little Old Woman had heard in her sleep the great rough, gruff voice of the Great Huge Bear, but she was so fast asleep that it was no more to her than the roaring wind or the rumbling of thunder. And she heard the middle voice of the Middle Bear, but when she heard the little, small, wee voice of the Little, Small Wee Bear, it was so sharp and so shrill that it awakened her at once. Up she started; and when she saw the Three Bears on one side of the bed, she tumbled herself out of the other and ran to the window. Now the window laws open, because the Bears, like good tidy Bears as they were, always opened their bed-chamber window when they got up in the morning. Out the Little Old Woman jumped; and whether she broke her neck in the fall or ran into the wood and was lost there, or found her way out of the wood and was taken up by the constable and sent to the House of Correction for a vagrants as she was, I can not tell. But, the Three Bears never saw anything more of her."

Activities:

1. Respond to questions posed in the Teacher Guide.
2. Transform an evil character in a fairy tale or story into a good person or vice versa. (S)
3. Alter one or two details in a fairy tale or story to change the story. (S)
4. Use different adjectives to describe key characters in the story or fairy tale. (K)
5. Have a famous person you know to be the one who tells the story. How would that change the story? (S)

6. Transplant a fairy tale or story from one geographic location to another and analyze how that would alter the story line. (A)
7. Introduce a new character into the story or fairy tale. (K)
8. Have students compile a glossary of terms used in fairy tales. (K)
9. Have students write a puzzle poem for a story or fairy tale. (A)
10. Create a new character who combines feelings, traits or attitudes of at least two characters in the story or fairy tale. (S)

ENTERING THE MIND OF CHARACTERS IN STORIES

An important reason for reading stories is learning the thinking processes of characters. Learning how others think enables individuals to learn more about their own self. A good book or story captures our interest not merely due to its plot, but due to its characters. Many people create visual images of characters in stories, and frequently express surprise when the story is made into a film because the characters don't fit the mental image created by reading. Following are suggestions to engage students with characters in fairy tales and stories.

1. What would be the favorite sport of the character in the story? ©
2. If the character was a student in the class, how would she/he act and think? (A)
3. Describe the type of person who would be a friend of the character. (A)
4. If the character taught this class, how would it be taught? (AN)
5. Describe the type of person the character would most likely marry. (AN)
6. What type of mother/father would the character be? (AN)
7. If the character was your brother/sister, how would they act to you? ©
8. If you met the character how would she/he act towards you? ©
9. Which movie or TV personality is most like the character? (AN)
10. If the character was President of the USA, how would she/he act or think? Identify an issue and explain the character's reaction to it? ©
11. In which ways is the character different or the same as a different character you read about in another story? (AN)
12. Change any aspect of the character's personality. Describe differences that would result from this change. (E)
13. If the character was alive today, what type of job would she/he have? ©
14. If you were asked to write something to appear on the tombstone of the character, what would you write? ©
15. What do you like best about the character? (E)

Dialogue With the Teacher

Fairy tales and stories invariably depict elements of conflict. Conflict is predicated upon the assumption that individuals, groups, and nations, have conflicting interests and goals which are the basis of disagreement. Stories can be an excellent source for students of learning why conflict exists and strategies to transform conflict into a positive experience for all. Conflict resolution is based on the assumption that a resolution is best accomplished when all parties in the conflict gain something. This lesson is designed to demonstrate how a fairy tale or a story can be used not merely to teach about conflict, but the basic components of foreign policy.

Concept: Conflict Resolution

Focus: Students will orally and in writing analyze conflict and express specific strategies to resolve a conflict.

Standards for the English Language Arts

Standard 2: Students read a wide range of literature from many periods to build an understanding of the many dimensions of the human experience.

Standard 5: Students employ a wide variety of strategies as they write and use different writing process elements to communicate with different audiences for a variety of purposes.

Teacher	Student
1. Hand out story of Snow White.	1. Students read.
2. Hand out examination of Snow White from a Conflict Resolution model which explains how each character has goals and a foreign policy.	2. Students read and ask questions about the process and method of analyzing the Snow White story.
3. Divide students into groups. Each group is to select a fairy tale or a story. The task of the group is to analyze behaviors of each character in the fairy tale or story based on the goals of the character and their foreign policy directions. The model is to be followed in the analysis process. a. Each group presents its analysis.	3. Students in groups of four select a story or fairy tale and analyze it according to the Snow White model. a. Group presents its analysis to class for comments.

4. Hand out model of how to analyze a conflict. Review and discuss all aspects of the model.	4. Students listen and ask questions about the conflict analysis model.
5. Students working in groups identify a fairy tale or story which contains conflict issues. The task of the group is to analyze the story based on the conflict model.	5. Students in group identify a fairy tale or story to be analyzed according to the conflict model. They present their analysis to the class for comments.

Assessment: 1. Students identify a story or fairy tale and analyze it with either of the two models.

2. Group work endeavors.

Multiple Intelligence: Logical Mathematical
Verbal Linguistic
Interpersonal

Hans Morgenthau: "The Future of Diplomacy"

Hans Morgenthau was a prominent writer who identified key ideas in conducting foreign policy based upon employing compromise.

His Four Fundamental Rules were:

1. Diplomacy must be divested of the crusading spirit.
2. The objectives of foreign policy must be defined in terms of the national interest and must be supported with adequate power.
3. Diplomacy must look at the political scene from the point of view of other nations.
4. Nations must be willing to compromise on all issues that are not vital to them.

His Five Prerequisites of Compromise:

1. Give up the shadow of worthless rights for the substance of real advantage.
2. Never put yourself in a position from which you cannot retreat without losing face and from which you cannot advance without grave risks.
3. Never allow a weak ally to make decisions for you.
4. The armed forces must be the instruments of foreign power, not the master.
5. The government is the leader of public opinion, not its slave.

Snow White: A Study In Foreign Policy

After the Snow White story is read, the following information is given students.

Wicked Stepmother: She is driven by an ideology that she alone possesses beauty and that anyone who seeks to challenge her beauty must be crushed and destroyed. Her foreign policy is based on the premise that only her concept of beauty can prevail in the world. Her enemy is Snow White and this person must be killed in order for the Wicked Stepmother's view of beauty to triumph.

Snow White: Her policy is to assume a defensive position when attacked and to flee from the enemy. She does not wish to engage her enemy, but seeks allies who can assist her in repelling the attack of the Wicked Stepmother. She gains temporary security from the seven Dwarfs who reinforce her desire to avoid against her enemy. In accepting the Seven Dwarfs as her allies, she places herself in geographic proximity to the Wicked Stepmother which leads to her eventually discovery by her enemy. Her alliance with the Seven Dwarfs nearly results in her death.

Seven Dwarfs: Their policy is alliance with Snow White. This alliance enables them to gain an ally with skills in housekeeping and cooking who helps them to obtain a happier life. They offer refuge to Snow White but they are basically concerned with their own national interests rather than to assist Snow White in the fight against her Wicked Stepmother.

Prince Charming: His main foreign policy goal is to find a beautiful princess to marry. Any woman who meets his criteria is a possible wife. He does not appear to waver in seeking to obtain his goal.

An Analysis Based upon Morgenthau's Principles:

There is no evidence in the story of anyone seeking to compromise. Neither Snow White nor the Wicked Stepmother ever broach a compromise. It is unclear what are the basic desires of either party which could serve as the basis of compromise. The Wicked Stepmother will not budge from desiring to be the most beautiful woman in the kingdom, and there is no evidence that Snow White is aware of this goal

Compromises and Consequences:

1. If the Wicked Stepmother accepts that her stepdaughter is the most beautiful woman in the kingdom, she gains: (a) a daughter; (b) a son-in-law; (c) an alliance with Prince Charming's nation. In order to obtain these benefits, she must surrender her ideological belief that she alone is the most beautiful woman in the kingdom.

2. If Snow White agrees to disfigure herself, she (a) gains a stepmother; (b) remains in the kingdom and has a relationship with her father. However, in reaching out to Stepmother, she will fail to meet Prince Charming and possibly fail to become Queen of a kingdom.

3. If the Seven Dwarfs make Snow White flee they lose a hard worker who is making their daily life a much happier one. They have the alternative of identifying ways they can assist Snow White in the conflict with Stepmother.

A Conflict Analysis Model

Title: Who is the Conflict between?

For example: "A Conflict Between Stepmother and Daughter Over Which One Is The Most Beautiful"

Background: In this section list all pertinent information about the conflict. How did it begin, what were the important events, etc.. The Background data is written in a factual and non-judgmental manner. For example:

1. Stepmother wished to be the most beautiful person in Kingdom.

2. Snow White was her stepdaughter.

3. A mirror told the Stepmother that Snow White was the most beautiful woman in the Kingdom.

4. Stepmother had woodsman kill Snow White.

5. Woodsman took pity on Snow White and did not kill her. Allowed her to flee.

6. Snow White took refuge with Seven Dwarfs.

7. Mirror tells Stepmother Snow White still alive.

8. Stepmother gives Snow White poisoned apple which puts her to sleep.

9. Stepmother dies.

10. Prince Charming arrives, kisses Snow White, she awakes, and they marry.

Treatment of Conflict: Describe how each party in Conflict handled the conflict.

1. Stepmother tries to have Snow White killed.

2. Snow White flees to Seven Dwarfs.

3. Stepmother makes second attempt to kill Snow White and puts her to sleep.

Results of Treatment: List consequences of how both parties treated the conflict.

    1. Snow White falls into a coma.

    2. Stepmother eventually dies.

Causal Factors: List all causes of this conflict. No attempt should be made in this section to discuss who is right or wrong. Simply list causes. In all conflicts both parties play a role in causing the conflict.

    1. Jealousy on part of Stepmother about issue of beauty.

    2. Beauty is highly valued in this society.

    3. Snow White is beautiful.

    4. Physical attributes of the Stepmother.

    5. Desire to have controlling relationship with father.

Alternative Treatment: List here all possible alternatives. Even list alternatives that probably could not work.

    1. Snow white could disfigure herself.

    2. Stepmother could accept idea she is second best in beauty.

    3. Father could be introduced for joint discussion about issue.

    4. Stepmother could arrange marriage for Snow White with prince living in distant kingdom.

Win-win Solution: Marriage with prince living in distant kingdom.

Dialogue With the Teacher

Writing is a skill that rarely in human history has captured the minds of the majority of people. People tend to write in order to communicate ideas, but this writing is more often directed at imparting information. E-mails are an interesting new form of writing and it probably is leading more people to share emotions in a written form than has previously been the case. The teaching of writing is not merely the responsibility of those teaching Language Arts and English since it should be embedded in every subject. Unfortunately, most teachers still consign teaching writing to Language Arts and English classes. This section offers a variety of ideas to stimulate writing.

Concept: Writing

Focus: Students will express ideas in written form.

Standards for the English Language Arts

Standard 8: Students employ a wide range of strategies as they write and use different writing process elements to communicate.

Teacher	Student
1. Introduce "Ideas to Stimulate Writing." Ask students to write "Opening Lines" and "Closing Lines."	1. Students working in pairs do "Opening Lines" and "Closing Lines" activity. Each team will share their ideas with the class. Class votes which team had the most boring opening lines, etc..
2. Introduce "Upside Down Writing." Ask students working in pairs to select two ways of writing Upside Down.	2. Students working in pairs select two Upside Down strategies. Share with class. Vote on who wrote the most interesting Upside Down way.
3. Introduce Oxymorons.	3. Students listen to oxymorons. Students working in triad create at least three Oxymorons to share with the class.

4. Introduce "Writing What I Like to Write About." Each student is to select one idea or add their own. If they wish allow using ideas from bad Opening Lines and Closing Lines as part of the writing activity.

5. Introduce "Collective Writing." Each Triad is to identify collectively write an Essay from list. The Triad has to write two versions. One is the worse and most boring essay and one is the most interesting.
   a. Hold class contest for most boring writing piece.

4. Each student selects an idea to write about. Students are placed in a Triad. After the individual completes the writing assignment, the other two people in triad give feedback.

5. Students in Triad write two pieces.

Assessment: 1. Students select a topic and write a boring or an interesting essay on the topic.

Multiple Intelligences: Verbal Linguistic
Interpersonal
Intrapersonal

Ideas to Stimulate Writing

A frequent complaint of students is that "I don't know what to write about." Every writer shares those feelings at one point or another. There is a simple strategy to get around being stuck – write something that is deliberately bad! If one knows how to deliberately write poorly then one is on the track to write interesting materials.

Opening Lines

The object of this activity is to deliberately write poorly. For example, the initial task is to write the most boring opening line possible.

Boring: I looked at the green leaf for a long time and the longer that I looked the greener it looked.

Cliché: It was a dark and stormy night when Madeline's car broke down in front of the evil looking castle.

Fantasy: The red hills of Torko turned black when its two moons disappeared from view in the early morning hours.

Closing Lines

Boring: She walked down the deserted street knowing she would never return to her childhood home.

Cliché: And John knew, that all's well that ends well.

Fantasy: As Mary's space ship broke through the gravitational pull, she saw her beloved planet disappear into a cloud of dust forever.

Upside Down Writing

There is nothing more interesting than to reverse things in life. We all enjoy seeing the weakling be transformed into Spider Man or Superman. Following are some writing activities designed to encourage Upside Down Writing.

1. Ask students to describe the feelings of an egg when placed in the frying pan.(A)

2. Ask students to write what the pet thinks about the family. (A)

3. Have students write about their school from the viewpoint of a school dropout. (S)

4. Have students write what darkness thinks when the lights go on. (A)

5. Have students describe a baseball or football game from the viewpoint of a baseball or football. (S)

6. Have students write a story in which cab drivers give traffic tickets to policemen. (S)

7. Have students write a story in which the principal does something wrong and has to go on detention. (S)

8. Have students write a story in which they are ordered to eat ice cream and candy by their doctor and parents. (S)

9. Ask students to write a story in which the TV set explains to parents why children should be allowed to watch as much TV as they desire. (S)

10. Ask students to write a story which explains why it became illegal to give students homework. (S)

Oxymorons

We inhabit a society in which the English language is continually abused by a host of advertisers as well as people in the ordinary walks of life. An Oxymoron is a statement that is inherently contradictory. Students can play with oxymorons to stimulate their ability to enjoy manipulating words.

Examples of Oxymorons:

1. New classic
2. Act naturally
3. Diet chocolate
4. Found missing
5. Soft rocks
6. Tight slacks
7. Alone together
8. Silent scream
9. Same difference
10. Living dead
11. Good grief
12. Almost exactly
13. Genuine _____
    (Add your own)

14. Extinct _____
    (Add your own)

15. Terribly _____
    (Add your own)

16. Definitely _____
    (Add your own)

17.   Advanced _____
               (Add your own)

Activities With Oxymorons

1. Ask students to write an essay containing at least ten Oxymorons. (K)

2. Ask students to identify examples in the daily media of Oxymorons. (K)

3. Ask students to use the Internet to find interesting examples of Oxymorons. (K)

5. Ask students to identify examples of Oxymorons in literature being studied. (K)

6. Conduct a contest for the "Worse Oxymoron That Can Be Written." (A)

Writing An Essay

On the previous pages students have been provided opportunities to experiment with differing strategies of writing. Following are several suggestions about topics for an essay. However, students should be encouraged to experiment by drawing upon previous activities. For example, "Write the Most Boring Review of a Movie" you can devise. Or, "Write About an Athletic Event Using Cliches and Oxymorons."

Activities:

1. A miniature submarine is wandering through your body. Write an essay describing what it encounters on that trip. (S)
2. Write a story about an animal that has been killed and is lying in the street. (E)
3. Write a story about what you like best about your body. Make that part of your body the hero in your story. (AN)
4. Write the most boring story that can be written about life in school. Use many clichés. (S)
5. Write about a problem you are encountering. In the story each time the problem is resolved describe how the solution creates a new problem. (AN)
6. Write a story about how you became dictator of America and how you behave. (E)
7. You are involved in a car accident with the teacher you most dislike. The judge orders the teacher to be your servant for one month. Describe what happens. (E)
8. Write a story from the viewpoint of your knees. How do they view life? (S)
9. You have just been appointed principal of the school. Write a story about what now happens in the school. (E)
10. Write a story about your encounter with a life form from another planet. ©

COLLECTIVE WRITING

Teachers know that most students fear writing. Students lack confidence in their ability to express ideas. Perhaps, writing a paper places students in the position of being entirely responsible for their actions. Collective writing is a strategy to reduce student writing anxiety by enabling a small group to collaboratively express ideas. Collective writing is <u>not</u> a substitute for individual writing, it is a support process, particularly for those who have writing anxiety. Authors are familiar with the support provided by editors who furnish concrete specific feedback regarding ways to improve a piece of writing. Collective writing can be viewed as another form of assistance.

There are several strategies to use in the implementation of collective writing. The simplest approach is pairing two students and asking them to collaborate on writing something. Another strategy is for the teacher to identify a topic. For example, "What does the bus driver think about when driving the school bus?" Each student is asked to write two sentences about this topic, but no name is to appear on the page. The teacher collects all sentences, and divides the class into groups of four. Each group receives four papers containing eight sentences. Their task is to write a two paragraph essay using the sentences they received as the foundation of their writing. After completing the two paragraphs, they are to write a third paragraph based on their collective input.

Several colleges are experimenting with web based collective writing. In one version of this model, a student writes an essay and posts it on the web page. Other students make corrections, can suggest sentences or thoughts for the essay, and provide concrete feedback. The original student is expected to rewrite the paper based on this input from peers.

Another approach to collective writing is for a student to write a paragraph. The teacher reads the paragraph and then writes his/her second paragraph. From this point on, the student is expected to complete the assignment.

A version popular with some teachers is for the teacher to identify a topic. The student in row one, seat one, writes a sentence about the topic and passes it to the student directly behind. That student adds a sentence and passes the material along until everyone in the class has added to the original sentence. Each student then receives a copy of all sentences and is asked to write a paper drawing upon this base.

Teachers frequently become upset if parents assist students in doing assignments. Nothing prevents making this a formal process. Ask students to have a parent, older brother or sister, aunt, uncle, etc...assist in the actual writing of the paper.

Students write for teachers, but rarely do teachers share their own writing with students. Why not give the class something you wrote and ask for their corrections or suggestions? This is psychologically important for students who believe that teachers know all about writing. Let them discover that the best of writers seeks help from editors and colleagues.

There are undoubtedly other approaches to fostering collective writing. For example, invite a newspaper reporter to class and ask her to discuss how a piece of writing goes through an elaborate editorial process before seeing the light of publication. Students who understand that asking for assistance is a positive sign will eventually become better writers.

Dialogue With the Teacher

There are many forms of writing taught in schools ranging from formal essays to composing letters. This book does not attempt to review what most teachers know about writing letters. Instead, this section explores aspects of letter writing ordinarily not covered in textbooks. We examine the interesting topic of writing "crazy letters." Randy Cohen, the humorist has made millions writing crazy letters to famous people. His books basically consist of his original wild letter and the responses received from famous people. For example, he suggested to the Mayor of New York that subways be converted to mobile red light districts and in 1980 he wrote presidential candidate Ronald Reagan requesting a list of his arguments against evolution as well as an autographed picture of Reagan with the monkey, Bonzo. He did receive the picture. The second example cited in this section is a variation of "Dear Abby" letters. Immigrant newspapers at the turn of the twentieth century invariable included a "Letter to the Editor" column in which people requested help regarding personal issues of their life. We provide examples. These letters constitute an invaluable source of information about daily concerns of people just as "Dear Abby" today provides a similar source.

Concept: Letter Writing

Focus: Students will verbally and in writing compose unusual letters to the Editors.

Standards for the English Language Arts

Standard 5: Students employ a wide range of strategies as they write and use different writing process elements to communicate with different audiences for a variety of purposes.

Teacher	Student

1. Hand out example of a "Crazy Letter." Ask students working in pairs to devise a similar type of letter to whomever they desire.	1. Students read letter. Discuss the letter with teacher and class.
	  a. Students working in pairs compose their own "Crazy Letter." Share with class.
	  b. Prize to best example of a Crazy letter.

2. Hand out example of letter from "Bintel Briefs." Discuss.
   a. "What do you learn about the lives of these people from their letters?"
   b. "Are any of you surprised if I said that most of these letter writers lacked formal education?"

2. Student responses to questions.

3. "Compose a letter which captures your emotions about a topic. Decide to whom your letter would be sent."

3. Individual student letter writing.

4. "During the next two weeks read letters sent to editors or Dear Abby. Select the most interesting such letter and bring to class.

4. Students identify letters and bring to class for discussion.

Assessment: 1. Write either a "Crazy Letter" or an emotional one.

Multiple Intelligences: Verbal Linguistic
Logical Mathematical

CRAZY LETTERS

A few years ago the author composed the following letter and sent it to the then Vice President. Unfortunately, he did not receive a response.

Vice President Daniel Quayle
White House
Washington D.C.

Dear Vice President Quayle:

    I read about your interest in playing golf and traveling in government planes to reach your favorite golf courses. I think you are doing a wonderful service to the American economy by showing such genuine interest in golf.

    Your critics fail to realize that every time you visit a golf course, some poor child in the ghettos is given an opportunity to caddy for you. It may well be that due to your frequent trips to golf courses that dozens of needy young people are given a chance to attend college. Your critics also fail to realize how many golf clubs and balls are needed when you play golf. This provides employment for thousands of deserving American citizens.

    I think your critics are unpatriotic. If it were not for your frequent trips to golf courses, the Japanese would probably take over the entire golf industry. You ensure that American golf companies make money and that keeps golf in America. It makes me feel real proud when I drive past a golf course that I can't afford to enter knowing that wonderful Americans like you are swinging away at the golf ball. Keep on hitting, and if you miss the ball, who cares, the important thing is that you are helping the American economy.

                                    Sincerely,

                                    Fred "Golf" Stopsky

Activities:

1. Ask students to write crazy letters to famous people. (E)

2. Have one student write a crazy letter to another student who must respond with a crazy response. (S)

3. Ask students to write Crazy Letters to school officials (warn them in time). (E)

4. Ask students to identify a silly local problem and write a crazy letter to the editor about it. (S)

5. Write a Crazy Letter to students instead of lecturing them about not doing homework. For example, "How Not Doing Homework Helps the Economy." (E)

Dear Abby

The invention of the penny newspaper in the 1840s enabled ordinary people access to daily reading materials. By the early 1900s dozens of foreign language newspapers catering to immigrants had "advice columns" aimed at immigrants to help them cope with the complexity of life in America. It is possible to learn about daily concerns of people by reading these columns. A famous example of this type of advice column was the "Bintel Briefs" which appeared in the Jewish language newspaper, the *Daily Forward*. Following are some examples from that column.

1906

Esteemed Editor

We were sitting in the shop when the boss came over to one of us and said: "You ruined the work; you'll have to pay for it." The worker answered that it wasn't his fault, that he had given out the work in perfect condition. The boss got mad and began to shout, "I pay your wages and you answer back, you dog! I should have thrown you out of the shop a long time ago."

The worker trembled, his face got whiter. When the boss noticed how his face paled, he gestured and spat and walked away. The worker said no more. Tired and overcome with shame, he turned back to his work and later he exclaimed: "For six years I've been working here like a slave, and he tells me, You dog, I should have thrown you out. I wanted to pick up an iron and smash his head in. I saw before me my wife and five children who want to eat."

Obviously the offended man felt he had done wrong in not standing up for his honor as a worker and as a human being. In the shop, the machines hummed, the irons thumped, and we could see tears running down his cheeks.

Did this unfortunate man act correctly in remaining silent under the insults of the boss? Is the fact that he has a wife and children the reason for his slavery and refusal to defend himself?

The Editor Responded:

The worker cannot help himself alone. To defend their honor as men, the workers must be well organized. There is no limit for what must be done for a piece of bread. One must bite his lips till they bleed and keep silent when he is alone. But, he must not remain alone. He must not remain silent. He must unite with his fellow workers and fight.

1906

Dear Editor:

   Last year I met a young man, a few years older than I, a businessman with a good income. He soon fell in love with me. He began to bring presents and begged me to say yes.

   Once he declared his love, my heart told me I would have trouble with him. I had no one here to advise me, and one time I wanted to leave New York to escape from him. But, I stayed and did nothing. As time went on, he began to introduce me to his friends as his fiancée. Then, he began to talk of renting an apartment. I want to state here that we are both free-thinkers, yet I didn't want to hear of just living together. But, he won out, rented an apartment, furnished it, and ordered me to move my baggage and possessions there.

   Dear Editor, its possible I should be scolded for my actions, but believe me I can't explain to myself why I obeyed him. I feel as if I'm losing my mind. I can't stand his bass voice, its as if a saw were rasping my bones. I hate him because he's a terrible egotist. When he starts talking or sits at the table with his cigar in his mouth or pokes a toothpick around his teeth after eating, I feel so disgusted that I fear I am going out of my senses.

   I have no tears left from crying. I want to save myself but I cannot. Often I choke from his talk but when he is near me I lost control and become his slaves. When he leaves, I feel disgust.

The Editor Responded:

The writer of this letter we believe can easily save herself. She could free herself if she really wanted to. By the 'really wants to" we mean if she had a strong enough character to accomplish it. The best move would be for her to free herself.

Activities:

1. Have students examine Dear Abby type columns and give their responses to the inquiries. (A)

2. Have students assume the role of an Editor and respond to letters written to the Editor of daily newspapers. (E)

3. Ask students what they learned about life in the early 1900s from these two letters. (K)

4. If the parents of any student subscribe to a foreign language newspaper, check to see if it has an "advice column." (K)

5. Assign two students each week to be the Editor. Students can write them about any aspect of what is being studied and they must respond. (S)

6. Have students pretend they lived in the past and were editor of a newspaper. For example, they lived when Columbus returned from America. One group of students pretends they were sailors on the Columbus ship and they write letters to the Editor. The other group of students responds to their letters. (AN)

7. Have characters in Fairy Tales or stories write letters to the editor. (K)

8. Allow students to write to you and you must respond. (E)

9. Ask students to assume a prominent person was the editor. They must respond to letters in the voice and manner of that person. (AN)

10. Check the Internet for foreign newspapers and investigate if they have advice columns. (K)

ADDITIONAL INQUIRY IDEAS IN LANGUAGE ARTS

1. Have students create an imaginary roundtable of authors ranging across time and cultures. For example, Shakespeare, Albert Camus, Toni Morrison, George Orwell, Thomas Mann, etc.. They could discuss a current topic.

2. Have students write dialogues related to current stories being read. For example, Cinderella talking with Holden Caulfield of "Catcher in the Rye.."

3. Have students select an episode in a text currently being read, and rewrite it from a different perspective.

4. Transform the genre of novel or fairy tale into a poem.

5. Rewrite a short story by introducing a new hero or heroine or villain.

6. Have older students rewrite a story they are reading so it can be understood by younger children.

7. Have students act as TV reporters commenting on a text being read.

8. Have students rewrite the ending of a book being read.

9. Have students create bumper stickers commenting on why people should read the book they are reading.

10. Have students write newspaper headlines about a book being read.

11. Have students write advertisements for unusual products.

12. Have students write a dialogue with their grandchildren in the year 2080 in which they discuss what they like about reading or writing.

13. Have students transform a book or story into storytelling.

14. Have students write a review of movies from a different era such as the 1930s.

15. Have students create "Daffy Definitions." For example:
    Curling Iron – An iron that curls steel bars

16. Introduce a character from the past into a modern situation.

17. Place a TV or entertainment character into something being read.

18. Find interesting dictionary definitions. For example:
    Orts –fragments of sentences or food left over

19. Have students review books from a different perspective. For example: Shaquille O'Neal reviewing a book currently being read

20. Have students create a class magazine using materials from classroom ssignments.

21. Have students maintain a current events journal about events concerning authors or poets.

22. Have students write: "The Lecture on Why Students Should Do Homework."

23. Have students review a fairy tale or story in rap.

24. Create "Amusing Dialogues." For example:
    A dialogue between a waiter and a customer who finds a fly in the soup.
    A dialogue between a parent and you as to why failing courses is good.

25. Write your interpretation of the origin of ordinary customs like shaking hands.

26. Create a dictionary that could have been written in the Stone Age.

27. Ask students to write the outline for a new course: "Self Esteem, How Not To Get It."

28. Have students develop a column entitled: "Nobody Asked Me" in which one comments on events. For example:
    Nobody Asked Me but teacher lounges always smell of sweat.
    Nobody Asked Me but short principals always look angry.

29. Ask students to write a sentence without using a specific letter of the alphabet.

30. Ask students to write their name in hieroglyphics.

31. Collect interesting memos sent in school. For example, the following is from a St. Louis middle school: "PLEASE check the XXXXX soda machine for long distance calls that are outstanding. Thanks, B.S."

32. Have students collect examples of jargon. For example, people no longer are fired, they are "downsized."

33. Have students write statements about a person beginning with the first letter of their name. For example:
    George Bush   Beltway's newest tenant.
                   Brother of another politician.

34. Ask students to create a dictionary containing euphemisms for Politically Correct. For example:
    Negative gain in test scores – Low test scores
    Temporarily displaced inventory – Stolen goods

35. Wilmont High School in order to toughen graduation standards now requires students to answer one last question before receiving their diploma. Ask students to devise that last test question.

36. Ask students to go to a garage sale and identify an object. They are to write an essay about that object.

37. Have students write a ghost story.

38. Have students write a mock interview with a person in the entertainment industry.

39. Ask students to bring in baby pictures and mix them up. Each person is to select a picture and write a story about the person in the picture.

40. Ask students to select a story in a newspaper and rewrite it.

41. Have students alter the personality of a character in a story and describe how that changes the story.

42. Ask students to identify a character in a story and imagine that individual is now part of their family. The task is writing about their family with its new member.

43. Have students write their Congressman or Senator about a current issue.

44. Ask students to write to their favorite author explaining why they enjoy reading this individual's books.

45. Ask students to identify a topic and then imagine how their favorite athlete would write about the topic.

46. Ask students to identify a topic and then imagine how their favorite TV or movie character would write about the topic.

47. Ask students to research old wedding superstitions. For example, an old Scottish belief is that good fortune for the bride is ensured if on the morning after her wedding, her mother comes to the door and breaks a currant bun over her head.

48. Ask students to give an explanation for the origin of their name.

49. Ask students to combine two TV series to create a new one. Their task is to then

outline a plot for the new series. For example, "Law and Order" combined with "Buffy the Vampire Killer" becomes…..?

50. Ask students to write their own dialogues for current cartoon strips.

51. Ask students to select a book currently being read and transform it into a comic strip. Some students can do the art work while others write dialogue.

52. Ask students to create art work depicting a book being read.

53. Ask students to transform a Shakespeare play into a cartoon strip.

54. Ask students to write the dialogue for a courtroom scene that is within a book. For example, the trail scene in "To Kill a Mockingbird."

55. Ask students to write a poem using a particular artist as a model. For example, following is a Cubist poem:

> othe
> mean
> womenw
> alkingsukps
> idedownth
> ethrongingbu
> usydissystreets
> indirtystreetsintown

CHAPTER 6

MULTICULTURALISM

Chapter Outline

1. Introduction
2. Contemporary Issues
   a. Issues Related to Moslem People
   b. Issues Related to Middle Eastern People
3. Issues Related to Hispanic People
4. Issues Confronting Irish and African Americans
5. Issues Confronting Italians in American history.
6. Issues Confronting Germans in American history.
7. Issues Confronting Jews in History
8. Slaves and Issues of Resistance
9. Multiculturalism for Younger Children

Chapter Questions are coded by Bloom's Taxonomy:
Knowledge   (K)   Analysis   (AN)
Comprehension: ©   Synthesis   (S)
Application   (A)   Evaluation   (E)

INTRODUCTION

"I want the winds of all cultures to blow freely about my house, but not to be swept off my feet by any."

Ghandi

Prior to the arrival of Europeans, a variety of peoples and cultures existed in the western hemisphere. Inhabitants of the Great Plains, forest, and arid regions of North America fashioned numerous societies in response to their geographical environments. The Navajo lived in a Hogan, the Sioux in a Tepee and the Iroquois in Long Houses. Further south, the Aztecs created a sophisticated urban society whose capital Tenochtitlan surpassed in beauty and population virtually all European cities. Still further south, the Incas constructed a marvelous road system extending 2000 miles. Multiculturalism was a way of life in this hemisphere years before Europeans arrived.

Europeans who invaded and conquered peoples of the western hemisphere came from different backgrounds, beliefs and cultures. America was populated with people with no common descent, no common system of law, no common language, and no common culture. Benjamin Franklin in 1752 warned his English compatriots of dangers posed by German immigration. "Why should Pennsylvania, founded by the English, become a colony of aliens, who will shortly be so numerous as to Germanize us instead of our Anglifying them, and will never adopt our language or customs any more than they can acquire our complexion."

The Swedes in Delaware introduced the log cabin, two people from Poland were among the original Jamestown settlers while Danes and Norwegians came to Dutch New York. Catholic Spain conquered vast areas of the western hemisphere and imposed Spanish values and beliefs. A boat load of Jews arriving in New Amsterdam in the 1650s battled prejudice while French Catholics coming to New England had to endure bigotry. Priests were executed in Puritan New England and the original Catholic inhabitants of Maryland lost their rights when Protestants gains a majority in the colony.

The term 'multiculturalism' is still without an agreed upon definition. The United States encompasses peoples from every part of the world. In the early part of the 20th century there were over 1,000 foreign language newspapers in America servicing the needs of millions of immigrants. Although there is undoubtedly an "American culture" people within this nation have consistently carved out racial, cultural, and ethnic enclaves. The expression "Melting Pot" derives from a play in 1908 by Israel Zangwill which depicts a Jewish boy and Catholic girl falling in love and encountering hostility from respective parents until they decide in America people of different backgrounds can marry and raise families. As early as 1915, Horace Kallen in the Nation magazine challenged the idea of a melting pot by coining the expression "cultural pluralism" which he believed envisioned "cultural individuality."

Multiculturalism emanates from the conception that our society encompasses varied patterns of behavior, cultural styles, and ways of belief. It recognizes that in a society of nearly three hundred million people, the umbrella is broad enough for people to play soccer or baseball, practice differing religions or none, eat at McDonalds or sushi and allow people to live together in separate neighborhoods or form multicultural living arrangements. This chapter addresses these issues.

DIALOGUE WITH THE TEACHER

In the aftermath of September 11th, many people of the Moslem faith or those whose ancestry is from Moslem societies, have encountered prejudice. This bigotry derives from exaggerated fears to misunderstandings of people whose origin is not Judaic-Christian. This lesson is designed to raise awareness of cultural differences. No "right" answer is presented in these case studies. The goal is to generate discussion regarding how people may practice different customs.

Concept: Cultural Differences

Focus: Students will be able orally and in writing identify at least three cultural differences that result in conflict.

Social Studies Standards:
Standard 1: Culture and Cultural Diversity

Teacher	Student
1. Teacher reads the case study of the Chador.	1. Students listen.
2. Students in groups are asked to identify at least two issues creating the conflict. After identifying these issues, the group is to list reasons in support or against the viewpoint.	2. Groups discuss and identify two issues and list arguments for and against. Share with class.
3. Teacher asks: a. "Can anyone identify an example in which someone who has different customs from most people in this classroom?" (AN) b. "Can anyone think of a belief you have that would create difficulty for other students in the class?" (AN)	3. Class responses.

4. Teacher hands out Case Study on "Modern American Crime."
   a. Conduct Mock Trial

4. In group, students identify arguments for or against parent behaviors. Share with class.
   a. Conduct Mock Trial

5. Teacher Poses: "Can anyone identify a belief or behavior you have that would be viewed as criminal in another society?" (AN)

5. Class discussion.

Assessment: 1. In essay form, respond to the following: "If an individual decides to live in America, they must be willing at certain points to abandon certain values or beliefs." Or, " Individuals have a right to keep their cultural beliefs if they clash with dominant American values." (E)

Multiple Intelligences: Verbal Linguistic

THE CHADOR

On Monday morning, three girls who have been raised in the Moslem faith entered Jefferson High School wearing chadors. The chador is worn by women in many Moslem societies. It is a headscarf covering hair, eyes, and neck of a woman and only allows the wearer's eyes and a small part of the face to be seen. Fatimah, Samira and Leila told the principal they wished to wear the chador in accordance with their religious beliefs.

The Koran's teaching on the subject of the chador is contained in two chapters entitled Light, and The Confederate Tribes. Verse 31 of Light says: "Enjoin believing women to turn their eyes away from temptation and to preserve chastity: to cover their adornments(except such as are normally displayed); to draw their veils over their bosoms, and not to reveal their finery except to their husbands, their fathers, their husbands' fathers, their stepsons, their brothers, their brothers' sons, their sisters' sons, their women servants and their slave girls and children who have no carnal knowledge of women. And let them not stamp their feet in walking so as to reveal hidden trinkets."

Verse 59 of the chapter of The Confederate Tribes says: "Prophets, enjoin your wives, your daughters and the wives of true believers to draw their veils close around them. That is more proper, so that they may be recognized, and not molested."

The principal, Mr. Harris pointed out to the girls that although himself an African American and sensitive to the rights of people, he had taken a strong stand against attempts by certain gangs to wear special hats and colors to school. He said if he allowed them to wear chadors, other students would wish to wear their own special headgear. Mr. Harris said public schools in America were secular institutions and religions could not impose their values upon the school. He pointed out that he already had banned Christmas trees and decorations and would not allow Jewish children to put up a Menorah. Mr. Harris gave the girls the choice of removing the Chador or going home. They decided to go home.

The next day, Mr. Harris and the Superintendent of Schools, Ellen Moskowitz were visited by a delegation of Moslem clerics who were accompanied by two rabbis. The groups insisted that chadors be allowed in accordance with the religious beliefs of students. The Moslem cleric were upset that Mr. Harris was forcing the girls to abandon their religious beliefs. Rabbi Goldberg backed this view and said the chador should be worn just as Jewish children had a right to wear a yarmulke. He argued that differences were part of the American multicultural heritage.

Questions:

1. List arguments for and against allowing the Chador in classrooms. (K)
2. Can you identify any similar issue about wearing clothes which is an issue in your school? (A)
3. Present an argument in support of either side. (E)

A Modern American Crime

Ahmed Gumel arrived in America last year after escaping from Iraq. He had opposed the government of Saddam Hussein and had to flee with his family. Ahmed and his family settled in Lincoln, Nebraska. His two daughters were sent to high school. They quickly became involved in school activities and made many friends. They had good grades and their teachers encouraged them to consider going to college.

Ahmed and his wife became very concerned about the behavior of their daughters. They spent time with girls and boys who were not of Middle Eastern ancestry. They went to parties, the movies, and engaged in many social activities. The parents were very concerned about the girls. In their culture, it was not proper for girls to date boys without permission of parents and a girl who had sexual activity prior to marriage would not be able to marry a boy from a good family. The parents feared that the freedom of American culture was ruining the lives of their daughters as well as getting them to abandon their cultural values and beliefs. They feared they were losing control over their daughters.

The parents met with other immigrants from Iraq who lived in Lincoln. Ahmed and his wife decided they would arrange marriages for their fifteen and sixteen year old daughters. They found two nice young men who had recently migrated from Iraq. One was twenty-six and one was twenty-seven. The parents paid doweries for each girl and the girls were married before a Moslem cleric a few weeks later. On their wedding nights, the girls slept with their new husbands.

The following week, both girls went to school. One of them mentioned to a counselor about getting married and being forced to sleep with their new husbands. The counselor reported the marriages on the hot line and the police were notified. The police arrested Ahmed and his wife as well as the two husbands. The two husbands were charged with rape and Ahmed and his wife were charged with assisting rape.

Questions:

1. List arguments for and against behavior of the parents. (K)
2. Is there any belief by someone in your family that others might claim violates American values or customs? (AN)
3. Present an argument in support or against either side in this conflict. (E)

Dialogue With the Teacher

During the past half century, immigration to America has shifted from European areas to those in Latin America and Asia. Chinese immigrants originally arrived in the 1840s during the California gold rush and the drive to construct a transcontinental railroad. The Chinese were the first people to arrive in America who had no connection with the Judaic/Christian heritage. Their dress, customs, and foods were outside the knowledge base of people from Europe. Many of the same complaints made against people of Hispanic origins today are reminiscent of what was hurled against Chinese and Japanese immigrants – they worked for low wages or worked very hard, etc...This lesson plan on multiculturalism focuses on the relationship between current criticisms and those frequently heard 150 years ago. Students should become aware that each generation of immigrants is charged with similar complaints – including the ancestors of students in your classes.

Concept: Enduring Prejudice in American History

Focus: Students will be able to orally, in writing, and visually list examples of how current prejudice and bigotry has historical roots.

Social Studies Standards:
Standard 1:   Culture and Cultural Diversity
Standard 4:   Individuals, Groups and Institutions
Standard 2   Time, Continuity and Change

Teacher	Student
1. Hand out "We Want Them But Don't Want Them." a. As groups report, teacher transforms list into a chart and categorizes reasons into economic, social, political factors.	1. In groups, students make a list of all reasons given to dislike people of Mexican background. Share with class.

2. Hand out cartoons on anti-Chinese feelings during the nineteenth century.
   a. As groups report, transform their comments into a chart.
   b. Pose to students: "Compare and contrast comments on both charts."

2. In groups, identify complaints about Chinese. Share with class.
   a. Class discussion.

3. Hand out dialogue between African American and Irish worker.

3. In groups, identify arguments raised by each person.

4. Hand out Case Study of lynchings of Italian Americans.

4. In group, respond to questions at end of case study. Share responses with class.

5. Hand out Dialogue about German Americans

5. In groups, respond to questions at end of Dialogue. Share with class.

6. Hand out case study on Jewish students.

6. In groups, identify discuss questions at end of case study.

7. Hand out visual images of Irish, Italians, Jews, and Japanese Americans.
   a. Create chart on ways in which these people are depicted.

7. In groups, identify issues raised by visual images.

8. Hand out Dialogue with Frederick Douglass.

8. In groups, students identify key points raised in dialogue by Douglass. Share with class.

9. Work with class to create a master chart indicates how various groups in the past and present have been the object of prejudice.
   a. Class discussion identifying what have been most common reasons for prejudice against groups.

9. Students participate in creating the chart.

Assessment:

1. Write an essay on: "Compare and contrast discrimination and prejudice encountered in American history by at least three ethnic, racial or cultural groups." (AN)

2 Interview at least eight people regarding their ideas about any cultural, racial or ethnic group. (K)

3. Develop an action plan to be submitted to the Principal or School Board regarding ways our district can confront racial, ethnic, or cultural prejudice. (S)

Multiple Intelligences: Verbal Linguistic
Visual Spatial

"We Want Them But We Don't Want Them"

Steve and Mary Macon decide to earn some money this fall in order to help pay for a car both are willing to share owning. Their parents told them they could get a car provided both earned $1,500 to help pay for car insurance. They went to a hardware store owned by a neighbor, Mr. Elliot, who they recently heard tell their parents he needed some help in the store. Steve and Mary entered the store and approached Mr. Elliot.

Steve: Mr. Elliot, Mary and I heard you say you needed help this fall on weekends. We would like to apply for a job.

Elliot: You both are terrific youngsters and I would like to help. In all honesty, money is tight and I need someone to work off the books.

Mary: What does it mean to work off the books?

Elliot: If I don't officially list you as working, I don't have to pay certain government taxes and I don't have to pay the minimum wage.

Steve: You mean we wouldn't get the minimum wage like they pay at McDonalds?

Elliot: Right. To tell you the truth, I just talked to a couple of Mexican guys who are here illegally and they are willing to work for half the minimum wage rate.

Mary: Gee, that's only about $3.50 an hour!

Steve: That's a very low wage. We need a lot more than that.

Elliot: I'm willing to hire both of you off the books at half the minimum wage. If you don't want it, I'll give it to the illegal immigrants. That night at dinner, Steve and Mary told their parents about the meeting with Mr. Elliot.

Mary: Steve and I went to see Mr. Elliot about a part time job, but he said he would only pay us about $3.50 an hour because he wanted to keep things off the book. He said he was hiring some Mexican workers who were here illegally.

Dad: That's terrible. You two live in this community, we pay taxes, and Mr. Elliot wants to get around the law by hiring foreigners who work for next to nothing. These Mexicans come here and take jobs away from decent Americans.

Mom:	I bet these illegal people work for a while and then go on welfare and collect money. What is this country coming to anyway?
Steve:	Yesterday in our English class we were reading some poetry written by an African American. In the poems he describes how African Americans were forced to work for low wages just to get jobs. Is it wrong for me to blame these Mexican workers?
Dad:	No, you are not prejudiced. People born in this country obey the laws. These illegal Mexican immigrants hurt everyone by working for low wages. I wish we never let these people enter our country. Every worker suffers because they refuse to obey the laws and work for minimum wages. It's not fair.
Mom:	I think people born in this country should have first call on jobs. It's our country and yet these foreigners come here and take jobs from Americans. I passed by the Walnut Creek area where they live. It is a filthy slum. I guess they'll be asking for a tax increase to pay for cleaning it up.

Questions:

1. Identify the main concerns of this family regarding Mexican workers. (K)
2. Identify a similar view you have heard expressed in your own community about certain people. (S)
3. Assume you were on a City Council in your area and the question came before the City Council of creating an area where people could gather and solicit work regardless if they were from your community or came from outside, how would you vote? Explain your reasoning. (A)

A Dialogue Between An Irsih Worker And An African American Worker – 1850s.

African American: Hey, Paddy B'Hoy, where are you going in such a rush? Here, have a drink with me.

Irish Worker: Whiskey, it is. Ahh. I wouldn't mind even drinking with the likes of you.

African American: Why do you talk to me like that? We both work here on the docks, we help one another. What bothers you so much about me being here?

Irish Worker: I got nothing against you in particular. You're a fine fellow. It's not you, it's the others. I mean, just imagine if they freed them slaves and they come up here in droves. What would become of me? And, by the way, what would become of you?

African American: I'd rejoice if slavery ended and my brothers and sisters were free from the bondage of slavery. If they came here, at least they would be free.

Irish Worker: Ah, so what you want is to make slaves of free white workers. If the slaves came up north, they'd work for slave wages. The bosses would use them to put down white workers and pay low wages. And, by the way, you'd also lose your job. As long as there are free white workers in this country, then there will be freedom for all.

African American: I was reading in the paper that one of your great Irish leaders, Daniel O'Connell said that no man should be a slave. He said no man can be free if another man is still a slave. He said he would not trade the independence of Ireland if it meant that blacks were still slaves in America.

Irish Worker: Daniel O'Connell is a great man and some day he will get Ireland it's freedom. America is a free country because its white workers are free and have the right to vote. If we end slavery, then thousands of slaves will come North and they will destroy the power of free white workers. Daniel O'Connell simply doesn't understand this country.

African American: But, your own Pope has come out against slavery! I don't understand your line of reasoning. You want freedom for

	workers. I'm a worker. You want America to be a free country. But, America has slavery which means it can't be a free country until slavery is ended.
Irish Worker:	B'Hoyo, B'Hoyo, its white workers that make this country free. If we freed the slaves they'd come north and take jobs from free white workers and end freedom in this nation. Slaves don't know how to act like free men, they are used to obeying orders. They would do as the boss ordered and soon we would all be slaves. A free white man acts like a free man. You are a decent fellow, but you really can't think or act like a free white man. You need free white men to make sure you still have your freedom. You mention the Pope. The Pope is an important man, but he lives in Italy and doesn't understand America.
African American:	I'm trying to understand you, Paddy. When you came here, most jobs in New York like barbers or servants were held by black men. Your people were so poor they took jobs for low wages and we black men lost our jobs. I know how you were treated. Americans treated you like dirt and look down on you. Since, you faced all this prejudice can't you at least understand how we black people feel?
Irish Worker:	You don't know what it's like to face prejudice. We Irish were the lowest of the low. They made fun of how we spoke. They called us black people and treated us like them. They made our women become servants because we were so poor. Look, my friend, the plantation owner wants your people kept in slavery. The only reason rich people in the north want to end slavery is so they can enslave the Irish workers.
African American:	Many of my fellow African Americans support freedom for Ireland. We want the Irish to be free of English rule. Why can't you back freedom for black people in America? We are all in this together, let's help one another rather than be separated.
Irish Worker:	The English treat the Irish people as though they are slaves just like they treated the colonists as slaves. We Irish fight back because we are free white people who will never be

	enslaved again. You black people can't help us. If slavery ended tomorrow in America, thousands, no, millions of former slaves would come north and take our jobs. If we lost our jobs we couldn't fight for Irish independence. I hate slavery. I don't want any man to be a slave. It's because I hate slavery that I don't want any man to be a slave. If slavery ended, white workers would soon become slaves of the bosses. The time is not right to end slavery. Maybe, you black people should go back to Africa. Then, you wouldn't be a problem to freedom in America.
African American:	So, you are saying since slavery would hurt the Irish and their desire for Irish independence, we black people should remain slaves. I was born in this country and I'm an American. I don't intend to go to Africa.
Irish Worker:	I'm not doing anything that will make white workers slaves in this nation. This great country will only be free as long as there are free white workers to defend its liberties.
African American:	I think you should listen to your Pope who wants to end slavery. Maybe, your people have suffered too much and you are too afraid. I don't know, I don't understand.
Irish Worker:	We Irish are not afraid of anyone or anything. There is only one thing on our mind and that is freedom for the working people of this country.

Questions:

1. Identify the main points raised by each person in this dialogue. (K)

2. Is it possible to dislike a group of people but like an individual from the group? (AN)

3. Is this discussion similar to discussions heard today? ©

A Case Study Of The Killing Of The Chielf Of Police In New Orleans

On the night of October 15, 1890, at 11:20 p.m., Chief of Police David Hennessy was shot several times at the front door of his home. A few hours later the police arrested Pietro Monasterio and twenty other people of Italian descent. Although most were later released, twelve Italian Americans were charged with the death of Hennessy. Trial date was set for February 28, 1891.

The prosecution charged that a man named Macheca had rented a shanty near the home of Hennessy for his friend Monasterio. The District Attorney said a boy named Asperi Marchesi was posted to notify the gang of Italians – Antonio Scaffedi, Antonio Marchesi, Manuel Polliz and Antonio Bagnetto – of Hennessy's arrival. The prosecution said that Asperi whistled to announced the arrival of the Chief of Police at which time the gunmen opened fire and killed him. The prosecution claimed Italian Americans had a secret whistle which was used in cases of crime.

The defense offered evidence indicating the men charged with the crime were elsewhere at the time of the shooting. The jury, headed by a man named Seligman, deliberated a few hours and on March 10, 1891 rendered a verdict of Not Guilty. Judge Baker examined the paper stating the verdict, grimaced in the direction of the jury to indicate his displeasure and announced the men would be held on other charges and remanded them to the parish prison.

Newspapers in New Orleans were furious at the verdict. They urged citizens to render justice in any way they deemed possible. A mob gathered around the prison which held the Italian Americans. Some boys in the crowd began to whistle claiming it was the secret Italian whistle. The boys shouted: "Who killa de chief?" to which they responded: "the Italians." Captain Davis who was in charge of the prison was told by a delegation they were coming for the Italian Americans. Speakers urged action. As one said: "When the courts fail, the people must act. What protection is there left when the very head of our Police Department is assassinated in our very midst by the Mafia Society and his assassins are turned loose on the community? Are there men enough here to set aside the verdict of that infamous jury, everyone of whom is a perjurer and a scoundrel."

The District Attorney told the mob: "When the law is powerless, the rights delegated by the people are redelegated back to the people and they are justified in doing what the law has failed to do." He then led the mob to the jail and demanded that Captain Davis turn over the prisoners. Captain Davis refused. The mob pushed him aside, entered the jail and began shooting the Italian American prisoners. For example, Jim Caruso was shot forty-two times. A few of the prisoners were hung on lamp posts. As the mob walked away, they were cheered by women and children gazing from balconies.

The New York Times, while deploring the lynchings, said the people of New Orleans had to use force to "inspire a wholesome dread to those who had boldly made a trade of murder. Compared to the Sicilian murderers, the American murderers were men of nobility." Its readers were assured that henceforth there would be greater respect among Italians living in New Orleans for law and order.

The Italian government protested the lynchings, but President Harrison said he lacked power to remedy the situation. He allocated a cash indemnity of $25,000 to families of the murdered men. Congress denounced his action and some congressmen threatened to bring impeachment hearings against the President. Harrison said the lynchings were an offense against law and humanity."

No one was ever brought to trial or punished for their actions or the lynchings.

Questions:

1. What do you find most surprising about this incident? (AN)
2. Based on information in this case study, what appear to be images held by some Americans in the 1890s regarding Italian Americans? ©
3. Do you agree or disagree with the District Attorney's statement that "the people" have a right to remedy what they consider to be a miscarriage of justice by courts? (E)
4. Are any of the images emanating from this case study still alive in contemporary America? (E)

German Americans And Temperance In Nineteenth Century America

Following is a hypothetical discussion that might have taken place in the 1860s between a German American and Mr. Dow, a leader of the Temperance Movement.

Dow: I have asked to meet with you to discuss how your people can begin to act more like Americans and end their Old World customs.

Schultz: I have heard many good things about you, particularly your work to end alcoholism in this nation among those under the influence of the demon rum. I am not a drunkard, I simply enjoy a good glass of beer. I regret if drinking beer bothers you, but it is an old custom in Germany.

Dow: Unfortunately for you, this is America, not Germany. Our Temperance Movement was making great progress until you Germans arrived with your beer. Your brewery is an evil place and does the devil's work. Don't you Germans realize that alcohol is ruining our nation and driving thousands to poverty? If Germans had a sense of decency they would destroy these evil beer breweries and join God fearing Americans in the fight to end alcohol.

Schultz: My friends and I drink beer because we like its taste and we enjoy spending time at the tavern talking and discussing issues of the day. On Sunday, our families gather at the tavern for social purposes. During these social times, we drink our beer, laugh and have a good time. This is a free country and each immigrant group has a right to live by its own cultural standards. I don't tell you what to drink or how to spend your leisure time. Please don't tell me.

Dow: This nation was founded by people who were not German. You are a guest in our land and as a guest you should abide by our culture and customs. You either become an American or leave this nation. You have brought evil to our nation with your beer. Your beer corrupts our youth who now spend time drinking

	beer rather than working. If you want to live as Germans, go back to Germany. If you want to live as Americans, then a bide by our customs and traditions.
Schultz:	First of all, there were Germans living in America two hundred years ago. But, that is not the issue. The issue is that each immigrant group has a right to bring its own customs and traditions and values to America. Manufacturing or selling or drinking beer is legal. My customs do not interfere with your life so why do you seek to interfere with mine? This is a free land and each group has a right to live in the manner it desires.
Dow:	We can never become an American nation if our lives are polluted by the customs of aliens living in our midst. You sit in taverns on Sunday, a day of rest and you drink beer. Even worse, your wives and children are at the tavern learning to become drunkards. We have a national problem with alcoholism and you people are making it worse. You should spend Sunday at church, not drinking.
Schultz:	Beer drinking and social gatherings go hand-in-hand among my people. We drink beer because it tastes good and it relaxes everyone. Oh, perhaps, sometimes an individual gets drunk, but that is the exception, not the rule. Look, if other Americans enjoy German beer, so be it. No one forces them to drink it. What I don't understand is why you welcome support of Germans in the fight to end slavery, but you hate us because of some of our customs. After all, we are among the strongest opponents of slavery, you are an Abolitionist, and yet you hate us!
Dow:	Of course, we welcome your support in the struggle to rid this nation of the cursed practice of slavery. I commend German Americans for their Abolitionist views. But, your beer drinking is also a curse upon this nation. One good deed does not eliminate the evil that you have brought to this great nation which gave you welcome when you fled Germany. If you wish to truly be an American, then adopt American values, customs and traditions. If not, I warn you that one day America will repay the ingratitude of Germans by inflicting pain upon you people.

Questions:

1. Identify the main issues between the two men. (K)

2. Mr. Dow claims that newly arrived immigrants should alter their customs and adopt those of America. Do you agree or disagree with this viewpoint? (AN)

3. Can you identify any contemporary examples of similar differing views? (A)

4. On one hand, Mr. Dow welcomes German support in the Abolition movement, but, on the other hand he hates their beer drinking. Have you ever encountered examples in your life of someone who likes one thing about a person, but hates them because of something else? (A)

5. In which ways did Mr. Dow's claim that revenge would be taken against German brewery owners come true? (AN)

Should We Let Them In?

The following dialogue might easily have taken place at an Ivy League college during the 1920s.

Dr. Hall: Gentlemen, we have much to do today. We have to reach final decisions on which students will be accepted for the next academic year. Before we begin let me emphasize that we have responsibilities to our alumni and to those who provide financial support to this institution. They want an entering class composed of young men of high moral and academic standards.

Mr. Anders: Let me begin with the individual who scored highest on our entrance exam. His name is Smelsky and he comes from the Bronx High School of Science in New York City. He was an "A" student, but we have little evidence he was involved in outside activities. In his letter, Mr. Smelsky claims he had to work after school and thus could not become involved with clubs and sports.

Prof. Essex: Ah, another one of the Jewish hard workers. The Hebrew people are an industrious race. They are always studying and trying to out perform other people.

Dr. Hall: It is important to maintain our standards. My question is whether this Mr. Smelsky understands the importance of team play and has good social manners to fit into our environment. We don't need academic grinds who spend their time studying rather than engaging in social activities.

Prof. Essex: There is something very unfair about these people like Smelsky. These Hebrews think only of grades and high test scores. I find these people very well prepared academically, but they lack social graces. Other students who understand that college is also a time to make the right connections in life are at an unfair disadvantage when confronted with the Smelskys of the world who ignore our clubs, our organizations and our sports; instead they spend their time studying. How can our men of high moral value compete equally with these creatures?

Mr. Anders: In fairness to Mr. Smelsky, his family is poor. They work in the garment district and he obviously works after school to help his family.

Dr. Hall: Isn't it obvious that if he came here, Mr. Smelsky would still have to work to make ends meet. He would never be accepted by any fraternity and would always be an outsider. You know, some of my friends are of the Jewish persuasion and I have even invited them to my home for dinner. But, they are refined and cultured Jews, not the foul smelling, poorly dressed and uncouth characters who fill the streets of New York or Boston or Chicago. We have to consider "appearances" in our selections. We have to be certain students will easily adjust to our culture.

Prof. Essex: That is an important point, Dr. Hall. My concern is that this young man will graduate with a degree from our prestigious institution and use it to get a job. He will wind up with some money-grubbing law firm or be involved in low class business activities. He will never contribute financially or socially to this college.

Mr. Anders: The Admission Office received a letter from a Jewish organization named Bnai Birth and they expressed concerns that our institution has a quota system that restricts the number of Jews admitted. They want to know if such a quota system exists and they threaten to go public about it.

Dr. Hall: That's just what I'm talking about. These Hebrews are trying to push their way into our lives. They are an aggressive race that seeks to compete against Christians. They view us as their enemies. I will not be pushed around by a group of foreign born people.

Prof. Essex: I am certain they would protest if we admit the child of an alumni who has lower test scores. They will probably yell discrimination. I think we have to take a stand in favor of the quota system. Our primary responsibility is to this institution and to our alumni. If we allow in every Jew who has a high test score this college will shortly become a Jewish college!

Dr. Hall: Absolutely! Our present system is very generous. We allow 2% of students entering to be Jewish. Mr. Anders, please inform this Bnai Brith organization that many colleges will not even accept one Jewish student, but we are very liberal. We are a democratic institution. Why, uring the nineteenth century we even had three Negro students who graduated. How dare they

	try to claim we are bigots. We have always been at the forefront in giving opportunities to minorities.
Prof. Essex:	As I understand this situation, if we accept this Mr. Smelsky we go over the quota limit for Jewish students. If we accept him that means the child of one of our alumni cannot attend. That is not fair. The other Jewish students we are accepting this year come from good Jewish families who have wealth and culture. We are a Protestant college and we already allow Catholics to enter. First Catholics, then Jews, who knows what will become of us. I guess the next thing will be requests from Oriental students!
Dr. Hall:	I think people like this Mr. Smelsky don't understand they live in a Protestant society. This institution represents the best in that society. We can not allow these people to flood into our college. We must take a stand. Enough. Now, let us turn to these fine young men who are children of our alumni. I am certain they will be a credit to this college.

Questions:

1. List the arguments raised by the Admissions Committee for their decisions about declining to allow Mr. Smelsky to enter the college. (K)

2. They raise the issue of protecting their alumni. Do you agree or disagree with the view that children of alumni should be given special preference in being accepted to a college? (E)

3. Do you find any modern parallels to this discussion in the 1920s? (AN)

AN INTERVIEW WITH FREDERICK DOUGLASS: AFTER THE FACT

This fictitious interview examines the topic of how do people enduring a horrible experience, cope with brutality.

Interviewer: Mr. Douglass, it has often been said that slaves lacked the drive to rebel. Except for a few cases, there were relatively few slave revolts. Why?

Douglass: We have to differentiate between "resistance" and "rebellion." There were some armed slave rebellions, but obviously, no successful revolt happened among slaves. However, millions engaged in resistance to slavery.

Interviewer: The reality is that only a handful of slaves took up arms to gain their freedom. Does this indicate the claims of slave owners that slaves welcomed slavery has some foundation in truth?

Douglass: I often heard such arguments in my lifetime. Slave owners claimed we black people welcomed the tyranny of slavery. Ridiculous. The first person killed in the American Revolution was a Negro. Negroes served in the Continental army under Washington. Over 200,000 served in the Union army during this past Civil War. We have always resisted oppression.

Interviewer: Why do you return to this idea of resistance?

Douglass: Critics unfairly criticize slaves. It was difficult for slaves to use arms to fight back. Guns and ammunition were difficult to obtain. If slaves used arms it meant they would have to flee to forests for safety. If large numbers fled, it would create serious problems of food and supplies. If an individual slave fought and fled, then his family was punished.

Interviewer: So, what do you mean by resistance?

Douglass: I was once a slave. I resisted every day. I slowed my work rate – that was resistance. We slaves kept our families healthy, took care of children, tried to be loving parents – that was resistance. The slave owners wanted us to act like animals. We refused. We kept our dignity as people – that is resistance.

Interviewer: But, is that really resistance? If you didn't like slavery, why not escape? After all, people like Harriet Tubman escaped.

Douglass: Ms. Tubman is a brave individual and did wonderful work helping a few people to escape. The journey to freedom was difficult. Unlike white indentured servants we could not easily blend in with other people. Imagine making a journey of 500 miles or more with your family. You travel at night, sleep in forests, scrounge for food and know that every white person will turn you in for a reward. If your child gets sick, what then? Remember, if I escaped and my family remained, they would be punished.

Interviewer: Yes, there were problems. But, if slaves really hated slavery then more should have escaped. People like Harriet Tubman prove slaves could escape. Perhaps, slaves were too passive.

Douglass: I have heard those comments throughout my life. Slave owners claimed we were passive or that we enjoyed slavery. They use those arguments to justify keeping people in slavery. We fought back. Many of us learned how to read and write—that was resistance. We had our own church services, we discussed important topics – all unknown to slaveowners. Interviewer: Aren't you the exception to the rule? After all, how many slaves resisted?

Douglass: History books ignore our resistance. Let me quote from Solomon Northrup who wrote a wonderful account of his life as a slave: Winding the lash around his hand and taking hold of the small end of the stock, he walked up to me and ordered me to strip. "Mr. Tiboats," said I, looking him boldly in the face, "I will not." He sprang at me seizing me by the throat with one hand, raising the whip with the other, in the act of striking. Before the blow descended, I caught him by the collar of the coat and drew him closely to me.. In the frenzy of my madness, I snatched the whip from his hand… I cannot tell how many times I struck him. Blow after blow fell fast and heavy upon the wiggling form. At length, he screamed and called upon God for mercy. But, he who had never shown mercy did not receive it.

Interviewer: But, isn't that an exception, rather than the rule. How many refused a lashing?

Douglass: There are hundreds of narratives written by people who were slaves. In virtually each one there are descriptions of resistance to brutality. For example, John Thompson in his narrative writes: One day the slaves were gathering corn which Ben was carting to the barn. The overseer thought Ben did not drive his oxen fast enough. The overseer struck Ben upon the head with the butt of the whip felling him to the ground. Ben sprang from the ground, seized his antagonist by the throat, and then jumping upon his breast, he commenced beating him until he nearly killed him… The master forbade the overseer from meddling with Ben.

Interviewer: It's difficult for some white people to accept that slaves resisted.

Douglass: White people wish to maintain the image of the passive slave. That image strips us of our dignity. It is part of the attempt to strip the black man and woman of their African culture. We maintained our African heritage in recalling stories and songs. The highest form of resistance is to maintain your dignity, your culture, and your values. Whites enslaved our bodies, but they could never enslave our minds.

Questions:

1. List the main points cited by Douglass regarding forms of resistance. (K)
2. Do you agree or disagree with the Douglass view that resistance doesn't have to mean fighting? (AN)
3. Are there any modern examples in which people experiencing oppression are accused of acting passive? (A)
4. In which ways in your personal life can you resist without using violence? (E)

DIALOGUE WITH THE TEACHER

Multiculturalism offers an amazing array of visual resources for teaching. Throughout history, groups, individuals, and situations have been portrayed in graphic visual terms. Our earliest sources of human communication undoubtedly are cave paintings by our Cro-Magnon ancestors. This lesson plan focuses upon the visual manner in which earlier Americans depicted immigrants from Asian societies. It has been estimated that of the 5,000 people lynched in America between 1865-1950 about 900 were people of Asian backgrounds – about twenty were Italian Americans. The only people to be specifically barred from entering America were the Chinese in the passage in 1882 of the Chinese Exclusion Act. (This lesson is for secondary students)

Concept: Visual Imagery of Asian Americans

Focus: Students will analyze visual materials that depict Asian Americans in nineteenth and twenty century America.

Social Studies Standards:
Standard 1: Culture and Cultural Diversity
Standard 4: Individual and Group Identity

Teacher	Student
1. Hand out sketches. a. Pose to students: "Which stereotypes of Asians are in these sketches?" "How do those stereotypes compare with what many non-Asians have of Asian Americans today?"	1. students in group identify main images emerging from sketches Share with class. a. Students respond.
2. Hand out sketches about Seattle and attacks on Chinese.	2. Students in groups identify key ideas in sketches. Share with class.
3. Hand out sketches about Japanese issues in San Francisco. a. Pose to students: "What do you find most surprising about these sketches?"	3. Students in group analyze sketches and identify key issues. a. Students respond.

4. Pose to students: "We have just examined sketches made about Asian Americans over a hundred years ago. Does anyone find today attitudes toward people of a group in America that is similar to what you have just seen?"

4. Students respond for class discussion.

Assessment:

1. Students respond to: "You have just examined stereotypes about people from a hundred years ago. Write an essay in which you explore any examples in your own mind of stereotypes about other people. In your essay, attempt to analyze why you have these feelings. You will not have to share this essay with anyone besides myself."

Multiple Intelligences: Visual Spatial
Logical Mathematical
Verbal Linguistic

THE TABLES TURNED.
How our Streets will look next Summer as the result of the Chinese invasion.

Multiculturalism ◊ 239

WHAT SHALL WE DO WITH JOHN CHINAMAN?
WHAT PAT WOULD DO WITH HIM.   WHAT WILL BE DONE WITH HIM.

THE MARTYRDOM OF ST. CRISPIN.

THE ANTI-CHINESE RIOT AT SEATTLE, WASHINGTON TERRITORY.—Drawn by W. P. Snyder, from Sketches by J. F. Whiting, of Seattle.—[See Page 145.]
1. Driving Chinamen on Board of the Steamer.   2. Marching under Guard to the Court-house.

Drawn by C. R. Weed.
CALIFORNIA LEGISLATOR: "I guess *I* know what an Alien is!"

OUR VISITORS.

JONATHAN. "Ah! Mister, and, pray, what can I do for you?"
JAPANESE VISITOR. "If you please, I would like to borrow a little of your light."

DIALOGUE WITH THE TEACHER

Following is a lesson plan about multiculturalism geared toward primary age children. It can often be difficult engaging young children with brutality and hatred because their life experience has yet to encounter things many adults have encountered. Actually, in their daily lives young children do experience many of the issues dealt with in multicultural education, but the lens and focus differ. For example, many in moving to a new school encounter the issue of "the stranger." If their family is of a differing ethnic, cultural or racial background than most of their fellow students, the result may be slights and remarks that hurt. Many children understand being "the outsider" when denied being chosen to play or not invited to a party. (This lesson plan is for elementary age students)

Concept: We are all strangers

Focus: Students will orally, visually, and in writing discuss the meaning of being a stranger or someone who is different from the majority as well as how today we eat, dress and play like people throughout the world.

Social Studies Standards:
Standard 1: Culture and Cultural Diversity

Teacher	Student
1. Hand out a sheet with the following foods foods for breakfast. Ask students: "How would you feel if your mom and dad gave you these foods for breakfast?" (AN)	1. Individual responses.
a. In groups, ask students to rearrange these foods for being eaten for breakfast, lunch and dinner.	a. In groups, students arrange list of foods to indicate which might be eaten for breakfast, lunch or dinner.
b. Pose to students: "Let's pretend we lived in the cold north like Eskimos. Which foods on this list would not be possible to eat because the animals that make the food can't live in the cold north?" (K)	b. Individual student response.

2. Hand out "The Horse and Giraffe."

3. Ask students to check the labels on their clothes. List on the blackboard names of countries that contributed to the clothes in the room.

4. Ask students to keep logs on food they eat over a one week time period. Work with students to identify origin of these foods.

5. Hand out "The Rabbit, the Squirrel and the Fox."

2. In groups, respond to questions and activities at the end of the story.

3. Individual responses.

4. In groups, make chart where the foods came from originally.

5. Students read story and respond to questions and activities.

Assessment:

1. In pairs, draw a picture story of a boy and girl who make friends with a new boy or girl who comes to school. (A)

2. Student comments during discussions.

Multiple Intelligences Verbal Linguistic
Visual Spatial

BREAKFAST AROUND THE WORLD

Jane eats caterpillars for breakfast.

Doug has a roll and piece of bologna for breakfast.

Alice has soup for breakfast.

Ibrahim has rice for breakfast.

Sally has eggs and toast for breakfast.

Suku eats friend pineapple for breakfast.

Nanu eats fish for breakfast.

Questions:

1. Select one of the above breakfast foods and explain why you would not eat it for breakfast but it would be OK to eat it for lunch or dinner. (AN)
2. Rearrange the foods and place them where in the day you would like to eat them. ©
3. If there is one food you would not eat, explain why you would not eat it. (AN)
4. In groups, create a new breakfast that no one has ever eaten before. (A)

The Horse And The Giraffe

Once upon a time there was a farmer who had a horse named Ben. He allowed Ben to wander around the pasture and eat the grass. The farmer was kind to Ben and let him wander around and play and eat all day long. The horse loved the pasture where he could eat the grass. He really enjoyed eating leaves that fell from the trees. Each day, he went out into the pasture, felt the warm sun on his body, leaned down and ate grass and leaves.

One day, the farmer got some interesting news. A cousin who lived in Africa decided to send him a giraffe as a gift. The farmer was happy to receive the gift and looked forward to receiving the giraffe.

A few weeks later the farmer went to the train station and there was his present — a giraffe! The farmer looked at the tall neck of the giraffe and noticed that when the giraffe smiled his smile was high up in the air.

The farmer got the giraffe home and the next day he let the giraffe go out into the pasture where Ben usually walked. Ben was in the pasture eating his grass and leaves. Suddenly, this strange creature came before his eyes. Ben thought it was a strange looking horse. He had never seen a horse like this one. The horse had a long neck. "What a strange looking horse," though Ben.

The giraffe walked by Ben and came to a tree. He reached his long neck up into the branches of the tree and began eating the leaves. Ben walked over to the giraffe. He raised his head, but could not reach the leaves.

Ben became frightened. The giraffe was eating all the leaves. Ben was upset because if the giraffe ate all the leaves none would fall to the ground.

Questions and Activities:

1. Identify all the problems that might come about between Ben and the Giraffe. AN)
2. Identify ways in which the horse and giraffe can live in peace and avoid having a conflict or argument over the leaves. (AN)
3. Draw a picture story – with words if you wish – that shows how the horse and Giraffe learned to live peacefully together. (A)

The Rabbit, The Squirrel And The Fox

It was a warm day and Dora, a black and white rabbit went out into the field for some food. She came across some nuts that had fallen on the ground. Rabbits usually liked to eat carrots, but Dora was a curious rabbit and decided to try eating a nut. It tasted delicious thought Dora. She went around the tree where she found the first nut and gathered up all the nuts she could find. "I'm going to take all these nuts back to my home and share them with my parents and friends," thought Dora.

Suddenly, a dark brown squirrel came up to Dora. "Excuse me, Ms. Rabbit," said the squirrel whose name was Mike, "you are taking the nuts that belong to the squirrels. We need those nuts for our food."

"Really," replied Dora. "I decided that I like nuts and I intend to take all these nuts. You will have to find nuts some other place. Just remember, I'm a rabbit and we rabbits are bigger and stronger than any squirrel."

"Well, it is not fair for you to take the nuts just because you are bigger and stronger than me. You rabbits can eat other food, but we squirrels need the nuts. You see, we squirrels gather nuts and store them away for the winter so we can have food when there are no nuts on the ground. I really would appreciate it if you would leave our nuts alone."

"Finders keepers is the old slogan," replied Dora. "And, since I am bigger and stronger than you, there is nothing you can do about it."

"Well, I'll get my other friends together and we can fight to keep our nuts."

"Yeah," said Dora, "just try it. I'll get the rabbits together and we can easily beat up you weak little squirrels. Get away from here."

Mike knew the rabbit was bigger and stronger and there was no way he could fight this tall creature. He hung his head down and went up the tree to tell his parents that there was a new enemy who was taking their food.

Dora had just about gathered all the nuts when she heard a noise. She turned and saw a red fox named Peter with sharp white teeth staring at her.

"What are you doing?" said Peter.

"I'm gathering these nuts for my family and friends," replied Dora.

"Hmm," said Peter. "Let me try eating one of those nuts." Peter reached down and took a nut from those Dora had gathered. "Wow, these are delicious nuts," said the fox.

"They really are," said Dora.

"I thought the squirrels usually ate these nuts," said Peter.

"Yes, they usually do, but today I decided that these nuts are just too delicious for squirrels to eat. I intend to give them to the rabbits.

"Really," said Peter. "Well, I think these nuts are just too delicious for rabbits to eat. I thank you for gathering them up. Now, I'll take them back to my fox friends."

"That's not fair," said Dora. "I worked to gather the nuts."

"But, I'm bigger and stronger than you," replied Peter. "From now on, the nuts belong to me and the other foxes. Leave these nuts alone from now on."

Dora was very unhappy, but the fox was bigger and stronger so Dora hung her head down and walked away.

Questions and Activities:

1. List all the arguments used by the rabbit, the squirrel and the fox why they should have the nuts. (K)

2. What is the main reason that the rabbit and the fox claim they can have the nuts? (AN)

3. In groups, write and draw a new ending for the story. In your ending, find a way for the rabbit, the squirrel and the fox to each have nuts and avoid being enemies. (A)

4. In groups, write a new ending in which someone else enters the story. Draw pictures of this new story. (A)

5. Identify something that happens in school that is like what happens in this story. Draw a picture story of this event and give it a happy ending. ©

ADDITIONAL IDEAS FOR TEACHING ABOUT MULTICULTURALISM

1. Do a search on Internet for Japanese American Internment in World War II and you will find excellent visual images, stories, cartoons, etc..

2. Do an Internet search of Harper's Weekly. This site has a selected collection of visual materials about prejudice in 19th century America.

3. If possible, access the original Life magazine which was published from the 1880s-1920. It contains vivid examples of anti-semitism.

4. Avoid using expressions such as "Native American" or "Indian" and substitute the original names of the groups – Navaho, Apache, etc...

5. Avoid classifying people by discarded customs. The Dutch no longer wear wooden shoes.

6. Access the rich sources available from Ellis Island.

7. Get students involved in studying their family history. There are many web sites which provide suggestions regarding getting students involved in family history.

8. Write a case study concerning a local multicultural issue. For example, a few months ago on Long Island two Mexican immigrants were attacked by a gang of local youth who objected to them seeking work in their area.

9. Have students research multicultural origins of American Presidents. For example, President Dwight D. Eisenhower was of German ancestry.

10. There are numerous web sites providing multiple versions of fairy tales. Use the fairy tales to examine ancient dress, foods, etc...

11. Use the Internet to learn more about Afrocentrism. Simply type that expression in as a search and you will discover many interesting sources including the debate about the concept, particularly between Asante and Leftkowitz.

12. Have students examine original locations of animals in the world and study how these life forms spread throughout the world. The horse is an example.

13. The 1930 Census is now available online. Have students use the data to learn about their grandparents.

14. In teaching social studies, devote time to the Hispanic presence in the New World. For example, while studying colonial America, examine what was happening in Hispanic Latin America.

15. Few contemporary multicultural programs examine prejudice against people of Polish or Hungarian or German or Greek origin. Have students select one of these groups to study.

16. Have students interview parents and grandparents about prejudice and find out from them about multicultural changes they have witnessed. For example, some of them lived during the desegregation of the armed forces.

17. Make a special study of desegregation of the armed forces.

18. If your school district has been around for years, the high school yearbooks offer rich sources of multiculturalism. Have students examine old yearbooks to examine changes in the student body in terms of multiculturalism.

19. Identify an invention, for example, the airplane. Have students study the cultural diffusion of the invention.

20. The film, "One Man's Hero" with Tom Berrenger depicts a forgotten incident in multiculturalism. It describes the story of a group of Irish American soldiers during the Mexican War who opposed slavery and discrimination. They deserted from the American army and fought as the San Patricio Battalion in the Mexican army. They have commemorated in stamps and celebrations by the people of Mexico. This could be an interesting example for students of moral dilemmas.

21. Have students examine the topic of anti-Catholicism. The author, Fred Stopsky, has a book on this topic which can be accessed on Internet.

22. Have students chart the multicultural origins of Supreme Court Justices. For example, when did the first Jewish or Catholic or African American or Italian supreme court justice first get appointed to the court.

23. Have students examine crime and multiculturalism. In the early 1900s, a group of Jewish and Italian youth formed the first multicultural gang under leadership of Meyer Lansky and Lucky Luciano.

24. Have students examine multicultural developments in sports.

25. Have students examine multicultural developments in entertainment. The famous actor, James Cagney, who was in many films from the 1930s-1960s describes in his autobiography that at age 18 he had three offers: the New York Yankees offered him a job in one of their rookie leagues, an Irish gang called the Westies offered him a chance to join them, and he had an offer from vaudeville. Obviously, he chose entertainment.

CHAPTER 7

CREATIVITY AND INQUIRY

Chapter Outline

1. Introductory Activities.
2. Brainstorming
   a. Morphological Forced Connections
   b. Design a New Cane
   c. Design a coat hanger
   d. Forced Relationships
3. Synectics
   a. Developing Analogy Skills
   b. Analogy Equation
4. Laser Thinking
5. Cross Matrix Thinking
   a. Cross Matrix Impact
   b. Literary Character in Cross Matrix
6. The Idea Tree
7. The Dig
8. Activities for Creativity

Creative thinkers are people who identify new patterns within existing problems in order to invent ingenious solutions. They alter conventional ways of thinking about problem solving by looking freshly at the situation. These individuals are found in all occupations whether it be butcher, grocer, mechanic, or college professor. It is not one's IQ so much as the manner in which an individual perceives the world.

In the 1950s, an inventive mind examined a round object and created the hula hoop which became an instant success. Everyone, at some point in time, reads about a new idea and exclaims, "why didn't I think of that?" The capacity for creativity lies within each human; the trick is unlocking what we already possess.

We are continually engaged in daily problem solving. Which color should be used to paint the living room? Which car should be purchased? If I mow the lawn, should I do it by going north/south or should it be done by moving in an east/west modality? People who mow lawns continually explore alternative ways in which to proceed.

Solutions to problems arise in unexpected times and places, and, most probably, even when not even thinking about the problem. Everyone has had the experience of awakening in the morning with an insight into a problem that has been vexing the awake mind for days. Creativity requires an "incubation period." Following is an example of the incubation process. Gave at an object in the room. Now, shift your gaze to an object that is several feet from the original object. Note, that while looking at the new object you can still see the original object in the "corner of your eye." Problems remain half covered in our minds for days and an occurrence can reawaken the festering problem.

Problem solving activities necessitate that students have opportunities to "walk away" from the task. Teachers who are bound by class periods and want creativity to occur in a specific time period go against every fundamental rule of the creative process. One must cease focusing on the problem and do something else in order to foster the creative insight.

We frequently "see" but don't see the nature of our problem. Examine the following figures which ordinarily disorient the mind at the initial viewing. As your mind plays with the objects a curtain will slowly lift to reveal new perspectives.

Solving problems begins with asking questions. Sherlock Holmes, the great fictional detective was famous for posing questions about the crime being examined. His questions to Dr. Watson were a means for him to proceed with his analysis of the case. Once students enter the Analysis Stage by posing a question they are ready to proceed on the road to solutions. Following are some action verbs that are frequently used in stimulating creative thinking:

Alter	Rearrange	Adapt	Modify
Substitute	Reverse	Combine	Transpose
Distort	Change	Eliminate	Invert
Flatten	Thicken	Squeeze	Add

Creative problem solvers believe anything can be related to something else. The easier part is having this belief, the hard part is identifying the other object. Since it is rarely self evident regarding the nature of the analogy, it is necessary to "play" with ideas that may at first glance appear absurd. A creative thinker understands that nothing is absurd if it helps to move along the path of solving problems.

A key component of creative problem solving is being able to "step outside" the boundaries of the problem. There are moments in creative thinking when one feels as though locked inside a room and hungers to step outside into the fresh air. This concept is best illustrated by the following simple problem: without lifting your pencil from the paper, draw exactly four straight connected lines that will go through all of these dots. You are only allowed to go through a dot a single time.

Noted creative thinker, Edward de Bono, terms his approach to creativity, "lateral thinking." He believes logical thinking more often than not results in digging a deeper hole rather than uncovering a new solutions. Select any major issue confronting American society and one is struck by the consistent solution offered is "more money." For example, the solution to drugs and crime is frequently linked to hiring more police, imposing tougher sentences or building more jail. De Bono points out how those solutions increase crime. If one hires more police, they capture more criminals leading to a higher crime rate and compelling the building of more jails. More criminals result in over crowded courts and tired police.

Anyone who has worked in education is bombarded by demands for more money to solve reading problems, discipline issues or attracting new teachers. New York City spends twice the amount per child as half the school districts in America, but probably has more problems. De Bono emphasizes the need for fresh thinking. For example, he suggests the easiest way to reduce crime is to focus on "decriminalizing" aspects of our society. Forty years ago it was illegal to be on lotteries or horse racing and those engaged in so doing were deemed to be criminals. De Bono notes that by decriminalizing betting, crime rates went down. De Bono once suggested to a police force they could save money by paying those convicted of non-violent crimes to stay out of jail. Ordinarily, it costs about $20,000 a year for jailing a criminal; he suggested paying non-violent criminals $5000 per year if they remained out of jail during the time they were supposed to serve. Your initial reaction is undoubtedly, "ridiculous." However, several states have moved to decriminalize small amounts of marijuana which is now lowering their crime rates. The author is not suggesting legalizing drugs, simply noting that de Bono's point is for imaginative new ways of dealing with existing problems.

There is an old folk tale about a merchant who was deeply in debt to a money-lender. The merchant had a beautiful daughter who the money-lender desired. The money-lender offered the merchant an opportunity to rid himself of the debt. The money-lender would place two pebbles in a badg a black one and a white one. The daughter would reach into the bag and pull out one of the pebbles. If she selected the black one, the merchant would not have to pay his debt, but his daughter would have to marry the money-lender. If she selected the white one, the merchant's debt would be cancelled and his daughter would not have to marry him. If she refused to select a pebble, the merchant would go to jail. The merchant and his daughter agreed to the test.

They were walking along a pebble strewn pathway when the money-lender leaned down to select the two pebbles. The daughter noticed that the money-lender had placed two black pebbles into the bag. Which alternative ways could she handle this situation?

1. She could refuse to select a pebble. In that case, here father went to jail.
2. She could open the bag and reveal the money-lender as a cheat. In that case, her father would still go to jail.
3. She could select the black pebble and marry the money-lender.

Is there a fourth or fifth alternative? Fortunately, the girl was a creative problem thinker. She placed her hand into the bag, and before the money lender could observe what she had selected, she dropped it among the pebbles on the path. She then exclaimed, "oh, I am sorry. I obviously selected the opposite of whichever pebble is still in the bag."

Children are natural born lateral thinkers because to them the world is filled with an infinite number of alternatives. The task of creative based education is to channel the child's inherent creativity in problem solving. The very idea of a "problem" is intriguing. Detectives when confronted with a case expend considerable time accumulating evidence in order to identify patterns. There are also "problems" because no one knows they have a problem. The individual who informs a spouse one morning, much to their surprise, of a desire for divorce is an example of this form of problem. McDonald's initially made a fortune selling milkshakes and hamburgers until someone suggested introducing a breakfast menu. Problems also arise as a result of creative thinking. Sam Walton, founder of Wal-Mart tried for years to persuade his employers to build small department stores in small towns before finally leaving and creating a vast commercial empire.

Anyone who observes children at play is soon fascinated with their imaginative solution to problems. Children in the Depression of the 1930s made footballs by rolling up newspapers and placing a rubber band around them to create an object which could be thrown. "Kick the can" was a poor child's version of baseball and was extremely popular for decades among city children. A stroll through urban streets in the first half of the twentieth century revealed thousands of children who took old cigar boxes, cut holes in them and engaged in games of marbles which required shooters to get their marbles in the holes. Teachers too frequently underestimate the intellectual and creative capacities of their students because today we have come to believe grades, IQ scores or test results identify creative thinkers.

Creative problem solving is found in all cultures and among children of all intellectual abilities. The "T" formation in football was invented by a coach who moved the quarterback three yards forward to stand behind the center and thus revolutionized the game. It took basketball players forty years before someone got the idea of shooting with one hand leading someone else to invent the idea of jumping in the air to shoot the basketball. Two young bicycle mechanics invented the airplane and Steve Jobs and his friends played around in a garage before creating Apple Computer Company.

Fostering creative problem solving requires teachers to establish an open environment which allows the free flow of ideas from all children. Creative thinkers engage in "play" because this form of human activity allows one to step outside the boxes of conventional thinking. Creative thinking does not emerge from a one session "lesson." It is the result of hard work, play, and opportunity to reflect.

DIALOGUE WITH THE TEACHER

Every teacher wants to foster a creative spirit within their students. The main question is how does one stimulate student creative thinking. The author believes that each child, regardless of IQ, has the potentiality for creative thinking. Creative thinking is basically the capacity to identify new patterns within an existing situation. This chapter is designed to enable each student in the classroom to engage in creative thinking. Most creative thinkers comment on the necessity to have fun while thinking in a creative spirit. The chapter activities are enjoyable ones for students as they have them proceed on the road to creative thinking. Many of the introductory activities allow students to create new objects which enables them to demonstrate creativity. (Elementary-Secondary)

Objective: Creative Thinking

Focus: Students will verbally, in writing, and visually demonstrate their ability to engage in creative thinking.

Teacher	Student
1. Engage students in the Introductory Activities.	1. Students in pair do Introductory Activities.
2. Introduce Morphological Forced Connections. Select an object appropriate to your grade level.	2. Students in group of four redesign object.
3. Introduce practice in Designing a New Cane.	3. Students in group of four redesign the cane.
4. Introduce Design a Coat Hanger.	4. Students in group of four design a new coat hanger.
5. Introduce Forced Relationships. Adjust words to fit your grade level.	5. Students in pair do Forced Relationships.

6. Introduce Developing Analogy Skills.

6. Students in triad do Analogy Skill activities.
   a. Each triad create 3 new analogies to share with class.

7. Introduce Laser Thinking
   a.
   b. Identify at least four ideas from Laser Thinking List.

7. Students in group of four identify
   a. Laser Thinking Problem they wish to explore using the model in the book.
   b. Students in group react to Laser Thinking Ideas.

8. Introduce Cross Matrix Thinking.

8. Students in group of four identify a problem they wish to explore using Cross Matrix Model. Share results with class.

9. Introduce Idea Tree.

9. Students in group do an Idea Tree on a current topic.

10. Option: Do a Dig.

10. Class engages in The Dig.

11. Select several ideas from end of chapter list of creative thinking ideas.

11. Students work in pair or in group on creativity ideas.

Student Assessment: Students are posed a problem being studied and asked to employ either one of the Creative Thinking Models in order to solve it.

Personal Assessment: Employ at least ten creative thinking ideas in this chapter during the coming school year.

Multiple Intelligences: Verbal Linguistic
Logical Mathematical
Visual Spatial
Interpersonal
Intrapersonal

BRAINSTORMING

Creative problem solvers draw upon brainstorming in order to generate new ideas. Brainstorming is best done in groups of four to six students in order to encourage the free flow of ideas. Brainstorming is predicated upon the concept that generating many ideas whether valid or not will eventually open the portal to exciting new ways of thinking. Ordinarily, there are four requirements for a brainstorming session:

1. Defer judgment. No one is allowed to criticize the validity of any ideas thrown out in the session. There are no "good" or "bad" ideas because one does not wish to impede individuals from speaking their minds.

2. Free-wheeling. Laughter and play are encouraged. Individuals are expected to be "silly." A good brain storming session is fun.

3. Tag-on is encouraged. If an individual says something, others are encouraged to build on the idea and take it in other directions.

4. Quantity is important. The more ideas, the more possibilities one will lead to a solution.

An initial brainstorming session with children should best relate to a problem they confront in their daily lives and about which everyone has an opinion. For example, a session on "improving the lunch menu" is bound to generate interesting responses. Prior to engaging students in a discussion of "pollution" or ways to solve a math problem, engage them with something that allows full participation of the class.

The open ended aspect of brainstorming allows children of all abilities to participate. No teacher knows who eventually will become the creative thinker. Edison and the Wright brothers had limited education. Billy Gates and Steve Jobs are college drop outs. Lincoln was home schooled, Harry Truman never went to college, and Franklin Delano Roosevelt was a "C" student in college. Several studies indicate the average grade of individuals who become millionaires is "C."

FORCED RELATIONSHIPS

A "new" idea ordinarily emerges from reordering past ideas. It took several experiments in burning wood to get hot air in order to lift the first balloon into the air before someone connected the existing idea of helium to use in balloon efforts. The automobile eventually gave birth to the tank. After all, people have been cooking chickens for centuries before Kentucky Fried Chicken persuaded others to allow someone else to cook their chicken. Examine the process of this creative endeavor:

1. People cook chicken at home.
2. People enjoy experimenting with cooking chicken to make it tastier.
3. Colonel Sanders has a recipe which friends enjoy.
4. Colonel Sanders opens a store to sell his special chicken.
5. Someone persuades Colonel Sanders to allow another individual to use his recipe and give him a percent of their profit.
6. The fast food franchise is born.

What is "new" in the above example? Actually, the "new" component is the idea of a franchise. The combination of existing ideas frequently leads to the invention of a new one. Examine the following list of words. The task posed students is combining any two of these words.

Hose	tire	hammer	shoes	ball
Window	rope	guitar	pencil	box
Bed	chair	bottle	stick	tie
Orange	wheel	chain	comb	radio

Assume a group of student selected "hammer" and "comb." The task of the group is examining this new combination — hammer-comb — in order to create a new object. Their thinking might eventually lead to the idea of a hammercomb which allows one to hammer away while keeping hair out of one's face. Perhaps, one might regard this as a silly idea, but that is not the point. One is encouraging students to think in a free and open manner as they invent new designs. By the way, the Swiss Army knife contains a host of implements which prior to its creation were never found on knifes.

Young children could be encouraged to combine animals. Present a list like the one above to a group of primary age children and ask them, working in groups, to connect two of the animals. They could then be asked to draw a picture of their new animal and decide what it eats, how it moves, etc.... This simple activity leads to creative thinking. Most importantly, EVERYONE in the class can participate on an equal basis.

REDESIGN THE COAT HANGER

Draw a picture of a coat hanger.

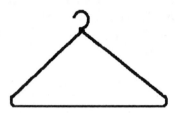

Ask students to imagine they are a coat hanger in a closet. Pose to students: What do you think about when a sweater covers your coat hanger body? How does it feel when pants are slung between parts of your body? What is life like in the closet? You may add additional questions to ask students to consider.

The task of each group is to select at least three words from the following list:

Shoe	glasses	pen	peanuts
Knife	paper	clock	chair
Dish	orange	ruler	lamp
Cup	envelope	book	gum

After students select three items – they can select more if they so desire – the group is to link their items to the coat hanger. After drawing a picture of the new coat hanger, the group is to explain how their items function as part of the coat hanger.

Draw a picture of the new coat hanger.

MORPHOLOGICAL FORCED CONNECTIONS

Don Koberg and Jim Bagnall in their book, "The Universal Traveler," describe a process which guarantees that any student will become a creative thinker. Their process is based upon the theory that inventions are simply new ways of combining bits and pieces of existing knowledge. There are three steps to this process:

1. List attributes of the situation.
2. Below each attribute, list several alternatives.
3. Make random choices across your list of alternatives by selecting one item from each list of alternative attributes. After choosing those items, draw a picture of it and describe how it functions.

Example:

Subject: Improve upon the automobile.

Attributes of the Automobile;

Metal	wheels	gas	wheel	glass	box shape

Alternatives:

Plastic	feet	solar	hand	cellophane	circle
Wood	suction	water	computer	shades	square
Paper	ski	electric	rudder	plexiglass	hexagon
Rubber	skates	nuclear	voice	open	pyramid

Invention: A pyramid shaped plastic car running on skis that utilizes solar energy and is directed by a computer with plexiglass type windows.

Your task: Select random set of words from the above list – or create a new list – and then draw a picture of your car. After drawing your picture explain the function and form of your new style automobile. If you wish, invent a new name to replace the word "automobile." Remember, the initial name for an automobile was "carriage."

SYNECTICS

The technique of creative problem solving developed by W.J.J. Gordon is known as 'synectics.' The word is from the Greek meaning the joining together of different and apparently irrelevant elements or ideas. Gordon's method draws heavily upon relating problems to analogues in life or from nature.

Einstein's recurring image of a man in a falling elevator led to his general theory of relativity. If the man dropped a ball while in an elevator, did the elevator's floor rise to meet the ball or was the ball pulled to the floor by some outside force? Brunel, the tunnel builder, based his ideas of construction from observing shipworms make their way through wood by removing material ahead of it by pushing it out through the rear of its body.

Adolf Hitler based his mass demonstration political rallies upon watching movies of American cheerleading and use of fight songs at football games. Willie Sutton, a famous bank robber, got his ideas for breaking into bank vaults with a cutting torch from his pervious job as a welder in a shipyard.

Gordon's work differs from the randomness of forced connections because it is based upon a purposeful connection of ideas in problem solving. Gordon was once asked by the owner of a potato chip company to discover ways of packaging them in a can. His synectics team drew an analogy between wet and dry leaves. Dry leaves are brittle and easily break. Wet leaves are not brittle. They utilized the idea of wetting potato chips, and placing them in cans where they dried out. A group was once asked to invent a new can opener. During their brainstorming session one man jumped on the shoulders of another man and shouted, "I am a can opener" while the other man shouted, "I am a can." From that encounter the idea of a flip top can opener was invented.

Gordon has developed extensive practice activities for students to enhance their analogy skills. The purpose of these activities is to stimulate minds to form connections between the natural world and problem solving.

Developing Analogy Skills

1. What in nature would have led to the invention of the safety pin? _____

2. What in nature would have led to the invention of the pencil? _____

3. What in nature would have given humans the idea for a zipper? _____

4. What in nature would have given humans the idea for dams? _____

5. What in nature would have given humans the idea for a drum? _____

6. What in nature would have given humans the idea for a flute? _____

7. What in nature would have led to the idea for scissors? _____

8. What in nature would have led to idea for a parachute? _____

9. What in nature would have led to a idea for a backpack? _____

10. What in nature would have led to idea for a smokestack? _____

Add Your Own Analogies

11. _____

12. _____

13. _____

ANALOGY EQUATION

Gordon uses analogies in order to focus attention upon uncovering ideas for problem solving. The purpose of the Analogy Equation is integrating components of brainstorming, analogy thinking, and problem solving into a single equation.

Problem Description:

How to prevent a new bike from being stolen.

Step 1: The Paradox

A bike is locked up, but thieves appear free to steal it.

Step 2: Analogue

Fish sometimes disguise themselves to avoid being eaten.

Step 3: Unique Activity

Some fish are edible, but appear poisonous to predators.

Step 4: Equivalent

Bike is valuable, but appears poisonous to thieves.

New Idea:

Make the bike appear "poisonous" by painting it an ugly color and design.

Adapted from *The Basic Course in Synectics* Books, Cambridge, 1981, pg. 51

LATERAL THINKING IDEAS

1. Redesign a teaspoon and identify new uses for the object.
2. Create a new design for a windshield wiper. You can also give this object new uses not currently performed by a windshield wiper.
3. You see a man pouring something into his gas tank from a can. List all possible things he could be doing.
4. Parking is a problem in most urban areas. Identify new ways to handle the parking problem.
5. Org is a visiting anthropologist from the planet of Kryton. Life form on Kryton are linked together with a central brain. How would you explain writing to org?
6. Atahauallpa was leader of the Inca empire in the year 1530. the Incas believed in the Sun god and their religious beliefs emphasized war and violence. How would you explain Jesus Christ or Buddha to him?
7. The rain fall in a particular area of Missouri averages 12 inches a year over the past fifty years. However, during the past three years, rainfall has increased to 18 inches per year. You are a farmer who has benefited from increased rain since it has resulted in higher harvests. Which of the following actions would you recommend to the farmer for next year:
    a. Continue raising the same amount of crops.
    b. Increase your crop production.
    c. Reduce your cop production.
8. Edward de Bono was once asked by the police of New York City to identify new approaches to reducing crime. He suggested the following two ideas: (1) Any criminal who commits a non-violent crime would be offered the option of receiving $5,000 per year to stay out of jail for the number of years which he was sentenced to serve. De Bono pointed out it cost New York state $15,000 per year to house such criminals. (2) De Bono suggested dividing New York City into grids and identifying the dominant criminal gang in each grid. These gangs would be paid a certain amount of money each year in which crime goes down in their area. The police rejected his ideas. Identify your own imaginative ways of dealing with crime in America.
9. Edward de Bono was once asked to improve traffic speed in New York City. He suggested that buses going across Manhattan be cut in half allowing people to jump on and off the bus. Identify your own imaginative idea to handle traffic problems in a large city.

10. You are called in the principal of your school and asked to identify new ways to improve school spirit. Identify an idea that has never been used in your school to improve school spirit.

11. You are a teacher who has a class clown in the class who continually interrupts to tell something humorous. Identify an approach to this problem that would allow the class clown to be funny every day and allow the teacher to teach without interruptions.

12. Students in your school have four minutes to move from class to class. Some students argue it is not enough time to get from one place to another. Identify a new way to handle this problem.

13. Many parents in your school are working and have difficulty attending school functions. Identify new ways to deal with this issue.

14. Some states are experimenting with building "circles" at intersections and eliminating traffic lights. Cars go around the circle until they reach the street upon which they wish to drive. Invent another way to deal with intersections in order to speed up the process of driving.

15. Several students who failed making the cheerleaders at your school argue there should be a different way of selecting cheerleaders. Invent a new way to deal with this problem.

16. Following is a problem faced by Eskimos prior to arrival of modern technology. Eskimos ordinarily fished for seals by cutting a hole in the ice. Seals have excellent hearing and can hear Eskimo footsteps on the ice. If they hear an Eskimo approach the open hole, seals dive deep into the water, and surface when Eskimos depart. Identify at least one way Eskimos solved this problem.

17. Draw a diagram of how the defensive and offensive teams line up against one another in a football game. Experiment with changing positions of people in this scheme in order to identify new ways of playing football. For example, in 1940 a football coach moved his quarterback who was stationed about two yards in the backfield up forward to stand behind the center. This was the origin of the "T" formation which most teams currently use. Invent a new football formation.

18. You are asked to develop new strategies in order to persuade teachers to work in difficult schools which have violence. Which incentives would you suggest?

20. Heavy snowfalls usually result in trucks with snow plows being called out to handle the situation. Invent new ways to deal with heavy snow falls.

LASER THINKING

You are called to the office of the principal and told that an angry group of parents is coming to see her. She says, "I want you to identify at least three ways I can handle an angry group of parents." You decide to brainstorm various strategies to handle this situation.

1. I will imagine I am one of the angry parents. What would reduce my anger?
2. I will visualize myself meeting with parents in which everyone is happy.
3. I will ask myself what people at school did to create this anger?
4. I will become "anger." What do I like about myself? What do I dislike about myself? What can someone do to become my friend?

This list has not yet solved the problem before the principal, but is the initial step toward uncovering a solution. Laser Thinking is an approach to creativity which incorporates elements of synectics and later thinking.

During the 1830s Charles Goodyear experimented with using rubber to make new products. He created a mailbag made out of rubber which proved a failure. Rubber fascinated him. He was intrigued that rubber became sticky in the summer and brittle in the winter. He wondered how to get rid of the smell of rubber. Goodyear continued experimenting with rubber until he ran out of money in 1839.

He decided on one final experiment. Goodyear heated the compound that had decomposed while he was making the mailbag. By mistake part of the compound fell on the stop top and solidified like leather. The compound had become transformed. Goodyear showed the results to colleagues, but they were not impressed.

He was not deterred. Goodyear dipped pieces of his compound into boiling sulphur, and it solidified. From these experiments arose the vulcanization process. The rest is history. This story illustrates several characteristics of creativity.

1. Goodyear worked on the basis of a hunch which motivated him to explore several directions.
2. He employed analytical and logical methods of experimentation.
3. Goodyear spent considerable time on the problem. He did not rush to a conclusion to meet specific time deadlines.

4. He experimented with several ideas.

5. Trial and error created conditions for an "accident" to occur which helped lead to a solution.

6. His solution came in a moment of "illumination."

7. Even after discovering an initial solution, years of additional hard work were necessary to complete his project.

Laser Thinking incorporates these seven steps of the creative process. It accepts the principle that "play" and experimentation are essential in the creative act. However, play should not be construed as meaning that logical analytical thinking are also not critical in any creative thinking process.

Laser Thinking Problem

Darwin Elementary School encourages students to engage in fund raising activities in order to support school programs and clubs. The Principal has received

Many complaints from parents that children are continually selling commercial goods within neighborhoods and to relatives. Some local business people are annoyed when children sell goods that are sold in local stores.

Dominant Ideas

After identifying the problem, the next step is to clarify which are the key issues emanating from this problem.

1. Darwin Elementary School is short of money to carry out several functions.
2. Children are used to solicit money to handle financial problems in the school.
3. Fund raising is conducted within the local geographic area.
4. (Fill in another dominant idea)_____

_____

5. (Fill in another dominant idea)_____

_____

Restructuring

Restructuring the problem requires viewing it from another perspective. It entails manipulating elements of the problem in a random fashion in order to uncover an "Emperor Without Clothes" perspective. For example, baseball managers faced with a

slump juggle their lineup in hope the new configuration of players will result in a different outcome.

1. Have parents sell commercial products to students.
2. Have students give away candies and cookies to people in the community.
3. Have commercial enterprises sell their goods in schools.
4. (Add another restructuring statement)_____

_____

5. (Add another restructuring statement)_____

_____

Play

Closely allied to the concept of Restructuring is that of Play. Imaginative play enables the mind to explore an infinite range of possibilities. Humans who engage in play temporarily suspend a tight control of their rationality. Play enables humans to return to those aspects of childhood when imagination held free reign. Most humans at one point or anther while involved in play uncover insights that escaped their attention when focused upon logical thinking. In the Laser Thinking model, a word is simply introduced into the problem in a random manner in order to jar the mind from its desire for logical thought processes. For example, in this problem, the word "fish" will be introduced.

1. Fish go under the water, but also swim on top of the water.
2. Fish swim in a school with other fish.
3. Fish find their own food but sometimes people give them food.
4. (Make a fish statement)_____
   _____
5. (Make a fish statement)_____
   _____

Analogies

Analogy plays a key role in Laser Thinking as it does in most creative thinking methodologies. An analogy occurs when two things correspond in some respects, especially in form or function, event though they are dissimilar in other respects. Analogies are best used to form connections between the problem and some aspect of the natural world.

1. Some animals hibernate, shed their skins, and put on new skins.
2. Some animals eat food and then pass it on to their own children.
3. When it rains, we use umbrellas.
4. A pack of tigers will share a newly slain animal.
5. (Add an analogy statement)_____
   _____
6. (Add an analogy statement)_____
   _____

New Insights

New Insights is an initial endeavor to identify new ways of examining the problem to be solved. The purpose of preceeding activities was to jar our minds from the logical thought processes we ordinarily resort to when confronting a problem. Analytical thinking is imperative in problem solving, but it always runs the risk of recreating past failures. This section of Laser Thinking is an opportunity to identify different approaches to confronting the issues being examined.

1. We need an approach which enables children to raise money while satisfying the interests of parents and merchants.
2. Money is a necessary evil.
3. One can engage in an activity which outwardly appears one thing, but in reality is another.
4. Fund raising is a means toward a desirable end which raises a question as to whether or not the means justifies the end.
5. (Add your New Insight statement)_____

New Design

The end goal of a creative thinking process is to identify solutions. The identification of several possible solutions enhances the probability that among these ideas at least one may be a solution to the problem. The statement of several solutions, even those which probably are not feasible assists thinkers to elicit from the host of ideas the kernel of an idea which can be an operational solutions to the problem.

1. Have each child be restricted to a specific geographical area in order to avoid duplication of efforts and thus avoid annoying adults with multiple solicitations.
2. Designate a certain percent of all money raised to be assigned to a local community agency such as the homeless.
3. Have a one day fair in which local merchants hire students to sell their products with profits being divided between merchants and the school.
4. (Add your New Design statement)_____

5. (Add your New Design statement)_____

CROSS MATRIX THINKING

Adults have ordinarily in their lives experienced the phenomenon of having a wish fulfilled that becomes a horrible event. Undoubtedly, people who marry and then undergo a terrible divorce have this feeling. Have you ever wondered why good things can lead to bad results? An important component of corporate planning entails understanding the consequences of any action such as a new product. There is no guarantee that we can see the future, but we can anticipate possible outcomes from any action which is taken. The essential components of Cross Matrix Thinking is making individuals aware of possible ramifications of any action will automatically trigger off several alternative actions. Let us illustrate this phenomenon with this example:

In order to improve discipline, these solutions are identified:

1. After school detention
2. In school detention
3. Parent conferences during the school day.

If option 1 is implemented it may trigger the following outcomes. A student in after school detention misses the school bus resulting in parents having to pick up the child. A parent at work is compelled to leave early from work to pick up their child. This can result in an increase in anger toward the child or an increase in anger toward the school. An increase in anger toward the school might result in a negative vote in the next school bond election. An increase in anger toward the child might trigger violence toward the child resulting in injury or it might lead to a dispute between parents regarding the best way to handle the situation. This dispute could result in increased tension within the family and impair the success of the marriage.

Perhaps, none of the scenarios depicted above will occur, but the possibility exists that one or several could happen. Cross Matrix Thinking is designed to familiarize minds with expected or unexpected consequences of any action. Let me illustrate this factor with an example from World War II. A decision was made in World War II to land American and British troops in France in order to defeat Nazi Germany. The landing of 250,000 men on the beaches of Normandy required 5,000 ships including thousands of landing craft. This meant American shipyards had to reduce their building of aircraft carriers which were needed in fighting in the Pacific in order to meet the needs of the Normandy invasion. Admirals fighting in the Pacific were furious at being deprived of the aircraft carriers they needed in order to invade Japanese islands. Fortunately, extensive Cross Matrix Thinking was conducted by American military leaders in order to minimize the consequences of their actions. They were aware that a European invasion would lead to anger among Pacific admirals and extensive time was taken to explain the consequences of the action. We may never be able to avoid problems arising from any action, but being aware of consequences empowers us to mitigate unfortunate consequences.

This is an important concept for young children to learn. Every parent understands their children do not initially grasp the concept of "limited resources." A family has "X" amount of dollars to serve meeting their multiple needs. Spending money for "B" means no money is left for purchasing "C." Cross Matrix Thinking is designed to assist youth in understanding that whenever an action is taken it has a ripple effect upon other possible actions and consequences.

Cross Matrix Thinking can be introduced in various ways. For example, Cross Matrix Thinking enables individuals to understand the emergence of trends in society. We can assume that if a particular idea is being discussed in a cross section of the American media it indicates this idea is capturing the attention of a significant proportion of the American population. Cross matrix Thinking introduces students to the difference between short and long term effects within society. If a particular idea continues to be examined in a variety of periodicals and media outlets over an extensive period of time, one can assume it represents a long term trend. On the other hand, there are daily occurrences of ideas which capture the imagination of Americans and disappear after a short period of time. "Pet Rocks" is one such phenomenon. Hair styles can be either short of long term trends. During World War II, American soldiers wore helmets and helmet design required uniformity so all soldiers were required to wear short hair. Short hair lasted until the 1960s when it was replaced by long hair.

In order to begin training students to grasp this societal ripple concept, initiate the following:

1. Identify one or three ideas: For example, Education, Hair Style, Media
2. Assign a pair of students to follow a specific periodical for six months.

3. The task of the students is to cut out any article dealing with Education and place it in the folder marked "Education." Or if they are collecting articles on several topics, then material for leach topic goes into its file.

4. Select the periodicals from a disparate collection. For example, Teen magazine, Business Week, Time, Vogue, Nation magazine, National Review, Scholastic, Entertainment, etc....

5. After students have collected materials from their own periodical and placed them in the Education file or other topic files, they will have collected a disparate body of information.

6. The class at the end of a period of time, examines their collection. If they discover certain themes being repeated in these various periodicals, it suggests the existence of a long term trend. On the other hand, they might realize that certain topics are restricted to specific age or interest groups.

7. A short version of Cross Matrix can be done with a topic such as a particular movie. Have students collect movie reviews from several sources and compare and contrast how each source regards the movie.

8. Another possibility is to use Internet sources to quickly grasp how different societies view the same issue. Internet contains English language periodicals from societies throughout the world. Select one topic and have students realize how the topic is reported in a dozen societies.

9. Cross Matrix Thinking can also be done on the basis of age or gender. Have students identify an issue and interview people of different ages in order to uncover if age impacts views about the topic.

10. Have students identify an issue facing their school district. They should interview different people such as teachers, principal, superintendent, etc... to uncover if the position influences perception of the issue.

Cross Matrix Impact

Following is a model to train students in understanding relationships between actions and consequences. We have identified the issue of "POLLUTION" to analyze through a cross matrix process. The Cross Matrix is organized in the following manner.

1. Students in groups identify five to ten things they believe will help solve pollution problems.
2. These pollution solutions are listed in the manner indicated below.
3. Students examine the matrix by proceeding along a single line. For example, in number one, "Electricity replaces gas" they examine the other four desires by asking this question: "Assume electricity has now replaced gas to fuel engines, how will they influence being able to attain the goal of "cars required to get 60 miles to the gallon?" In other words, will electricity replacing gas have a positive enhancing impact on reaching the second goal of 60 miles to the gallon or will it have a negative influence?
4. After discussing the second goal, students then proceed to the others.
5. After completing the first goal, students are then asked: "Assuming cars get 60 miles to the gallon will that make it more or less likely that electricity will replace gas as fuel for cars?"
6. Students are asked similar questions about the other desired goals.

Pollution

	1	2	3	4	5
Electricity replaces gas					
Cars get 60 miles to gallon					
Hydrogen used as fuel for cars					
Railroads built to substitute for car travel in cities					
Only electricity driven cars allowed in major cities					

LITERARY CHARACTER CROSS MATRIX

The purpose of this activity is to cross reference several components in literature and media that span different genres. In the process of shifting characters and events across time, new insights are offered about traditional aspects of the curriculum.

Students initially are confronted with the following:

Television Shows	**Novel Jane Eyre**	**Romeo and Juliet**
Friends	Jane Eyre	Romeo
E.R.	Edward Rochester	Juliet
Melrose Place	Bertha Mason	Tybalt
The Simpsons	Aunt Reed	Friar Lawrence
Seinfeld	Blanche Ingram	Capulet

Students select any combination of characters and TV shows. They are to assume that all other characters are also in the new configuration. Following are some questions that can be posed about the future setting:

1. How has the "future" changed the character's opportunity for an education or career?

2. How has the future changed the character's social life?

3. How has the future changed the character's method of handling conflict?

4. How has the future affected the final outcome of the character's life?

For example, the hateful arrogant Blanche Ingram could meet her match in the even more hateful and arrogant Amanda on Melrose Place or Romeo and Juliet could be saved by doctors on E.R. Create a scenario in which Homer Simpson is now in the play Romeo and Juliet.

Another possibility is to completely mix genres. Bring together a character from Seinfeld with a character from Jane Eyre and Romeo or Juliet. Imagine Juliet sitting in the diner with Jerry, George, and Kramer and have here discuss her problems with Romeo.

THE IDEA TREE

The Idea Tree is a technique which visually demonstrates how each decision generates a series of consequences. Initially, an issue is identified. Students are asked what would happen if a specific solution was adopted to solve the problem. At this point, a branch is drawn from the tree trunk with the proposed solution. Students are then asked what would be the consequences if this solution became a reality. At this point, branches are drawn from the initial branch to represent each proposed solution. For each solution, additional branches extend out.

Issue: Pollution

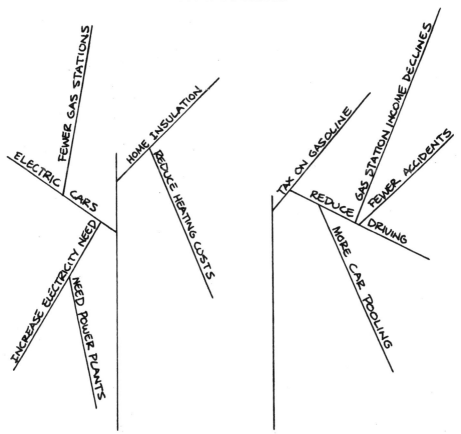

THE DIG

Archeologists devote their lives to the pursuit of uncovering mysteries of the past. They dig into layers of earth in hope of finding a fragment of some past artifact that will illuminate past civilizations. In a sense, archeologists engage in a combination of logical thinking and creative interpretations. "Doing the Dig" is an opportunity for students to replicate the thought processes of archeologists.

The "Dig" activity can be restricted to a single class or it can encompass a grade level or even an entire school. Participants are divided into two teams. Team "A" creates a civilization with artifacts representative of that civilization. For example, eating utensils, games, chairs, tables, toilet seats, etc... A written description is provided for each artifact which describes its form and function. The artifacts are then buried in an outside area. In the meantime, Team "B" studies how archeologists function and the methods they employ to understand the purposes of artifacts. Team "B" then digs up artifacts buried by Team "A."

The purpose of the activity is engaging students with creative problem solving. Both teams are engaged in creative thinking. For example, Team A has to conceive a civilization, but more importantly, identify artifacts that would be an integral part of this civilization. Team B also had an arduous task of doing speculative thinking about the function of an artifact. For example, imagine if you didn't know the purpose of a toilet seat and came across one lying on the ground, what would be your initial speculation as to its function? Take a moment and reflect upon this issue.

David Macaulay's Motel of the Mysteries turns the Dig activity upside down. He hypothesizes that our present civilization had a calamity and was lost to the world. Centuries later archeologists from the future stumbled upon the remnants of our civilization. They would have to hypothesize the meaning of artifacts they found. For example, assume they uncovered the meaning of some words and came across an artifact that had "Washington" upon it. It might be logical for them to imagine this was the site of where people washed their clothes.

The Dig is an opportunity for each student to fully participate in the creative thought process. Howard Gardner's Multiple

Intelligence theory can be used as a take off point to draw upon the various skills of students in creating artifacts digging them up and interpreting what is found. Students could even create musical or art pieces as artifacts.

The Dig can be completed within a few weeks or an entire semester. It is an enjoyable and exciting opportunity for all students.

IDEAS FOR CREATIVITY

1. Write imaginative stories about:
   a. The teacher who doesn't talk.
   b. The duck that doesn't quack.
   c. The monkey who likes ice cream.
   d. the cow that brays like a donkey.

2. List all things one could do with an old shoe box.

3. List all problems that might arise when you take a bath.

4. Using a series of dots, transform the dots into an object.

5. Problem: Some children fight on the playground. Brainstorm ways fighting on the playground could be halted or made less dangerous.

6. List all possible origins of the flexible ice cube tray. For example, a shoe is left outside in the cold and ice forms on it.

7. How can you make four nines equal one hundred? You can do anything with the nines.

8. Introduce a commonly held assumption such as "Children with high IQs receive high grades." Turn it around to see if it applies. "Children with high grades have high IQs." Identify another assumption and play with it.

9. Place yourself in an unusual situation. For example, Jim Carey, the movie actor, has been asked to mediate the dispute between Israel and the Palestinians. What would happen?

10. Identify a problem where nothing exists. For example, students are served pizza twice a week in the school cafeteria. Transform this into a problem.

11. Identify an ordinary puzzling event to be examined. For example, every time we have a storm, our cable TV blanks out for at least an hour.

12. Work backwards. Identify a current problem, and retrace its origin. Identify such a problem.

13. Make a list of crazy inventions. For example, a microwave that both cooks and freezes food. Identify your own example.

14. A miniature ship is inside a bottle. List all possible ways it got there.

15. Design an unusual packaging scheme for a product. For example, Hamburgers are packaged in flip top cans. Identify your own examples.

16. Ask a question to challenge a perspective. For example, "Why don't candidates for president, wear beards anymore?" Identify your own questions.

17. Invent a new life existence system. For example, you have reached the planet of Moros where life forms sleep 22 hours a day and are awake four hours a day. Explain how life functions on the planet. Identify you own example.

18. Identify a topic about which you know very little. Pose a question. For example, "why can't people playing soccer use their hands?"

19. Pose a "what if" question. "What if television had not been invented? How would my life today be different?"

20. Reverse the order of a sentence.
    Bill played with his bird. The bird played with his bill.
    John went to Disneyland. Disneyland went to the john.

21. Assume a famous movie or TV star taught your class. For example, how would Oprah teach your class?

22. CNN is at the Constitutional Convention. How would they report it?

23. Invent a new rule for playing basketball that would help short people.

24. Invent something totally useless. For example, tiny umbrellas to cover shoes in the rain.

25. Imagine a specific animal was announcer for a football game. For example, how would a lion report a football game? Identify your own example.

26. Identify a picture. Write anything you see happening in the picture. Ask a question about the picture which can not simply be answered by looking at the picture.
    a. List as many things as possible that could have caused the action in the picture. You may cite things that happened prior to the actual action depicted in the picture.
    b. List as many things as possible that may occur as a result of what is happening in the picture.

27. Share with students an example in which you engaged in creative thinking.

28. Set aside each week a ten minute time slot for practice in brainstorming. Students could identify topics for the focus of the session.

29. Ask students to observe a cat or dog or bird and analyze how they solve problems.

30. Ask students to redesign a game and create new rules.

31. Show students a video from a popular sitcom in which a problem is solved. Engage students in a discussion of the thought processes of the characters or how students would have handled the situation.

32. Invent a character from another planet and provide it with characteristics and skills. Pose a problem for the alien to solve. Students working in groups can explain how the alien solved the problem.

33. Use creative thinking to handle classroom discipline situations. For example, assume Mary, Deborah and Susan have difficulty playing with one another. The girls are to devise a solution to their problem. Perhaps, they decide to have a nickel place in a jar by one of their parents each time they cooperate. When the jar is filled, they can spend it on a cooperative activity. (This idea came from Elizabeth Stopsky, age 10)

34. A mysterious phone call:
    "Hello, is this 493-1484?"
    "Yes, who is calling?"
    "Don't you recognize me? My mother is your mother's mother-in-law."
    "Huh?"
    Who is on the phone?

35. Grandmother likes coffee but hates tea, she likes apples but not oranges; she likes it cool, but not hot; she likes fall but doesn't like spring; she prefers cookies to cake and prefers mommy to daddy. Which of the following would grandma select?
    Summer or winter   muffins or bread
    Ann or Joe   pear or tangerine

36. Arrange ten ornaments in such a way that there are four ornaments in each row.

37. Alternate uses: We frequently find uses for things that originally were intended for a specific purpose. For example, children use old boxes to keep toys or make it into a doll house. Ask students to identify new uses for: automobile tires, newspapers, empty jars, shoe boxes, etc… During the Depression of the 1930s New York City children rolled up newspapers and made them into footballs. Encourage your students to be creative.

38. Create a new activity that might enter the Guiness Book of Records.

39. Create a new physical activity. For example, "pinky lifting."

40. Subway Problem Solving. Youngsters in the city's subways are stealing light bulbs. The subway company cannot afford to hire more security guards. Ask students to identify at least one way in which this problem could be solved.

41. The Snowball Problem: At a football game, spectators in the stand began to throw snowballs which hit members of the band and cheerleaders. The public address announcer asked them to halt but they continued. Identify at least one way the problem could be handled.

42. Consequences: Everyone is aware of consequences, some intended and some unintended. We are unfamiliar with consequences of unusual situations. For each of the following situations, identify as many consequences as you possibly can:
    It is daylight 24 hours a day.
    Humans have a third hand.
    (Add your own)

43. Using 13 cars make 5 groups of 5 cars each.

44. Identify a common object such as a can. Cut out the top of the can and ask students to identify what is the piece and from whence does it come.

45. Collect logos from a variety of products. Give students your logos and ask them to identify the products.

46. The Tower Problem: A tower is 50 feet high with an opening at the top. It is made of heavy wood and has smooth sides all around. Inside, at the bottomof the tower is a bag which has $25,000. your task is to get inside the tower to get the money. All you have are 20 feet of rope, a box of nails, and a box of matches. List as many ways as you can how to get the money.

47. Name the eight vegetables that make V-8 juice. Invent a new vegetable in order to sell V-9 juice. Describe the vegetable, its taste, how it grows, etc...

48. A riddle from Lewis Carroll: A Russian has three sons. The first he named Rab who became a lawyer. The second he named YMRA who became a soldier. The third became a sailor. What name would the father have chosen for this son?

49. Make sense from the following by adding punctuation marks:
    time flies you cannot they fly too fast

50. From which of the following could you most likely make a needle:
    cabbage   spice   steak   paper box   fish

51. Identify the name of the sport or game concealed in each of the following sentences:
    His foot got caught in the ball and chain.
    Annin has a tendency to do poorly in spelling.
    Sally put the socks in her mother's drawer.

52. Pyramid Power: Place a letter of the alphabet in each of the 15 blocks that form a pyramid. You may not use the same letter more than once in any horizontal row of blocks. After completing this task, make a list of all words that can be formed from letters within the pyramid. Identify another physical object and create a similar or different task.

53. Draw an envelope with one continuous line.

54. Use twelve matchsticks to form five squares – one large and four small ones. Can you rearrange them to form six squares? You can move the sticks in any manner you desire.

55. Create symbols to stand for the ideas expressed in the following statements:
    Ring the bell.
    Take a test.
    Answer the telephone.
    Mow the lawn.

56. Solving Problems by Taking Another Look: identify which of the following statements is right or wrong:
    The Statue of Liberty holds the torch in her right hand.
    A record on a record player turns in a clockwise manner.
    The stripes on a zebra's legs are horizontal.
    Most pencils have eight sides.
    Lincoln's head on the penny faces left.
    (Add your own)

57. The Doctor Problem: Jane was riding her bike near her home when she was hit by a car. Her father put her into the car and raced to the hospital. They wheeled Jane into the operating room. "Oh no," cried the surgeon, "I can't operate on this child. She is my daughter." Explain the situation.

58. The House Problem: A child arrives home after school and discovers the house is locked and he forgot his key. His parents have been delayed by an accident and are on their way home. List all possible ways the child can enter the house without breaking anything.

59. Take a dollar bill and a quarter. Balance the quarter on the edge of the dollar bill. You can't use any extra props.

60. Place five little rolled up pieces of paper in the palm of your hand. Blow them off the palm, but you can only blow one piece at a time.

61. How many ways can you turn a glass of water upside down without spilling the water?

62. What comes next?
    a. A,B,C,D, E, ____, ____, ____
    b. A,B,A,C,D, A, ____, ____, ____
    c. A,D, G, J, M, ____, ____, ____
    d. M, T, W, T, ____, ____, ____

63. How can a cake be cut into 8 equal pieces with only three cuts?

64. IV = 1 1 1 + 1 1 1.
    Change this into a correct equation by only moving one match.

65. Someone has been fishing in your private lake. He left two fishing poles, and apparently will return to resume fishing. Instead of calling the police, think of an interesting way to shock your unwelcome guest.

66. Someone parks in your assigned parking spot at work each day. Instead of having the car towed away, think of something that will ensure the culprit does not repeat this action.

67. Go the a garage sale and find an item that is unusual. Invent an explanation of how the item was used by its original owner.

68. A Sherlock Holmes Walk: Take students on a walk in the park. They are to assume they are Sherlock Holmes. As they walk, their task is asking Sherlock Holmes type questions. For example, "how did this twig get broken?" or "Why is this shoelace here?" Based on what students find and ask, they are to divide into groups in order to write a mystery story using their data.

69. Have student ask a garage owner what type of invention would best help him in his occupation. The task of students working in groups is to create such an invention.

70. The Categorizing Game: Psychologist Jerome Bruner developed the "Categorizing Game" to help children learn to categorize. A group of students are given (a) three string loops; (b) nine shapes including three each of squares, ovals, and triangles, and each set includes one white, one black, and one striped shape. Students are told to place all triangles in one loop, all black shapes in another loop. Any shape that fits both categories is placed in the center. Any shapes that do not belong to either category, are left out.

71. How many objects can be made from these circles?

    0   0   0   0   0

72. List every conceivable problem that could occur when one takes a bath.

73. Design a new bath that meets a variety of needs.

74. Redesign the wall calendar for some new purposes.

75. Ask students to invent a new use for an everyday object such as a rubber band.

76. Identify an ordinary object – the plastic top on soda bottles. Ask students to brainstorm alternate uses for this object.

77. Ask students to invent a new type of Kleenex.

78. Today, adults insist students perform well on examinations in order to prove they are learning. Ask students to develop a "New IQ Test" that measures intelligence differently.

79. Pose the following to students. "Summer vacation is ordinarily two months. Why did this come about?" After discussing this topic, ask students to redesign the school year – including vacation and break weeks – for the 21st century.

80. Connect two totally different objects or ideas. For example, a glass and a chair. Students are to brainstorm ways of combining these objects to create something new.

81. Sneakers increasingly are manufactured in different styles and uses. Students are to design a sneaker that has unusual features.

82. Students are to identify an object that makes a sound. Their task is to create a musical piece using that object to make appropriate sounds.

83. The task of students is to design a new approach to speeding travel across bridges.

84. Unusual definitions:
    a. The key of a minor — a latch key
    b. An obsolete beverage in the south — cotton gin
    c. A tender poise — porpoise
    (Add your own)

85. Below are animals arranged in a Matrix:

	Frog	Pig	Squirrel	Robin	Ant	Lion	Coyote
Cow							
Bear							
Snake							
Elephant							
Ostrich							
Shark							
Tiger							

Students are to link two or three animals on the matrix and draw a picture of what this new animal looks like. For example, a cow from the left column combined with a Squirrel's head. After drawing a picture of this new creature, students will explain how the animal functions and what it eats, etc…

86. Transform the following dots into something:

....

....

....

....

....

87. Design a new type of hat that functions well in winter or summer.

88. Young people today wear many forms of body ornaments. Invent a new form of body ornament people of your own age.

89. Pose the following to students: "Your task is to invent something that will reduce use of drugs by young people."

90. Pose the following problem to students: "Santa Claus is stuck in the chimney. How can we help him get out?" A student in one class when asked this question, responded: "Have the elves tickle him." Ask students to brainstorm all possible ways to get him out.

91. Have students invent a new cheer to use at their athletic events.

92. There are many action heroes depicted in the movies and television. Have students create a new action hero. The action hero has to have special qualities or characteristics.

93. Have students invent an unusual hobby.

94. Below is an example of how an object can be transformed into a face. Create your own.

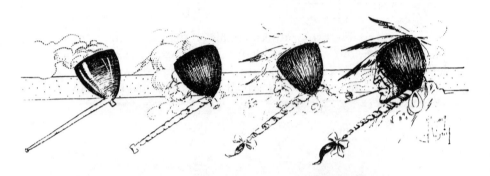

95. Below are examples of handwriting from Benjamin Franklin and Oliver Cromwell. Ask students to image how an important figure would sign his or her signature and then check out if their prediction is accurate.

96. Following are hair designs from the 18th century. Ask students to create outrageous hair designs for important people today.

THIS IS SUPPOSED TO BE A CARICATURE OF A HEAD-DRESS WORN IN 1780. IT IS UNDERSTOOD (SAYS THOMAS WRIGHT) TO REPRESENT THE CELEBRATED MARY ANNE ROBINSON. IT IS NOT UNLIKE THE MUSHROOM HATS WORN TO-DAY.

A DUDE OF 1772.

97. Following are pictures of games played by children in medieval Europe. Ask students to play a modern version of these games.

98. Following is a visual response from 1910 why a woman did not wish to wear a hobble skirt. Ask students to write a modern visual response why they don't want to wear a particular piece of clothing.

Why She Won't Wear It

She will not wear
a hobble skirt; she
says the style is much too
pert, and that no woman of good taste
would so deharmonize her waist; besides,
she says she thinks the style will last
for but a little while, because to any
one it seems the fad is going to extremes.
Whene'er her hobbled sisters pass she only
sighs and says: "Alas! How can a
lady of good sense incase herself in that
pretense! Just see her trip and wobble
by! Would I appear in that? Not I!
And how the horrid men-folks stare at
her as she goes here and there! Oh,
if she knew just what they said I
know she'd blush a rosy red. Besides the style is awkward, too,
I don't care if they claim
'tis new." And so she carefully explains her preference
for fuller trains, and for a
petticoat that's wide, and
will not be with giggles
eyed when she is trip-
ping down the street
—Besides you
see she has
LARGE   FEET!

Wilbur D. Nesbit

99. Below is a "short hand portrait" of figures from the past. Ask students to create a short hand portrait of some modern people.

MARK TWAIN

ROOSEVELT

ROCKEFELLER

100. Following is an object found in a prehistoric dig. Ask students to identify all possible uses that our ancestors could have made from this object.

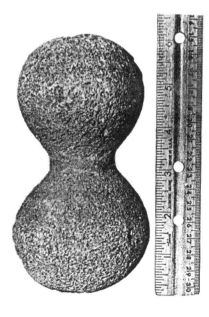

AND

Guidelines for Creative Problem Solving:

a. Don't settle for a first solution. Generate a host of solutions and select from the most interesting.

b. Suspend judgment. Don't evaluate solutions according to criteria of "good" or "bad." Allow solutions to soak into your mind and play with them.

c. Work with a team on problem solving.

d. Approach any problem from multiple perspectives. Put yourself in another person's shoes or in another time in history.

e. Allow time to "incubate" an idea. Treat "time" as an ally.

f. Allow the playful part of your personality to be prominent in creative problem solving.

CHAPTER 8

INQUIRY AND INTERACTING WITH TEXTUAL MATERIALS

Chapter Outline

1. Restating Information
2. Dialogues
3. Tips for Interacting With Textual Materials.

Restating Information

Although we live in the age of computers, textbooks and other textual materials continue to dominate the school curriculum. The first textbooks known to humanity were found in ancient Sumeria and they describe students memorizing and doing homework. The modern textbook is an eighteenth century invention to provide a population with limited access to books a summary of information. Textbooks are a means toward an end, they are not the end. Textbooks are a "book," nothing more, nothing less. There is nothing intrinsically bad or good about a book, it is the content which is critical and uses made of that content.

The most common use of textbooks is providing students a summary of a vast array of information. The attempt to cover this data ordinarily results in resort to generalities and selection by authors and publishers as to what is deemed worthy of being in the book. Students ordinarily confront textual material without a strong data base and thus are compelled to forge understandings from information presented. Examine the following passage from a textbook on American history:

"From Puritan days economic ventures in America had manifested a strong individualistic bent. By the 1820's and 1830's the laissez faire concept of government was so strong that President Jackson was able to accomplish what Jefferson had tried to do but failed – to give others besides the wealthy and privileged few the chance to pursue their economic goals. Jackson did this by preventing the rechartering of the Bank of the United States, which he considered a 'monster' because of its control over the national economy and its conservative lending policies made it difficult for the 'common people' – western settlers, farmers, and urban workers – to borrow money for their enterprises."

This passage contains several complex concepts that require extensive background knowledge to understand. It is an excellent summary, but essentially is meaningless to 99% of students – and quite a few adults. Many textual materials follow this pattern –making the simple very complex, and, in so doing, creating confusion in the mind of students. Teachers can assist students by examining textual materials and presenting reworded versions of complex passages. For example:

"The absence in America of government owned enterprises has led to individuals establishing their own businesses. The right of individuals to own their own business is termed, "laissez-faire" from the French meaning "to leave alone." Presidents Jefferson and Jackson believed in this idea. Jackson in the 1830's decided to abolish the Bank of the United States which was where the government kept its money. He was concerned that the Bank of the United States loaned money to wealthy people and made it difficult for a beginning businessman or a farmer to get a loan. Jackson had government money deposited in state banks to help poorer people get loans for farms and business."

Note the same number of words are used, but in the second example, students have an easier time understanding what is being stated. Clarity and conciseness make difficult material easier to understand. Teachers obviously can not rewrite an entire text, but they can select key passages and rephrase. Here are several suggestions:

1. Rewrite chapter headings. For example: "The Progressive Era" and be restated as: "Preventing wealthy business leaders from controlling the economy and efforts to reduce government corruption."

2. Write an introductory and a concluding paragraph for each chapter to ensure that main points are clear to your students.

3. Write your own summary of the chapter.

4. Write a one sentence key idea for each page in the chapter.

5. Ask students working in groups to summarize key ideas.

6. Preview the chapter and identify examples of jargon or complexity <u>before</u> students read the material. <u>Anticipate</u> reading problems.

The above list may not necessarily be accomplished in one year. Each year select at least one focus for your work in making textual materials understandable to students. Remember, YOU BEST UNDERESTAND YOUR STUDENTS. Textual materials are written for an amorphous group of students. Anticipation of reading and comprehension problems avoids difficulties and provides evidence to students that their teacher is continually thinking about their individual needs.

DIALOGUE WITH THE TEACHER

Textbooks were invented in the 18th century and continue to be a dominant piece of equipment in the education of children. The expression "textual materials" as used in this chapter refers not only to textbooks, but to stories used in teaching or handouts containing information. Teachers continually confront issues of reading abilities when using textual materials since it is rare for everyone in a class to be at the same level of reading comprehension. This chapter is designed to assist in making certain that students understand what they read and to use textual materials in order to foster inquiry learning. It is extremely important in using textual materials that students express their ideas in their own words to ensure recall of information. (Elementary and Secondary)

Objective: Understanding Textual Materials

Focus: Students will be able in writing, verbally, and visually to demonstrate their understanding of material assigned for reading.

Teacher	Student
1. Select a paragraph in a reading selection and rewrite it in words that allow all students to understand the material.	1. Students listen. Ask questions.
2. Select a chapter heading and rewrite it in terms students could understand.	2. Listen. In groups, students rewrite chapter headings in their own words.
3. Examine the example, "The Civil War as Discussed in the Cheers Tavern." Create your own model for a chapter or story to be read. In your dialogue include mistakes about what is contained in the reading selection.	3. Students in group use the Dialogue and find each mistake in the reading selection.
4. Prior to handing out a reading selection, anticipate what in the reading selection may cause comprehension problems for the reader. Write a dialogue in which you anticipate the reading problem, and then explain the material in terms that everyone can understand.	4. Students in group read material and develop list of items they find difficulty understanding. Present to teacher who will review these items.

5. Assign each group the task of taking a part of the reading selection and writing a dialogue which explains the material. They can use any characters in their dialogue.

a. Each group selects a different portion of the reading selection and writes a dialogue containing mistakes.

6. Review ideas for developing questions that stimulate inquiry in reading textual materials.

7. Create your own questions for the reading materials. Include in your questions examples of: Recall, Analytic, and Divergent.

5. Students in group create dialogues.

a. Students in group create dialogues with mistakes. Present to class which is to identify the mistakes.

6. Students in group are assigned a portion of the reading selection. The group is to create new questions for the material to be presented to class.

7. Students individually respond to questions.

Student Assessment: Students are to write three questions about reading materials given for a homework assignment. These questions will be asked of the class.

Personal Assessment: During the coming year write your own questions for reading materials rather than relying upon those provided by a publisher.

Multiple Intelligences: Logical Mathematical
Verbal Linguistic
Interpersonal

Dialoguing With Textual Materials

The author was recently teaching high school students and in reviewing their world history text concluded several chapters were confusing. A majority of his students came from working class backgrounds and were not immediately going on to college. They were bored with social studies which they found bewildering and difficult to understand. The author noted that when material was restated in other than textbook terms, student interest dramatically increased. Prior to reading a chapter, students were provided a short dialogue which raised key ideas being discussed in the chapter. The dialogues frequently were written in a humorous manner such as the following:

The Civil War As Discussed in the Cheers Tavern

Norm: Pour me a libation while I make sense out of my son's homework assignment about the Civil War.

Cliff: Now, wait a second. I am known at the Post Office as the leading authority on General Hubert Grant, the Civil War general.

Norm: Cliff, I think you mean Ulysses Grant. But, if you know so much, answer this question – what caused the Civil War?

Cliff: Well, my ma told me his name was Hubert. You see, there were these tax laws that upset the American people.

Carla: Look knucklehead, you got the Revolution confused with the Civil War. Everyone knows the South wanted to keep slaves and wanted to take their slaves out west. So, Lincoln, told them couldn't go west with slaves.

Norm: Slaves, taxes, going west, who cares. Give me another libation.

Cliff: Carlah, my dear, you are confused. The North wanted to tax stuff coming into America and the south didn't want those taxes.

Rebecca: I don't know if I am right or wrong, but actually Cliff might have a point. I thought since the North had more factories they wanted to tax manufactured goods coming from other countries to keep American factory goods at a lower price. The tax is called a tariff. And, the South didn't want those high tariffs.

Sam: Wait a second, I'm no brain unless we are talking about women, but I thought the Civil War started when a lot of people from Boston got mad because people in the South beat up on slaves.

Carla: Yeh, Sam, the way fans at the ball park beat up on you when you came in as a relief pitcher.

Cliff: Carlah, as one well versed in this topic, I can way without hesitation the Civil War started when that great Southern general, Alfonso Lee invaded the North to capture runaway slaves who were living in the capitol which in those days was in Philadelphia.

Carla: Cliff, get a frontal lobotomy. The South attacked Fort Sumter in Carolina. Then President Lincoln sent relief ships which couldn't get through. That's how the war started.

Norm: Another libation, please......

This dialogue served two purposes. It provided students a simple, clear statement of basic causes of the Civil War and, secondly, it contained several factual errors which they could clarify by working in groups. After they completed discussing and reviewing this dialogue, they read the chapter. Their next task was to work in a group and select one piece of the chapter to present to their classmates in the form of a dialogue. They could select characters from their favorite TV show as focal people in their dialogue. The class voted on which was the most humorous and informative dialogue. The end result was the chapter was read and student interest in its content was much higher than following normal procedures of reading a chapter.

Dialogues don't necessarily have to be humorous. They can also be data based. The key quality in any dialogue is presenting complex information clearly. Many people have discussions with neighbors about a household problem because the other person may be skilled and able to clearly explain how to handle the problem. Everyone has probably at one point or another had a dialogue with someone in which something they did not know was clearly explained. It is important in writing dialogues to anticipate what your students will not understand when asked to read a particular textual material. For example, the following was written to explain a chapter that dealt with Adolf Hitler:

Student: Ms. Lopez, I don't understand why people didn't stop Hitler in the 1930s.

Lopez: Notice the chapter tells about a Depression. This means the economies of most countries collapsed and millions of people were poor. For example, one out of three Americans was on

	welfare. England and Germany had similar problems. People were so concerned about their own situation, that they failed to pay attention to what Hitler was doing in Germany.
Student:	Yes, but he said he would conquer the world. Didn't that concern people?
Lopez:	Good point. Actually, at the beginning, Hitler just focused on Germany to improve its economy. Sometimes, he would make demands and threats but he usually backed away from actually going to war. He was clever. He claimed he wanted peace, but kept on building up Germany's armed forces.
Student:	But, didn't people get upset when he began killing Jews?
Lopez:	At first, he said he didn't want to kill Jews, but wanted them to leave Germany. He also knew there was a great deal of prejudice against Jews even in countries like the United States. He gradually increased the severity of his actions against Jews. What we will learn in the coming days is the process he followed to kill Jews and attempt to gain world control.

The above is a portion of a dialogue but it illustrates how a teacher can transform complex material in a textbook into terms that any student can understand. The adult mind frequently forgets how much we as teachers bring to the page; an information background which is not present in the mind of students. We read words differently than students since our minds fill in blank spots or draw upon other things we have read about the same topic.

Dialogue can be used for students of all ages. For those still learning how to read, a puppet show is another way to explain what is being discussed. However, for students in elementary school who have the basics of reading, dialogues can be used to foster their critical thinking. In the following dialogue there are numerous factual errors from the Cinderella story. Students working collaboratively examine the dialogue to identify mistakes.

Stepsister:	Cindy, I want to thank you for doing my chores. It gave me time to get dressed to go to the ball. Now, I can go with you.
Cindy:	Well, I didn't think it was fair for you always to do the chores.
Stepsister:	I know. I guess my mother likes you better than she does me.
Cindy:	I guess so. You know, she is going to introduce me to the Prince when we get to the ball.

Stepsister:	I hate to tell you this, but I met the prince a week ago. He told me he wants me to go on a date.
Cindy:	Wow! That's terrific.
Stepsister:	My main problem is not having a good dress for the ball. I am going to ask my fairy godmother to make me one.
Cindy:	I wish I had a fairy godmother.
Stepmother:	Cinderella, you work too hard. I think it is only fair if other people in this house do some of the chores. Come on dear, get ready for the ball.

Dialogues enable students to learn through means of a conversational style instead of the traditional paragraph form of imparting information. They are particularly effective in clarifying and explaining. A teacher used the following dialogue to assist her fourth graders to more fully understand the story entitled, "The Little House." This is a story about a house living in the country who yearns to live in a city. Eventually, urbanization catches up with the house and it finds itself inhabiting a stifling urban environment. The house is saved by children of the owners who bring the house once more back into the country. The following dialogue was created to focus attention on issues raised by this story:

Teacher:	Little House, what do you like best about living in the country? What do you least like?
House:	It's nice seeing children play and laugh and have a good time in the open fields, but then they grow up and move to the city. I lose all contact with them.
Teacher:	Do you remember when cars came and then gas stations and houses?
House:	Oh, yes. At first it was fun to have all these neighbors. But, then everything got dirty.
Teacher:	What did you miss most about living in a city?
House:	Fresh air, and daisies and watching cows wander around meadows.
Teacher:	Did anything else bother you about city life?
House:	I don't like those big buildings which block out the sun.
Teacher:	Do you have any regrets about being back in the country?
House:	Not really, but.......

After students read this dialogue, they worked in groups to complete the last sentence which completed with a "but." Then, they wrote a modern version of the story about a house in the country which wants to be part of a city.

Writing Dialogues is a relatively easy task. For example, if you were to write a dialogue dealing with the Snow White fairy tale, it would be necessary to complete the following practice exercise.

Practice Exercise

Step One: Which key ideas are discussed in the dialogue?

1. _____

2. _____

3. _____

Step Two: Who will conduct the dialogue? (The dialogue can be conducted by anyone or any animal or even an object like the house)

List Characters in Dialogue: _____

_____

Step Three: What will be the tone of the Dialogue? Humorous, Serious, Satirical.......

Step Four: Will the Dialogue contain elements of mystery for students to uncover?

Step Five: What will be the setting for the Dialogue?

Step Six: Write your Dialogue about Snow White?

Students generally connect reading textual materials with being required to recall what they have read. It is not uncommon for students to read end-of-chapter questions and then find the answers within the chapter. This results in being able to answer questions without ever have to read the entire chapter. It is important for individual teachers to create their own textual questions to supplement those provided by publishers. Of course, one need not merely write questions. Posing a "mystery" requiring students to employ analytical thinking is the best guarantee they will actually read textual materials. The book "Manchild in the Promised Land," by Claude Brown depicts a young Harlem boy being raised in the 1940s and 1950s. A teacher posed the following task to her students about the book:

"If Claude Brown was viewing 'The Godfather' with you in a movie theater, what would he comment about the film?" Brown in his book describes how gangsters in the 1950s dumped large amounts of drugs upon Harlem which fits into a key scene in the movie which depicts this action.

She also posed this question: "If Claude Brown were alive today, how would he respond to Affirmative Action programs?" There is no "right" or "wrong" answer to the question. The teacher was mainly interested in the thought process a student employed in order to react to the question.

The Chinese version of "Little Red Riding Hood" is entitled, "Lon Po Po." In the Chinese version, three children named Shang, Tao, and Potze, are home alone when the wolf (who pretends to be their grandmother) knocks on the door. The wolf enters and soon the children realize it is a wolf rather than their grandmother. The wolf comes out and begs the children to get some nuts which are high up on the tree. The children persuade the wolf to get into a basket which they will raise high enough for the wolf to get the nuts. The wolf complies and when he is high in the air, the children drop the basket and kill the evil wolf. This brief synopsis raises interesting questions and tasks students could be posed about the fairy tale.

1. Who am I? I used clever questions to figure out it was not my grandmother but a wolf. What was my name and how did I save my brothers? _____

2. I am a very clever wolf – or at least I used to be. Explain my smart moves in this story and the mistakes that led to my death. _____

3. In groups, rewrite this story so that no one dies.

4. (Add your own question or activity) _____

_____

_____

_____

Interacting with textual materials does not necessarily require extensive rewriting or creating new materials. A simple rewording can also suffice. For example, in a science class a teacher slightly altered a question at the end of the chapter in order to stimulate student inquiry. The question read: "List the components of the energy chain in an automobile." Instead, the teacher posed: "Write a dialogue between two or more components of the energy chain in an automobile in which they discuss how they interact with one another." Instead of a recall response which students could have obtained by simply going back into the chapter to get the necessary information, they had to employ critical thinking to properly respond to the question.

ADDITIONAL TIPS FOR INTERACTING WITH TEXTUAL MATERIALS

1. Prior to introducing a text, review the entire book by discussing the table of contents and explaining the connections between chapters. This provides the reader an overview regarding what will happen in the book.

2. After completing a chapter, discuss how material in the following chapter connects to the chapter just read. Prior to beginning a chapter, discuss its content and its relationship to other parts of the book.

3. Present students material from another textbook in order to emphasize that textual materials are the views of authors.

4. Redo questions. For example, a question at the end of a chapter in Dickens' "A Tale of Two Cities" asks: "What was the method of execution used to kill aristocrats?" Redo the question this way: "Assume you are the guillotine, how would you think as your sharp blade cuts into the heads of aristocrats?

5. A question in a health book asks: "List the four main food groups." "Pose a question like this: "OK, we all know the four food groups, in groups invent a new food group that contains elements of each of the four food groups."

6. Question in a math textbook: "What is the answer to the problem 4X4?" Play with the question this way: "Assume four and his friend four met two strangers who are named four and three. What would they say to one another?"

7. Ask students to select a character in a textbook and have them comment about a current topic.

8. Create a meeting in which characters from three of more books meet to discuss a topic such as: "What I like or don't like about teenagers."

9. Rewrite questions in textbooks to shift from the passive to the active mode. For example, an HBJ Science textbook asked this question: "The surface of a mirror is always (a) smooth;(b) very rough; (c) made of silver." Pose the following: "Which of the following is most like a mirror?" (a) an ice pond; (b) city pavement © a lake. Explain your answer."

10. Prior to having students examine a textbook which contains visual elements, ask students working in groups to examine only the visual components of a chapter list what they learned from just examining visual elements.

11. Divide the class into groups. Each group has its members identify words they do not understand in the chapter. These words are explained in clear

terms. Each group's work is collected and collated to produce a mini-dictionary of words and terms to assist the reader.

12. As students read a textbook chapter, halt, and help them focus on visual images of what is being read. For example, "We are reading about triangles. Form an image of a triangle in your mind. Where in your house can you see a triangle? Imagine the triangles are a dance team. See the triangles dance. Open your eyes and gaze around the room until you find a triangle."

13. Assign students to research the textbook author. Has the author ever taught at the elementary or secondary levels?

14. Encourage students to identify examples of ethnic or gender bias in the text.

15. Select a topic from the textbook. Have students use Internet or the school library to research the topic. Their task is to identify new or different aspects to the topic.

16. Have students do their own illustrations for a chapter.

17. Have students create illustrations for a book that has none.

18. Encourage students to identify questions about what they are reading.

19. Organize a "quiz show" after each chapter. Each time a different group of students is selected to participate on the show.

20. Discuss with students any concerns you have with a particular chapter or topic covered in the textbook.

21. Ask students to write headlines to identify the main idea in a chapter.

22. If you are daring, try teaching one year by teaching backwards. Begin with the last chapter and work yourself backwards.

23. Invite another teacher who teaches the same topic. Engage in a dispute about a topic handled in a chapter. Let students listen and hear two professionals engaged in an intellectual discussion about a textbook.

24. In social studies, find a textbook written in a different language which deals with a topic covered in the textbook. For example, a textbook from Mexico which discusses the Mexican War with the United States.

25. Include questions on tests from prior chapters – make certain students know you will do this. The questions should be connecting the prior chapter to the present one being studied.

26. Have a character in one novel ask a question to a character in another novel.
27. Discuss with students the process by which textbooks are selected in their school district.
28. Provide an argument about a specific topic in the chapter. Explain why you disagree with the manner in which it is presented.
29. Present an example from a professional journal in which an author disagrees with ideas expressed in your textbook.

CHAPTER 9

INQUIRY ON THE INTERNET

Chapter Outline:

1. Introduction
2. Suggestions on Using Internet

AN INNOVATIVE EDUCATIONAL TOOL

Educators have always dreamnt that new technology would enable schools to vastly improve their effectiveness in teaching. Throughout the twentieth century, a host of machines ranging from phonographs to movie projectors to tape recorders have not only been a source of enjoyment but have been used in many facets of our society. However, they have had limited impact on the average classroom.

A growing number of educators are heralding the Internet as the way to enliven education and stimulate critical thinking. But, even a cursory glance at past encounters with technology reveal that after an initial burst of enthusiasm, classrooms return to the familiar pattern of an adult in front of the room and students sitting in chairs listening. If Rip Van Winkle awoke from his two hundred year sleep, the only familiar sight he would find is the school classroom.

Today, the Internet is welcomed as an innovative tool that will alter education. The Internet is and will be used, but its mere use does not necessarily guarantee that inquiry learning will be fostered. Abundant evidence exists that the Internet is being utilized as the latest manifestation of the textbook. It appears to be following a pattern established by use of other technologies. Many teachers show films and ask students to regurgitate what they saw which transforms film into textual material. It is very common for teachers to use the overhead as a means of transmitting data just as videos serve as visual textbooks.

The Cyber world can be a force of educational transformation or it can become yet another linear mode of education. In theory, the shift from written textbooks which few use as an interactive device to entering the Internet with its multitude of options should produce dramatic new ways of education. However, most Internet assignments still require students to gather information from Internet sites, synthesize the data, and report it either in written or oral form.

Many educators tend to draw upon their experiences with textual material in determining Internet tasks. An assignment requiring students to investigate a topic and report factual data could equally be accomplished in a library. The Internet's greatest impact upon education will not lie in providing efficient access to information. The Internet for the first time in human history affords an opportunity for students to investigate multiple sources of ideas, to compare and contrast, and to engage in original source research.

A central issue of the Internet lies in differentiating between information and knowledge. Information pertains to accumulating discrete pieces of data whereas knowledge involves extrapolating broad concepts from the information. The interactive features of the Internet and its capacity to access virtually unlimited sources make it an interesting medium for inquiry and the creation of knowledge. It can not be emphasized enough that students engaged in gathering and summarizing data are not "constructing knowledge." They are "summarizing information."

The challenge is to use the fabulous resources of Internet in the quest to stimulate inquiry. An inquiring mind needs information, but it uses the information to uncover understandings and insights. Following are several strategies to shift from information accumulation to inquiry.

Activities

1. Students are asked to check the home pages of the Immigration and Naturalization Service (INS) and secure a copy of the test given prospective immigrants. Each student takes the test, and then working in groups, they devise the test they would like immigrants to pass in order to qualify for citizenship. Their new test is e-mailed to the INS and to their local congressman with requests for comments.

2. Students identify a current topic. It could be anything from a Chinese space probe to a new movie or the latest fashions or to a world conflict. They click on "international newspapers" and investigate how the topic is handled in newspapers from at least four nations. In their compare and contrast of the materials, students make note of omissions, wordage, interpretation and bias. Their report is reported both in written and chart form.

3. Students are given the names of five artists. Each group has a specific artist whose home pages are checked. Each group creates a visual presentation of the work of their artist, but they also provide the teacher a written summary indicating their artist's approach and ideas about art. As each group presents, the remainder of the class is given five handouts and their task is to identify from the art work being presented which artist is being depicted. At the completion of these presentations, each group's task is to create a piece of art that incorporates the ideas of the five artists.

4. Students working in groups are each assigned a Supreme Court Justice. Their task is to check their Justice's home pages and learn about his or her

philosophy and ideas. The teacher presents a summary of a case that will appear in the coming months before the Supreme Court. The task of each group is to hypothesize how their particular Justice will rule on the case. After the group writes their hypothesis, it is e-mailed to a clerk working for their Justice who is asked to comment on their hypothesis. After the case is decided, each group discusses their hypothesis and how the Justice actually ruled.

5. Each student is asked to identify an occupation they wish to enter. Students then use homepages of the United States Census Bureau to gather pertinent information regarding their occupation. The task of each student is to research using Internet sources information concerning their occupation in order to determine which geographical location affords the best opportunity for obtaining work in that occupation.

6. Students are asked to read at least three versions of the fairy tale, "The Snow Queen." Each group then writes a modern version of the fairy tale, but shifts its locale from an environment containing snow to one which lacks snow. They also do illustrations for their new tale.

7. Students working in groups check the web site of the Yellowstone National Park. After taking the test about their knowledge of Yellowstone, the group identifies an environmental issue facing the Yellowstone National Park. The group then examines parks within their geographical area in order to identify which environmental issues these parks are confronting, and, if possible, find one having a problem similar to one faced at Yellowstone. The group then contacts their local park to inquire if it is aware that their issue is similar to that of Yellowstone. The task **of the gro**up is to establish contacts between at least two parks having similar environmental issues in order to facilitate exchange of information and ideas about solutions.

8. The web site of the Library of Congress contains maps from different eras in history. The web site of the Department of the Interior also has numerous maps. The task of students working in groups is to identify maps from these sources that trace the evolution of their particular geographical area over at least two hundred years in terms of geographical characteristics, which changed, population density, animals, etc....

9. Students working in groups identify an issue from American history that involved at least one other society and the United States. For example, the Spanish American War or the American Revolution. Each group has the task of contacting a school within that society in order to establish communication with teachers and students. The goal is to obtain from these students or their teacher how the topic is covered within their school and society.

DIALOGUE WITH THE TEACHER

A key question to pose any teacher is whether or not the task being assigned on Internet could just as easily be accomplished without Internet sources. Can one use existing library resources for the task? Another question one can pose is, "how can my existing assignment be transformed into something different by relying upon the Internet?"

The internet is a fascinating development in human history that offers an incredible data bank of information. No teacher can replicate that source of information. However, teachers possess one quality that few computers can equal – our ability to pose interesting and unusual questions. Elie Wiesel, the Nobel Prize winner, once said it is the questions asked, not the answers given, which distinguish the wise person from the fool. The Internet's most revolutionary influence on education is its impact upon our questioning capabilities.

Educators can proceed on the path of imparting information without regard to the attainment of wisdom, although in doing so, we function as inefficient computers. Or, we can accept the challenge of the Internet and alter student assignments to engage them in developing the spirit of inquiry. The Internet will never become a revolutionary tool until we dramatically change our questioning strategies and our requirements both inside and outside the classroom.

Concept: Climate in the World

Focus: Students will be able to visually and in writing demonstrate understanding of the relationship between climate and life.

Social Studies Standards:
  Standard 3:   People, Places and Environment

Teacher	Student
1. Students are divided into groups and informed a zoo space ship has crashed on Earth. Each group is assigned a planet in our solar system. Their task is to gather geographic and climate information about their planet from Internet web sites.	1. Students work in groups gathering data on their planet from Internet web sites.

2. Each group is to create a life form that is consistent with the data they have gathered about their planet. For example, a life form from Venus would thrive if placed in areas that are hot. The task of the group is to visually depict their life form.

3. Each group is to identify places on Earth where their life form would be able to live.

4. Entire class works to create a world map on which they will place their life forms.

2. Students in group use data to create a life form and visually depict it.

3. Students in group use climate maps of world to find places in which their life form could live.

4. Class works on world map collage.

Assessment: 1. Evaluation of group's life form and how it is placed on Earth.

2. Evaluation of group's reasoning why they created the life form and why they placed it in specific locations.

Multiple Intelligences: Logical Mathematical — reasoning must be used to identify places On map.

Visual Spatial — Visual creation of their life form

Interpersonal — Working together in group

Web Sites on Climate

This site contains information about climate in the world
www.worldclimate.com

This site has excellent data about climate
www.greeningearthsociety.org/climate

This site allows access to world climate records
www.nhes.com

This site contains weather and climate maps
www.worldbook.com/fun/atw/climates/index.htm

This site contains information on climate changes including historical data and maps
www.sunysuffolk.edu/mandius/lia/index.html

This site is organized by the World Wildlife Fund and has reports on climate and species
www.panda.org/resources/publications

This site has information on climate changes including data about deserts
www.geo.Arizona.edu/news/F98/atacam.html

This site is organized by the National Geographic and lists climate and regions
www.nationalgeographic.com/wildworld/

This is an interesting site containing information on what it requires to bring life to Mars by altering its climate
www.sciam.com/1999/0399space/0399mckay.html

This site has information on biomes
www.blueplanetbiomes.org

This site has information on world Weather
www.weatherbase.com

Dialogue With the Teacher

Concept: The United States Supreme Court

Focus: Students will verbally and in writing identify the thinking processes of Supreme Court Justices pertaining to their decisions in upcoming cases.

Social Studies Standards:
Standard 5: Individuals, Groups, and Institutions
Standard 6: Power, Authority and Governance
Standard 10: Civic Ideals and Practices

Teacher	Student
1. Students are divided into pairs or triads depending on size of class. Each team is assigned a Supreme Court Justice. The initial task of the team is to investigate web sites pertaining to their Supreme Court Justice and gather information about the ideas and beliefs of the Justice.	1. Each team gathers information in written form.
2. Each team is to formulate an hypothesis regarding what is the philosophy of their Justice. This is shared with the teacher to receive feedback about the accuracy of their hypothesis.	2. Each team prepares a written document in which the philosophy of their Justice is described.
3. Each team is given a digest of a case currently being reviewed by the Supreme Court. Each team is to present their hypothesis regarding how their Justice will rule in the case.	3. Each team presents a written document which explains how they think their Justice will rule in the case. This is discussed with teacher to help clarify their ideas. a. Each team emails their hypothesis to a law clerk in the office of their Supreme Court Justice. They are to request feedback from the law clerk if they would provide it regarding the logic of their hypothesis.

4. After the Supreme Court decides in the case each team reviews how their Justice actually decided and compare and contrast their hypothesis with the actual decision.

4. Each team analyzes how their Justice actually rules as contrasted with their hypothesis. Class discussion.

Assessment: 1. Evaluation of written report developed by team. The evaluation focuses upon the reasoning used by the team and it is unimportant if the team was right or wrong.

Multiple Intelligences: Logical Mathematical — analyzing thought process of Justice

Verbal Linguistic — the team's verbal and written explanation

WEB SITES ON THE UNITED STATES SUPREME COURT

This site contains information about current cases before the Supreme Court
    http://Jurist.law.pittt.edu/supremecourt.htm

This is a virtual Supreme Court site which allows students to learn about a particular Justice, their philosophy and their decisions. Simply type in the name of the Justice in the appropriate place.
    http://law.penn.edu/fac/bwordhou/use/breyer.htm

This site provides information about how the Supreme Court functions
    www.law.cornell.edu/rules/supct/overview.html

This site contains information about court decisions over the years
    www.fundlaw.com/casecode/supreme.html

This site has biographical information about Justices and their decisions
    http://supct.law.cornell.edu/supct/justices/fullcourt.html

This site has information about current cases
    www.washingtonpost.com

This site has information about justices, biographies, and their philosophy
    www.1;.findlaw.com/supremecourt/justices.html

This is a help center for Social Studies teachers and their student about the court.
    www.socialstudiesHelp.com

ADDITIONAL IDEAS FOR INQUIRY ON THE INTERNET

1. Students identify a topic being studied. Each group gathers five original source documents related to the topic. Their task is to develop questions and activities using the documents.

2. Students working in groups identify a piece of clothing. Their task is to trace how this piece of clothing is made from the original raw materials. In their study of this piece of clothing the group is to identify use of child labor to make the clothing, working conditions and pay at each step in the process. At the conclusion of their report a visual depiction of how the clothing is made should be presented.

3. Students working in groups identify a fairy tale from Europe. Their next task is to identify a fairy tale with a similar theme that is found in another society. The groups compares and contrasts the two versions of the fairy tale. The group can also write a contemporary American version of the fairy tale.

4. Ask students to compare and contrast calendars in at least five societies and time periods. Each group gathers its information and all work together to identify similarities and differences as well as the current date from five views.

5. As a follow up to the above, each group is assigned a planet in the universe. The group's task is to gather information and pictures about their planet. After gathering that information, the group creates a calendar for their planet with accompanying illustrations for each time period.

6. Organize a 'child's view of the world." Have students research materials written by children all over the world. Identify from the material issues that impact children in every corner of the world.

7. Have students research mathematical and scientific ideas among the Incas, Aztecs and Mayans of the New World. Their task is to hypothesize how these ancient math and science ideas could be applied to modern issues or problems.

8. Have students research lighthouses around the world. Their task is to identify materials used to build the lighthouses, function of lighthouses, height, etc.. and then construct on their computers a modern lighthouse.

9. Ask students to working in groups to identify a food. Their task is to trace the manner in which this particular food spread throughout the world. After obtaining this information, groups are to chart the manner in which the same food is prepared and eaten in different societies. At the conclusion, they are to devise a new way to use the food.

10. Have students working in groups identify a natural resource and study its uses. Their task is to invent a new use for the natural resource.

11. Students working in groups are to identify web sites which teach how to play a musical instrument. The task of the group is to develop a teaching plan to teach the musical instrument to another student in the class.

12. Students working in groups identify three fairy tales from three societies. The task of each group is to: (a) identify what they learned about geography of the society which produced the fairy tale; (b) what they learned about law and government in the society; (d) what they learned about clothes and fashion. Each group is to explain to present a chart containing the above information and then explain each society's values. As part of this discussion they are to compare and contrast the society's values with contemporary American values.

13. Have students identify proverbs from various societies. Their task is to draw upon these proverbs to write modern proverbs.

14. Have students research flags from at least ten societies. Their task is to resdesign a new American flag. They are to create on the computer a new version of Uncle Sam.

15. A zoo ship containing life forms from planets throughout the universe crashes on Earth. Each group is to create a life form consistent with a planet. For example, a bird from Venus that needs fire to live. After making their creation, the group is to identify which part of planet Earth is most conducive for this animal to live.

16. Students collect original source documents written by soldiers in at least three wars. Their task is to compare and contrast issues raised by these soldiers.

17. Ask students to identify three sports. Each group selects a sport. The group task is to create a chart indicating place of birth of athlete. After charts are developed and shared, each group formulates an hypothesis regarding relationship of geography to sport.

18. Divide class into groups. Each group is provided a poet whose web pages are examined. The group collects information about their poet which is presented to the class. The group also writes a poem using the style of the poet. The task of the class is to connect the new poem to information provided about the various poets.

19. Have students working in groups check their local congressman or U.S. Senator's web pages for information concerning a particular topic. Each group is to develop a position paper concerning a current topic related to their state, nation or the world. This position paper is e-mailed to the office of their congressman or Senator and a response is requested.

20. Students are divided into groups and assigned a river to investigate. Their task is to collect information about the route of the river, vegetation, climate, trees, and products found near the river. After gathering the information, each group is to identify an environmental issue facing the river and write a position paper on the topic. This position paper is then e-mailed to the Department of the Interior or the state department of the interior in order to inquire what is being done about this environmental issue.

21. Assign groups to research web pages related to following three American presidents: Theodore Roosevelt, Woodrow Wilson, and Harry Truman. The group task is to gather information about their president including original source documents. Each group is to present to the class analysis of how their findings about the president compare and contrast with what their textbook says about the president.

22. Have students compare and contrast hotel prices in at least five cities. They are to develop a chart depicting these variations and an interpretation as to why prices are higher or lower in particular areas.

23. Have students click on home pages of the Census Bureau. They are to gather information concerning life expectancy in at least four geographical areas. The task of the groups is to formulate an hypothesis as to why life expectancy is higher or lower in a specific geographical area.

23. Students working in groups are assigned to investigate the climate in at least five geographical areas of America. They are posed the following problem to solve: "If you wished to build a home drawing upon solar power, in which area would you build and in which area would costs be lower?"

24. Students working in groups are to identify snow conditions in at least five geographical locations in the world. Their task is to identify how snow impacts life in these geographical areas and develop a chart depicting their findings. Their chart might include data on sports, dress, housing, foods, drinks, etc...

25. Students working in group check web pages devoted to the artist, Picasso. The task of the group is to hypothesize what type of art and which subjects would Picasso focus upon if he were alive today.

CHAPTER 10
FOSTERING INQUIRY THROUGH MEMORY POWER

Chapter Outline:

1. Introduction
   a. Recall information from previous time period.
   b. Tic-tac-toe activity.
2. Explanation of short and long term memory.
   a. Recall numbers
   b. Recall lists
3. Visual Imagery
4. Recall Through Linking
5. Memorizing Textual Materials
6. Recalling Data
   a. Names of state capitols
   b. Names of states
7. Memory Activities

Enhancement of Memory Retention

Critical thinking depends upon information, and information depends upon memory. Students are continually criticized by adults for failure to recall information, but few schools offer any form of systematic training in memory. A student who is able to recall data is not only more prone to successfully problem solve, but will perform at a higher rate of success on standardized examinations. This chapter presents interesting ways to enhance the memory retention of what is taught.

The first written description of memory in western civilization dates back to ancient Greece. The poet Simonides of Ceos was called away from a banquet hall, and during his absence, the ceiling collapsed crushing all the guests. The corpses were so mangled it was virtually impossible for relatives to identify which body belonged to their family. Simonides was noted for his memory power and he was able to recall where each person was seated thus making it possible for bodies to be identified. His memory technique consisted of placing things in a sequence and surrounding them with light. All memory experts utilize, in one form or another, some strategy to help retain information.

"I can't remember this stuff" is a frequent complaint of students. This attitude leads to feelings of personal inadequacy or disinterest in material being studied. Educators can either focus on blaming or they can switch to a proactive stance of training students to attain high standards of information retention. Actually, virtually all students have untapped memory power which if utilized would provide them the means of being superior performers in their courses. Attempt the following brief experiment – "You are asked to close your eyes and return in a split second to the house or apartment you consider to be your childhood home. Explore the kitchen, see the stove, open the refrigerator or ice box (if you are of my generation) and if there is a window in the room gaze outward at what you used to see as a child. Go to the bedroom and see your bed, examine the pillow and cover, open a closet door where once were your clothes and finger them in your mind's eye. If there was a window in your bedroom look outward at what were once familiar sights. Go anywhere else in that house and apartment." The vast majority of people can successfully conduct this experiment and within a minute recall an incredible storage of data. Why can people remember within a moment information learned ten, twenty, thirty, forty or even fifty years ago?

We recall best when the subject is connected to visual or emotional factors within our lives. We more readily learn when what is being taught is connected to what we already know. Teachers for years have been teaching children how to spell the word "piece" by having them associate the word with one they already know – "pie". Most students readily learn the shape of Italy when told it is shaped in the form of a boot. Or, the old familiar way of teaching names of the Great Lakes is to have children recall the word "Homes" – Huron, Ontario, Michigan, Erie and Superior.

The greatest mistake made in education is failing to acknowledge the power of an individual brain. There is not a computer in the world that matches the number of inter-connections within a single brain. The following exercise enables you to become more intimately connected to your own brain:

1. Write all incidents you recall from the past six hours.
2. Draw at least three visual images of anything you recall.
3. Shut your eyes and totally relax.
4. After a few moments, you are to assume you have become a movie director. Create a movie which links all the incidents that you recall.
5. Shut your eyes and relax.
6. Recall something that was not part of your original movie.
7. Analyze why you now recall information that originally was not part of your movie.
8. Sit quietly in a chair, play classical music and relax.
9. Again become a movie director and create a movie depicting the past six hours.
10. The next morning when you awake, take a moment to shut your eyes, and recall those six hours.
11. Shut your eyes, relax and take some deep breaths.
12. Once again, recall your movie. Chances are what you now recall is in more depth and quality than what first appeared as your movie.

Dialogue With The Teacher

In our concern about test performance and attaining standards it is frequently forgotten that the easiest way to achieve these goals is by enhancing the memory capacities of students. Why do we include in this book about inquiry an emphasis upon memory? Ironically, memory experts are among the world's greatest proponents of using inquiry. In this chapter, you will encounter interesting and unusual approaches to fostering good memory strategies among your students. A former student has taught her students memory strategies and prior to her tests, there is a class memory session. Test scores are higher, virtually every student in her class passes the exam and everyone is happy. If you teach students how to memorize it is a GUARANTEE that more students will pass your examinations and perform better on standardized tests. (Secondary-Elementary)

Objective: Enhancing Learning Through Memory

Focus: Students will verbally, in writing, and visually recall information that was taught.

Teacher	Student
1. Ask students to recall what they remember from the previous three hours. a. Select a student. Ask the student to go back to the moment they arrived at school. Ask them to recall leaving the bus or car and ask them what they saw walking from that place until they entered the school. Ask them to recall walking down the corridor. As students do this activity they will discover they remember more details than what they initially wrote on their paper.	1. Students individually recall.
2. Ask students to do Tic-tac-toe activity.	2. Students in pair do tic-tac-toe.

3. Introduce concept of short and long term memory.
   a. Ask each student to recall what is on a penny.
   b. Do recall of numbers.
   c. Read first list of words. Students must wait until completion before writing list in exact order it was given. Read second list of words. Insert in the middle of the list a word that would arouse instant memory among your students. You are demonstrating that a word which has Visual power is more readily recalled. Ordinarily, people best recall the beginning of a list of words and those at the end. They experience greatest difficulty with words in the center unless it is visually impacting.

3. Students listen.
   a. Recall penny
   b. Recall numbers
   c. Listen and write

4. Do "Exploring an Orange."
   a. Do the Planet Exercise to demonstrate how to learn information through visual means. The Planet exercise teaches location of planets from sun of each planet.
   b. As a follow up, work with class on visualizing names of Presidents. For example: "Shut your eyes and see yourself walking through a forest. You come to a stream and see a group of women washing a ton of clothes. uddenly, a naked man walks out of the forest like the first Adam, he comes to you and says, "have you seen my son Jeff, I'm mad about my son. Then, you notice a man rowing a boat. In the boat is another naked man like Adam and he shouts out, "have you seen my son Jack?" OK,

4. Students visualize
   a. Listen and visualize.

   b. Students in triad do activity and share with class.

up to this point, we have Washington, John Adams, Jefferson, Madison, Monroe, John Q. Adams, and Andrew Jackson. As practice, have students begin with the current President and work backwards. Emphasize to students the importance of transforming a name into a visual image. For example, President Reagan, is visually ray-gun.
c. Select some material that should be memorized for an upcoming exam. Have students use this approach in memorizing the material.

    c. Students in group develop memory strategies.

5. Do Linking activity.
   a. Assign a body of information being studied. The task is to link the material in a story and to use the postman delivering technique for recall.

5. Students listen.
   a. Students in pairs create link story. Individually memorize placing material on their block.

6. The Memorizing Textual Material is best done at the beginning of a course. However, at any time, you can have students exam the chapter headings and then review what they have learned and what they will be learning in future chapters.

6. Students listen.

7. Do "Recalling Data" activity.
   a. Select some material currently being learned and ask students to use this technique.

7. Students in groups complete task.
   a. Students in group use this memory device.

8. In preparation for a test, state an item. For example, "photosynthesis," and give students a picture of the item – or draw on board. Ask students to take a picture

8. Individually do picture in mind.
   a. In triad create rhyme.

of the drawing and place in their mind. As they do so, the student is to exaggerate the size and give it color.

9. Present information to students. Demonstrate on board how the material can be made into symbols or visual images. If you are teaching information that is linked, draw a diagram that links connections between the items.
   a. Ask students to do similar task for information that will be on a test.

9. Listen and observe.

   a. In groups, create images and draw connections between items.

10. Read information students are to learn. After reading a page, ask students to create a visual image about what they just read. Read another page, ask students to link what was on the second page with the first.

10. Listen.
    a. In group create linkages.

11. Select a passage that contains difficult material. Either yourself or a student you trust is to read the material cracking jokes about it.

11. Listen.

12. Present information you wish students to learn. Ask them to find something in their lives that is similar. For example, "triangles."

12. Students in group form linkage to their lives. Students give examples of where they encounter triangles in life. Ask them to draw a relationship triangle.

13. Prior to next test, have 20 minute "memory practice session."

13. Students in group, use any memory strategies to study for test. Each group shares their ideas with class.

14. Select items from end-of-chapter suggestions to use with students.

Student Assessment: Ask student to identify memory device they used to study for a test and explain why it helped or did not help. If it didn't help they are to revise strategy to make it work for next test.

Personal Assessment: Read a book on memory. Jerry Lucas has an excellent book for teachers. He formerly was a star basketball player for the New York Knickerbockers.

Multiple Intelligences: Logical Mathematical
Verbal Linguistic
Visual Spatial
Interpersonal
Intrapersonal

According to some memory experts, theoretically, virtually all information can be recalled. This may or may not be true, but everyone can enhance his or her ability to remember the past. Old fashioned teachers often emphasized that "practice made perfect." Memory experts tend to agree with this belief. Following is a simple exercise to provide practice in recall.

1. Draw a large tic-tac-toe graph on a paper. Each box should be about 3 inches square.
2. Pair up with a friend. If doing this exercise in class, have students pair off.
3. Person "A" fills in his or her tic-tac-toe with X's and O's without allowing person "B" to see their design.
4. Person "A" allows person "B" to see the design for a split second and then covers it.
5. Person "B" must then recall what was seen.
6. Each person takes several turns doing this activity. It is simply practice in training one's eye to recall a bit of information.

Humans do not have a problem remembering, the issue is recalling information on demand. A modern human is subjected to different stimuli than our ancestors. Consider life in the forest. What would people living in forests train their minds to remember? What type of oral or visual stimuli would most capture their attention? There is abundant medical evidence our hearing is not as proficient as that possessed by ancient peoples. However, regardless of the time era in which one lives, the basic structure of memory remains the same. Following is the classic description of the memory process:

Stimulus → Sensory Register → Short Term Memory → Long Term Memory

If something we encounter never registers on our senses, we are unable to recall that event. In your drive to work or walking along the street an infinite number of events or scenes occurred and theoretically you should be able to recall them. However, 99.9% never registered on your senses and thus are lost to your life history. For example, yesterday on your normal drive to work someone suddenly stopped and you hit their rear bumper. There was an exchange of insurance cards, and you left fuming at the incident. This event definitely registered on your senses and if you continue to grumble about it and become furious it may well enter your long term memory. On the other hand, yesterday, someone in front suddenly stopped and you <u>nearly</u> hit their bumper. Perhaps, you cursed for a moment and then drove on. That incident may or may not enter your short term memory, but most definitely it will not become part of your long term memory. People who were in their teens or older vividly recall the day President John F. Kennedy got shot. They will even go into minute detail about what happened that day.

The Kennedy example illustrates the power of an emotional event upon our memory. The day you got married – or divorced – lives on vividly in your mind. If you are a sport fan, an important World Series game or football play may be firmly embedded within your memory. On the other hand, try this experiment: Shut your eyes; and relax. Take yourself on a trip through memory lane of your school career. Begin with kindergarten and stroll through your years in school until high school graduation. Who or what do you recall? Notice that some classes or teachers are alive within our minds while others never made it to our long term memory. Why?

We recall that which is important – TO US. Teachers have been declaiming and preaching for years that what is being taught IS IMPORTANT! Unfortunately, each student decides what is important to secure a home within their long term memory. Teachers through threats and punishment have limited control over what enters short term memory, but long term memory is only within the province of an individual.

Try the following exercise. Shut your eyes and recall every piece of information found on an ordinary penny. After you have written down what you recall, examine a penny and discover what you forgot. Generally, virtually everyone recalls the color and shape of a penny because that is what they focus on when using pennies. Few people when using a penny examine its date or glance on the back to examine visual material. A rule of memory is: "What we use, is what we recall."

It has frequently been claimed by memory experts that the human mind most readily retains up to seven individual pieces of data at any single moment. That is why telephone numbers only have seven digits. Try the following exercise: Read the following list of numbers and memorize it within three minutes. Do not read what is below the list of numbers until you have completed the exercise.

```
5 9 4 2
7 1 3 4 6
3 9 8 1 4 7
2 5 7 3 9 1 8
1 3 6 2 8 4 1 5
5 2 7 3 9 1 4 6 8
8 3 9 2 4 3 6 1 3 2
```

The typical reaction is to memorize each of the 49 numbers as a distinct piece of data. Actually, there were seven numbers to memorize — 5,942, 71,346, 398,147, etc.. This activity leads to another rule of memory: If we "chunk" information it is easier to recall the data than learning discrete pieces within the chunk. You undoubtedly have used chunking throughout your life. Students have to be taught how to chunk and cluster data for improved memory retention. In preparing lesson plans, consider how you can chunk what is being taught in ways that make learning easier.

Human minds adhere to particular patterns in their encounter with learning. Reflect for a moment about your behavior as a student. At which points during the class period did you most focus upon what was being presented –beginning, middle or conclusion of the lesson? Following is a short exercise in recall of data. Ask a friend to read the following list to you. Immediately after list one is read, write the names of the items in the exact sequence in which they were presented. Then, have the second list read, and write the sequence.

* eggs, butter, cookies, hamburger, shoe, pepper, chair, pepper, onions, bread, pickles, peanuts

* lettuce, book, orange, oatmeal, gun, Playboy, apples, rice, table, steak, prunes, car

Ordinarily, a majority of people do best on recalling the initial item and the last item. Their greatest difficulty is recalling information in the middle of a sequence of data unless a visual image such as "Playboy" is presented. In opposition to education experts who argue for introducing lessons with a powerful activity or image, memory experts argue the most visual compelling portion or the most exciting part of a lesson should be in the middle of the class period. After all, most students are conditioned to pay attention at the beginning of the lesson and at the conclusion when assignments or homework is given.

A theme of this chapter is that memory strategies are effective in assisting students to recall information. Memory theory draws extensively upon the old adage that "a picture is worth a thousand words." Visual imagery plays a powerful role in recalling information. For example, suppose on your next trip to the supermarket your shopping list included the following items: milk, carrots, peanut butter, potato chips, spinach, cider, roast beef, bread, and fish. The list can be transformed into a visual image.

> *Visualize two pieces of bread and spread peanut butter on them. On top of the peanut butter place a piece of roast beef. See that image. Next to this sandwich see carrots and spinach. Seated at the end of a table see a giant red fish sitting in a chair. Before the fish is a glass of milk and a glass of cider. See the fish eating potato chips.*

Yes, this is a silly visual image but it contains the items on your shopping list. In the following pages there will be specific examples of teaching information through use of visual imagery.

Practice in Visiting Our Brain

Sit in a comfortable chair and shut your eyes. Go immediately to the right side of your brain and wander around. How does it feel? What does it look like on the right side of the brain? Is it light or dark? Walk from the right side and head to your left side of the brain. In order to reach the left hemisphere, you must cross an arched bridge called the Corpus Callisum. Come to the center of the bridge and sit quietly. Arise and move to the left side. Does it look or feel the same as your right side? Is it dark or light? After spending a few moments, walk back to the bridge and sit in the exact center. Just relax.

Exploring an Orange

Sit in a comfortable chair and shut your eyes. See an orange inside your head. Slowly peel off the outer skin of the orange. Look carefully at the bare skin. What is the color of an orange once the outer skin is removed? Break the orange in half. What do you now see? Take a piece from one half and have a bite. What does the remaining half look like? Identify specific aspects of this orange. Is there anything you once saw while eating an orange? Look for small details. Now, begin the process of putting the orange back together again.

These visualization exercises are practice in developing keen observation powers. Just like any famous detective, pay attention to small details in order to gain understanding of the big picture. Develop your own visualization exercises for students. Remember, these visualization exercises are meant to be done in one or two minutes. There is no need to spend considerable time from your class period in doing these exercises.

THE PLANET EXERCISE

Sit comfortably in a chair and shut your eyes. Take yourself to a favorite park or forest. It is a beautiful pleasant warm spring day. Birds are chirping as you stroll through the forest or park. Your hear the sound of crunching branches as you walk. You come to a brook and sit down. You lie back and doze feeling the warm sun on your face. You awake feeling refreshed. You resume your walk. You soon come to a lush green meadow. You notice something in the center of the meadow. As you approach, you discover it is an old silver Mercury car. Take a moment and see the silver Mercury car. As you stand there, there is a noise on your right. You turn to see a beautiful blond haired woman – it is the Goddess Venus. She comes up to you, smiles, opens the door of the Mercury car and sits in the driver's seat. As you gaze at Venus sitting in the car, you hear a sound on your left. You turn to find a beautiful black skinned woman approach. It is the famous singer, Eartha Kitt. Eartha smiles at you, opens the back door and sits in the seat. You notice that Eartha has a bag. Eartha reaches into her bag and pulls out what looks like a ten pound Mars bar. See Eartha unwrap the Mars bar and take a bite. Just at that moment you hear the sound of approaching feet. A giant appears stamping on the ground. It is the God Jupiter. Jupiter approaches you standing by the Mercury car, smiles at you, and jumps on top of the car. Venus turns the ignition key and the Mercury car begins to move. As it goes by, you notice the back license plate. It reads S U N. The back license plate is flashing S U N over and over as it moves. In your mind words appear – Saturn, Uranus, Neptune. Suddenly, you hear the sound of a dog barking. It is Pluto and he is chasing the car. Woof, woof, goes Pluto as he runs after the back of the car with its flashing S U N back license plate.

This exercise is used by teachers in primary grades to teach children names of the planets from the sun outward. The exercise should be repeated once a week for three weeks in order to be memorized. Nothing prevents an imaginative teacher from adding to the above by relating atmospheric characteristics to the planets in this story. For example, one could add, "as Venus approaches, flame is shooting from the top of her head." If interested, rework this story with additional pieces of information. Or, create a new version to teach something about planets.

The same information could be taught using a different memory technique. A simple sentence containing the same data might read: "M̲en V̲ery E̲asily M̲ake J̲ugs S̲erve U̲seful N̲ightime P̲urposes." An inquiring mind faces interesting challenges in creating memory strategies to enhance learning. The most important aspect of any memory device is a "yes" answer to the following question: "Does it work?"

Association is important in memory work. And, memory success depends upon visual imagery. Actually, a touch of humor or the ridiculous are positive factors in helping people to recall past events and information. Generations of children were raised on the image of George Washington throwing a coin across the Delaware River. Of course, this event never happened, but for millions it is deeply embedded within their minds as a true event. If I wanted you to remember the words "Balloon" and "House" my memory strategy would be to have you visualize a Giant black balloon sitting on top of a red house. Shut your eyes and see that image. It is now part of your memory. If during the coming hours anyone says the words "balloon" or "house" there is a strong likelihood you will see the image just presented.

Linking

The Planet Exercise is an example of Linking information through means of visual imagery and storytelling. Virtually any piece of information can be recalled through this simple, but effective, process. Memory experts Harry Lorayne and Jerry Lucas emphasize that Linking is more effective if:

* Items are seen out of proportion
* Size of items is exaggerated
* Items are given action
* Items are given color

Following is a list of unconnected words. They will be implanted in your mind through means of storytelling, visual imagery, and application of these four rules.

car, sunglasses, orange, pen, marshmallow, paper, tree, clock radio, airplane, fire

"You are seated in a <u>car</u>. As you look through the front window you notice it is shaped in the form of sunglasses. At the end of the hood is a giant <u>orange</u>. Sticking into the orange is a large blue <u>pencil</u>. On top of the pencil is the largest white <u>marshmallow</u> you have ever seen. The wind is blowing. Suddenly a piece of yellow <u>paper</u> gets stuck to the marshmallow. Whenever you hear the word, "paper" think of a <u>tree</u>. See the tree. Hanging down from a branch is a black <u>clock</u>. Hanging down from another branch is a green <u>radio</u>. Suddenly, you look upward and see at the top of the tree a purple <u>airplane</u>. You climb up the tree, come to the airplane, and open its door. Out comes <u>fire</u>."

If you wish to use this story in training, repeat the words you wish memorized in order to assist students in the memorization process. This technique can be practiced with students who are preparing for a test. Divide students into a group of four. Ask students to select pieces of information that will be on the test and create a story which links the data. In developing the story, the group is to adhere to the four rules. This memory device requires practice so dramatic results may not be forthcoming on their initial attempt.

A.R. Luria, a Russian psychiatrist, wrote a famous memory book in the 1920's entitled, "The Mind of a Mnemonist." It describes his work with a Russian newspaper reporter who was suffering from the disease of not being able to forget. He literally recalled everything from sight to sounds to smell. A favorite technique of the patient was to memorize material by connecting what he wanted to recall to a street on which he lived. He imagined himself a postman delivering the information to houses and places on the street. Prior to using this technique, students are asked to identify a street they know very well. The technique would proceed in this manner if we wanted to have students recall the prior list of words:

"I am a postman walking down my street. As I approach the Smith house, I notice an red <u>car</u> sitting atop their basketball pole. I walk to the front door of the Smith house and find on it huge pink <u>sunglasses</u> which contain black eyes within each rim. I proceed to the next house and find as I reach the mail box there is a giant <u>orange</u> with a smile. I then proceed to the Museed house. As I approach the house I notice a large blue <u>pencil</u> sticking into the front yard. On top of the pencil is a giant <u>marshmallow</u>. On top of the marshmallow the words "<u>paper</u>" "paper" are being flashed over and over again. I shake my head and walk toward the Henry house. I notice as I draw closer that their large elm <u>tree</u> has been cut down and is lying on the ground. I shake my head and move on to the Schwartz residence. As I draw near their fence I notice on top of the gate a large black <u>clock</u> with hands moving around and around the clock. Suddenly, I hear a noise. I turn toward the Hernandez house and see a large green <u>radio</u> on top of the lamp post and it is playing music. I listen to the music for a moment and then go to the Phillips house. I notice that their children, June and Mike are playing with a large brown <u>airplane</u> which is flying through the air. Just at that moment, I hear the word "<u>fire</u>" and turn to see flames shooting out of the Sontag family home."

A variation of this technique is first having students deliver these words along the street on which they live. Once they have made their trip, they are asked to walk backwards and pick up the words in reverse order. This is a simple trick many memory experts utilize in order to memorize going forwards or backwards. Some teachers working in primary grades have students place what they wish to recall around their bedroom. For example, they can visualize Sleepy the Dwarf in Snow White lying on their bed sound asleep. Or, they can place the four food groups around their room. On top of their bureau is a glass of milk, a giant carrot is hanging down from the ceiling, etc...

Perhaps at this point, you are wondering how can teachers actually use these strategies to teach information being presented in their classroom. Following is an example of teaching students names of American presidents in the exact order in which they appeared in history.

"You are walking through a forest. Soon you come to a river where a large number of women are <u>washing</u> what appears to be a <u>ton</u> of clothes. As you stand there watching them, there is a noise on your left. Out comes a naked man who reminds you of the original <u>Adam</u>. He approaches you and asks: "Excuse me sir, but have you seen my <u>son Jeff</u>. I am <u>Mad</u> about my <u>son</u>." Just at that moment you see a <u>mon</u> <u>row</u>ing a boat. In the boat a naked man stands up, just like the first <u>Adam</u>. He shouts out to you, "have you seen my <u>son, Jack</u>?" As you listen to him, something is happening behind you. You turn to see a <u>van</u> drive up, it parks, the back door opens, and out comes a <u>bureau</u>. You notice a sign on the van which reads, "<u>Harry and Son</u>."

Let us halt the story for a moment. We can also tell this story backwards.

"I am walking in a forest when I come to a <u>bush</u>. Just at that moment a truck drives up with a sign on the side that says, '<u>Clint and Son</u>." The truck is picking up dead <u>bushe</u>s in the forest. The driver of the truck uses a <u>ray gun</u> in order to remove dead branches in the forest He then places them in a <u>cart</u>. I heard his fellow worker say, "<u>nix on</u> that way of doing it." The driver asked him if his <u>son John</u> could help them tomorrow and the man replied that his other son <u>Ken</u> might but he was busy that <u>day</u>."

OK, you get the picture.. Students who engage in such activity are utilizing critical thinking in creating the stories and uncovering ways of recalling information. The act of inventing new memory devices is a creative one that stimulates students to become interested in the topic being studied.

A body can be used with younger children, or even older ones, to assist in recall of information. For example:

1. **The top of my head.**
   In attempting to recall an automobile, transform the automobile into a hat and place it on top of your head.

2. **Your forehead.**
   Convert your forehead into a billboard which flashes information in bright lights.

3. **Your nose.**
   Transform your nose into a vending machine which spurts out information to be recalled.
4. **Your mouth.**
   Transform it into a tunnel. As you enter the tunnel, information is flashing from the walls. "H 2 O" is flashing as water runs down the wall.
5. **Your throat.**
   Transform it into an elevator. As the elevator stops at a floor, and the elevator door opens, one sees a particular cluster of information. On the English floor a clerk comes up and says, "I am Ms. Verb, what is the subject of your inquiry?"
6. **Your chest.**
   Make it into a wardrobe. Open its doors and place information on a tray.
7. **Your hips.**
   Place information on your hips and have it jiggle and move.
8. **Your knees.**
   Envision yourself kneeling before the information to be learned.
9. **Your feet.**
   Envision yourself standing on information to be learned.

Any system of retrieval depends upon a process. Assume you were asked by the police to recall your whereabouts two weeks ago. Where were you last Wednesday? Which memory system would you employ in order to have an answer to that question? Consider the following:

* Your appointment calendar.
* Receipts from something purchased that day.
* Weather records.
* Car mileage records.
* Recollections of a friend.
* TV Guide for that day.

Ask students to create a system that enables them to recall what they learned in all their classes on a particular day of the week.

Memorizing Textual Material

In the prior chapter, several ideas were raised concerning interacting with textual materials. Following is a focus upon the memory process of reading textbooks and other materials in classes. Students need a memory system to assist in reading for effective recall. There are several key principles in memorizing textual materials.

* Review the Table of Contents with students and discuss each chapter title in terms of how it relates to the overall content of what is being studied.

* Encourage students to read an entire chapter prior to taking notes. Then, go back over the chapter and do note taking.

* Encourage students to make subheadings for each section of the chapter. Under each subheadings should be key words or expressions.

* Prior to beginning your lesson, ask students to read their subheadings, and then shut their eyes and recall whatever they can.

* Ask students to make a visual diagram of the chapter. If there is a character in a novel, have arrows pointing from the character to key events in the chapter or significant people. A visual expression of the chapter ensures better retention. Even before this activity is done, devote some time demonstrating how to make a visual diagram of action in a chapter. The entire class can work on this project with you.

* Before beginning a test on a chapter, ask students to take out their notes and visual diagrams and review them.

* Outlining a chapter is essential to any memory system. At the beginning of the semester, provide examples of how you would outline chapters. Students need models and one cannot assume they have learned outlining in prior classes.

Memorization of material is assisted when students have visual images to bring what is being read more dynamically into their minds. Visual imagery can be related to virtually any topic. For example:

* In studying rectangles, halt at a particular point. Ask students to shut their eyes and visualize the rectangles. Have them make the rectangles move or dance. Ask students to open their eyes and find a rectangle in the room.

* As students read a novel, ask them to halt at particular points and envision a character or event. Implant the visual image within their minds. If it is a character ask students to imagine the character was in their home sitting at the dinner table. What would the character say?

* As one comes to a key point in the chapter, engage students in visual acrobatics. For example, ask them to envision a triangle. They are then to envision the triangle become transformed into a straight line. The straight line then turns into a triangle. Or, in reading a social studies textbook, one comes to passage of the Dawes Act which established Indian reservations. Ask students to visualize Indians walking through a gate which has a large sign on top reading, Dawes Ranch. Or, in reading a novel, ask students to shut their eyes and imagine what will happen to a particular character in the next chapter.

* As a homework assignment, ask students to write a dialogue with a thing or character being studied. Mr. Square is at your dinner table tonight. Ask him a question. You have just seen a picture in class today of Picasso's famous painting of Guernica. Shut your eyes and imagine you are speaking to Picasso, what would you ask about this painting? You read the story of Cinderella. Imagine Cinderella is eating dinner with you tonight. What would you say or ask Cinderella?

Visual imagery can become integral to teaching. Assign students to a group of four and ask them to play, "Simon Says." Each person states a visual image and the task of other members of the group is to implant that visual image within their mind. For example, Joan says, "Snow White is eating a large red apple." All members of the group have to envision that scene. The next student states a visual image about the Snow White story and that becomes part of everyone's memory. This is an excellent strategy in preparing for a test. For example, in dealing with causes of the American Revolution, the initial student could say, "I want you to see a large wall on top of mountains and on top of the wall in huge numbers are 1763." This refers to the Proclamation of 1763 which forbade western settlement past the Appalachian Mountains. The next student might say, " I want everyone to see a five foot tall postage stamp on a piece of paper and a man is shaking is head." This refers to the Stamp Act.

Throughout this chapter we have emphasized several key ideas about improved memory. Success in memory development depends upon practice. It is a skill just like playing baseball or tennis; unless one devotes time to perfecting essential skills, there is scant likelihood of future success. Following are the basic skills of memory programs

* Establish strong associations between items being memorized.

* Memory retention improves when on employs humor, the ridiculous or even the absurd.

* It helps to be dramatic in establishing memory associations.

* Chunk information into groups or cluster for better retention.

* Utilize color, diagrams, pictures or movement.

* Memorize during many short periods of time over a long time period.

Recalling Data

Social studies teachers frequently insist that students recall pieces of data. For example, many remember fearful days in which one was expected to spit out names of capitals and states. After all, there are fifty states and fifty state capitals. How does one recall this data. Individuals find it relatively easy to remember movie stars or averages of athletes, why not names of states and state capitals. We remember when it is fun to remember. Following is a strategy to use in persuading students that it is easy to remember a body of information – turn the recall into a mystery!

Example: Small, plus a type of music.
           Little   Rock → Little Rock, Arkansas

1. Holy man plus a dog's foot → St. Paul, Minnesota
2. Wealthy plus a small hill → Richmond, Virginia
3. Coiled metal plus a meadow → Springfield, Illinois
4. Trick someone out of money plus three musical notes → Concord, Mass.
5. Summer month, plus a short vowel → Augusta, Georgia
    → Juneau, Alaska
6. You come from behind to win → Raleigh, North Carolina
7. Face card plus what's up during the day → Jackson, Mississippi
8. 1920's dance → Charleston, South Carolina
9. What a monster does with his teeth, plus a small French town → Nashville, Tenn.
10. Many girls like them → Boise, Idaho
11. Majorette's equipment plus make-up → Baton Rouge, Louisiana
12. Angry plus not one's son → Madison, Wisconsin
13. Talk show host plus a large town → Carson City, Nevada

14. Animal's home plus _____ → Denver, Colorado
    (add your own)

15. Part of a foot plus _____ → Topeka, Kansas
    (add your own)

16. Vegetable plus _____ → Pierre, South Dakota
    (add your own)

Names of States

1. Name of a French King plus woman who helped king of Siam → Louisiana

2. Another name for prison plus a stuck up person → Pennsylvania

3. A vowel plus what you say when greeting a person → Ohio

4. What you do when entering a doorway plus famous English princess → Indianna

5. Where you dig coal plus what you like to drink → Minnesota

6. What you place around a dog's neck plus what you use to make bread → Colorado

7. Boat Noah traveled on plus _____ → Arkansas
   (add your own)

8. Name of unmarried woman plus _____ → Missouri
   (add your own)

9. What children like to kick plus _____ → Kansas
   (add your own)

10. A common question plus _____ → Wyoming
    (add your own)

Activities:

1. Use these memory strategies to assist memorization of countries, physical characteristics, temperatures, etc...
2. Create a "memory detective" with certain reasoning powers who solves mysteries about names of states or cities or countries.
3. Divide students into teams and assign each group a baseball or football team. Their task is creating an approach similar to the above for the team.
4. Ask students to use this strategy in memorizing names of famous people.
5. Try this approach with names of paintings. For example, Mona Lisa.

Memory Strategies:

1. The "latch on" game is played by having one person name an item to be memorized; the next person repeats that item and adds another, and so on until everyone in the group has presented an item.
2. Prior to presenting information to the class, give students an outline about what you wish to cover. If possible, draw diagrams connecting points. Use color pens.
3. After completing the outline, underline and capitalize key words or ideas. A larger sized item is more readily recalled than a smaller one. For example, COAL = POLLUTION.
4. Encourage students to relate what they study to popular songs. For example:

    The Brain Song
    Oh, the spinal cord connected to the brain stem,
    The brain stem connected to the cerebellum,
    Dem brains, Dem brains, Dem split brains.
    Oh, the brain stem connected to the thalamus,
    Oh, the thalmus connected to the hyperthalmus
    Dem Brains, Dem brains, Dem split brains.
    Oh, the thalamus connected to the limbic system,
    Yeh, the thalamus connected to the limbic system,
    Dem brains, Dem brains, Dem split brains.
    And, everything connected to the cortex,
    Yeh, everything connected to the cortex,
    Dem brains, Dem b rains, Dem split brains.

5. Create memory audio tapes. A memory audio tape is created by placing information to be recalled on the tape. At frequent intervals, interrupt the information with selections from classical music. Students turn on the tape prior to going to sleep.

6. After teaching some information, ask students to go to sleep with their heads on the desk. Put on Baroque Classical Music and recite once again in shortened form the information you wish them to recall.

7. Encourage students to form visual associations. For example, in studying President Franklin D. Roosevelt's conflict with the Supreme Court ask students to visualize a giant frankfurter beating on the head of a judge.

8. Encourage students to relate physical features of prominent people to their name. For example, my name is Stopsky and I have a large nose. In gatherings I urge people when they see my face to envision my nose as a ski slope with the word STOP at the bottom of the ski slope.

9. Rhymes are an effective strategy to remember information. A Cheerio Box recently had this ditty:
> The vitamin called A has important connections
> It aids in our vision and helps stop infections
> To vitamin C this ditty now comes
> Important for healing and strong healthy gums.

10. An interesting strategy to assist young athletes is use of visualization. Ask students playing basketball to shut their eyes and see the basket leave their hands and make an arc in the air and descend into the basket. Many Olympic athletes use visualization practice.

11. Encourage students to keep a pad and pencil next to the telephone. After completing a phone call, they should write time of phone call, date, a synopsis of what was said and any further messages. This is excellent practice in keeping records.

12. There are numerous memory strategies to recall where one has placed an item. For example:
   a. Draw an Object Map of each room and indicate where specific items are usually placed.
   b. As you place an object on something, imagine you are sending a picture of where you placed the item to a satellite up in the sky.
   c. As you place an object on a surface, create a visual image between the object and the surface. You just placed some pliers that were being used in the garden on a chair as you rushed to answer the phone. In the split second that occurs when the pliers hits the surface see the pliers dancing a jig on the surface. You will not forget where you placed the pliers. Remember, this is done in a half second.

13. When going shopping, chunk items. All dairy items go together as do meat items.

14. Primary age children frequently forget where they place keys or other such items. Have these children identify the right pocket as number 1 pocket and the left as number 2 pocket. As they place an item in the pocket they should say to themselves, "number 1" or "number 2."

15. Students frequently forget the page they reached before closing a book. Tell them as they close the book to make the page number huge – 30 and have it flash in red lights on their forehead. This should take a moment.

16. An effective way to recall names is to create a substitute word for the name. For example:

    Barry → berry
    Carson → car son
    Daniels → dan yells
    Eaton → eat a ton

17. Teach young children a simple expression to explain changing clocks during the year:

    Spring ahead in the spring
    Fall back in the fall

18. Remember shopping lists by using a linking sentence.

    Let us turn up tomorrow and beat them into the cellar.
    (lettuce) (turnip) (tomato) (beet)   (celery)

19. Prove to yourself you have a great memory. Attempt to forget something you know.

20. Each morning as you awake, take exactly one minute and make a mental list of what you have to do that day.

21. When learning something new, associate it with something you already know. For example, this morning I read about a civil war in Africa. I related this war to the American Civil War and identified two connections.

22. The use of substitute words is an effective technique in aiding children to remember information. Following are some examples to link states with their capitol cities.

    Boise → A boy seeing an Idaho potato.
    Little Rock → A girl throwing little rocks at an ark.
    Helena → Helen climbing a mountain.

23. Similar to the above is creating a riddle to help students remember capitols.

    "Come from behind to win" → Raleigh
    "A saint and a cat's paw." → St. Paul
    "Water in a field." → Springfield

24. Select an object like a telephone, desk, radio, or TV. Examine the object very closely for a few minutes. Shut your eyes and draw the object. Compare and contrast your drawing with the actual object.

25. Pair students into teams. One team selects a picture and shows it to the other team. Their response is to quickly draw what they saw for a split second. Later, teams reverse roles.

26. Ask students to draw a map of the United States and place the following on the map. San Francisco, Boston, the Missouri River, Lake Huron, the Columbia River, the Rocky Mountains, New Orleans, and the Erie Canal. After students draw the map from memory. After completing it, students examine an actual map and compare and contrast their own map with it. After viewing the actual map, students once again draw a map from memory. This is practiced several times in the year.

27. Take students on a field trip to a zoo. Ask them to shut their eyes and listen to sounds of the animals. Their task is to correctly identify the sound with the correct animal.

28. Present the following words to students and ask them to memorize the list.

Book	magazine	spoon	pen
Wine	ink	fork	bottle
Pencil	knife	plate	pepsi
Newspaper	eraser	ice	video

Then, present the following method of remembering the list by means of classification of the items.

Book	pen	fork	bottle
Magazine	pencil	knife	ice
Newspaper	eraser	plate	wine
Video	ink	spoon	pepsi

29. Each day ask a student to leave the room on an errand. The task of the remainder of the class is to accurately describe the student.

30. An important factor hindering recall of information is the presence of negative attitudes. Athletic coaches understand the importance of fostering positive attitudes prior to the onset of a game. As a topic is introduced emphasize the ease of learning. "Today, we are going to learn about pollination. It is among the easiest topics in our science book." Accentuate the positive and eliminate the negative.

31. Kim's Game: Rudyard Kipling invented a game to train people in becoming more proficient in observation and memory. Place several objects in groups of three or four on a table. For example, one group could include an orange, pear, banana, and grapes. A second group might include a pen, pencil, notebook, and eraser. Cover your objects with a sheet for twenty seconds, uncover them and ask students what they recall. If students do well, they can be given additional groups to memorize. In the second sequence, mix up the groups so everything does not fall into the same category. These exercises can be repeated.

AND

DON'T

FORGET

* Create strong associations with material to be memorized.
* Images should be comical and absurd.
* Exaggerate the size of images.
* The more an association has personal meaning, the greater the ease of recall.
* Chunk information.
* Invent codes.
* Use diagrams.
* Draw pictures.
* Rhyme when possible.
* Create funny stories.
* Repetition works.
* Use color.
* Sing songs about the information

A FEW LAST SUGGESTIONS

1. Be Emotional.
   In the process of remembering a piece of data, invest emotional energy. For example, you wish to recall the formula H2 O. First, visually yourself pushing hard against a door shaped like the letter "H." for four seconds become angry at the H. See the number 2 on the door of H. Envision yourself punching the door and see the word "O" floating in the air like words in a comic strip.

2. Reward Yourself for Remembering.
   In the process of recall, each time you remember something, give yourself a treat. It could be something as simple as a piece of apple or lying on the couch for five minutes. As you partake of the treat, say inside your head, "It's great remembering X."

3. Be Logical.
   Transform your mind into a library. You have just read "Pride and Prejudice" by Jane Austin. Shut your eyes and envision the librarian opening the catalog file for "P." See the librarian place "Pride and Prejudice" in the file and notice a large letter "A" on the card as it goes into the drawer. File information under any system you wish to devise.

4. Use All Your Senses
   As you begin the process of remembering information, utilize all senses. Transform the data into a visual image, become furious at the information, and place it in your mind's library.

5. Be Aware of Your Mood
   We recall best when happy, sad, angry or fearful. Stop right now and recall something during the past few weeks that infuriated you. See how easy it was to recall the data. It's OK to be fearful in a class when attempting to recall information. Ironically, if angry or fearful, you will recall much better.

6. Categorize Tasks
   Divide daily tasks into groups and assign a part of your body to be the focal point of the category. For example, place morning tasks on your forehead. As you assign the task have your forehead become a billboard flashing the task in red lights. For example, tomorrow morning you are going to pick up donuts. Place the donut task on your forehead and have it flash DONUT in red lights. Your task coming home is to pick up medicine at the drug store. Assign early evening tasks to your foot. At the tip of your foot envision in large green letters, MEDICINE.

7. Listen when people talk to you and ask questions. This is important.

CHAPTER 11

INQUIRY AND SCIENCE AND MATH

Chapter Outline:

1. 110 ideas to stimulate science inquiry and math inquiry.

110 Ideas to Stimulate Science Inquiry and Math Inquiry

1. Snow White has the personality of a circle. She is talking with her stepmother who has the personality of a triangle. Write the dialogue between them based on these personality characteristics.

2. Historically, land in America was divided on the basis of a square. How would American history be different if land had been divided on the basis of a triangle.

3. A numerator and a denominator are seeking jobs. What type of job would each be good at?

4. An amoeba and a paramecium are sitting on a park bench. They observe some children playing. Write the conversation between them in which their comments derive from their function and purpose in life.

5. An amoeba and a paramecium meet and have a discussion of their love life. How would they differ in regard to love and interpersonal relationships?

6. Give a personality to a square, a rectangle, and a triangle. Identify an issue they will discuss based on their characteristics and perception of life.

7. Imagine that a miniture submarine is wandering through your body. Write their account of what they see as they meander through one part of your body.

8. An insect emerges from the egg with the same defenses it will have at death. Alter this reality by introducing another reality that allows the insect to learn. Write this scenario.

9. Pose this problem to students. "Genetically, at the age of 45 I am not the same person I was at the age of five. Explain changes that would normally have occurred to make this statement accurate."

10. Ask students to select an item from everyday life. For example, chewing gum. Pose this problem: "Without consulting any further reference, hypothesize how chewing gum would have come into existence."

11. Ask students to imagine they are attending a conference called by bacteria who live within their body. Students are to identify issues raised by the bacteria and, if possible, identify a strategy they will employ to make them sick.

12. Pose this problem to students: "In the early days of antibiotics, bacteria had difficulty coping with these new enemies. What happened that enabled bacteria to survive and prosper?"
13. Students are to imagine the dinosaurs were not wiped out and continued to exist. Pose to students: "How would life today be different?"
14. Ask students to compose "dinosaur poetry." In other words, if dinosaurs emerged being able to read and write, what type of poetry would they compose? The poetry should be consistent with the type of dinosaur that is doing the composing.
15. Ask students to create a dialogue between all components of the photosynthesis process in which they discuss what they are doing.
16. Pose the following to students: "The planetary system emerged differently. The sun only comes out five hours per day. How would this have changed life on planet Earth?"
17. Divide students into groups. Each group is given one planet. Their task is to invent clothing and footwear for their planet. They are allowed to invent new materials.
18. Pose the following to students: "Planet Earth never physically separated. How would life today be different as a result of that one alteration?"
19. Pose to students: "Your task is to identify the physically largest animal on each continent and create a chart indicating differences."
20. Prior to technology, "power" was generated by humans, animals, the wind, or water. Students are to identify which areas of the world would have had the greatest "power" based on the animals existing on their continent.
21. Students are to imagine they were with the first Europeans who arrived in the western hemisphere. Their task is to identify what about plant and animal life would have been most surprising to these Europeans.
22. Students are asked to create a menu for one week that only includes foods native to the western hemisphere.
23. Students are asked to create a menu for one week that only includes foods not originally native to the western hemisphere.
24. Pose to students: "It is the year 1780 and you wish to fly. Your task is to identify how you might fly but you are restricted to ideas and materials available in this time period.

25. Pose to students: It is the year 1880. Which inventions must emerge before you could invent a heavier than air flying machine?
26. Ask students to create a planet with an environment. Their next task is to create animals that would be able to exist within the environment.
27. In order to demonstrate how a virus infects people, divide class into four groups. Each group is provided a different colored powder. Students then move around the room visiting with other students. Each student who visits must deposit some powder to the person visited. After this process is completed, have students graph the progress of each group's virus.
28. Divide class into four groups. Each group is given some fruit. Their task is to formulate an hypothesis as to how many sections are found in each fruit. Their final products are two graphs, one is the original hypothesis, and the other is a graph of the actual number of sections.
29. Divide students into four groups. Each group is provided data on weather and the environment of several areas of the world. Students are also provided a list of animals. Their task is to identify which animal would best be able to disguise or camouflage itself in a particular environment.
30. Provide students with disassembled skeletons of several life forms. Their task is to correctly assemble the skeletons.
31. Ask students to provide the most interesting new law of physics they can devise.
32. Ask students to create examples of "cartoon physics." For example:
a. All principles of gravity are negated by fear.
b. As speed increases, objects can be in several places at once.
c. Any body suspended in space will remain in space until made aware of the situation.
d. A sharp object will always propel a character upward.
33. Ask students to create a dialogue between a neutron and a proton.
34. Pose the following to students: "A science teacher is now in charge of the school. How would the school be organized and what would be its curriculum?"
35. A science teacher is now the President of the United States. Select any current events topic and devise the question this person would ask about the problem.

36. Amoeba Follies: Draw a picture of the following:
    a. Amoeba vaulting a high fence.
    b. Amoeba with bow and arrow.
    c. Amoeba with a flashlight.
    d. Confused amoeba.
    e. Amoeba with an umbrella.

37. Paramecium Follies. Draw a picture of the following:
    a. Shocked paramecium
    b. Paramecium with glasses.
    c. Paramecium juggling an amoeba.
    d. Paramecium lifting weights.
    e. Paramecium hiding behind a desk.

38. Ask students to invent a planet, give it physical characteristics, and devise new laws of chemistry for the planet.

39. Ask students to devise new laws of physics for their planet.

40. Ask students to imagine a scientist from another planet has arrived on Earth, which questions related to science would this life form pose?

41. Have students create DNA Personal Ads
    a. I've been single-stranded too long; lonely ATGCATG would like to pair up with congenial TACGTAC.
    b. Uninhibited virus seeks reason to make me shed my coat protein.
    c. Mature cell seeks same who still enjoys cycling and won't go apoptotic on me. Let's fight senescence together.
    d. Highly sensitive, orally active small molecule seeks stable well-structured receptor who knows size isn't everything.

42. Create a science joke. For example:
    > 2 hydrogen atoms bumped into one another yesterday
    > One said: "Why do you look so sad?"
    > Other said: "I lost an electron."
    > Concerned: "Are you sure?"
    > Response: "I'm positive."

43. Pose a problem or old joke and ask how various scientists would respond: "Why did the chicken cross the road?"

    Einstein: "Whether the chicken crossed or the road or the road crossed the chicken depends upon your frame of reference."

Werner Heisenberg: "We are not sure which side of the road the chicken was on, but it was moving very fast."

44. Write a science song: The Complex Number Song
    Mine eyes have seen the glory of the Argand diagram
    They have seen the i's and thetas of De Moivre's 2/16/2003
    Now I can find the complex roots with consummate élan
    With the root of minus one
        Complex numbers are so easy
        Complex numbers are so easy
    With the root of minus one

45. Ask students working in groups to select a dessert. Their task is to present their dessert to the class in its chemical form. Winning team which stumps the class gets the dessert.

46. Pose to students: "Cats are from Venus and Dogs are from Saturn." Each group is to attribute characteristics to a cat or dog which are related to physical and environmental factors on their planet.

47. Divide class into two groups. One group becomes, "Dr. X-File" and the other group's task is to pose questions about aliens on Earth such as flying saucers. The task of the X-File group is to explain the phenomenon in logical scientific terms.

48. Ask students working in groups to create a spoof of an X-File episode which includes scientific mumbo jumbo.

49. Ask students to create a history of canal building on Mars – including photos.

50. Ask students working in groups to identify a movie action hero or heroine. Their task is to explain scientifically this individual's flight behavior in a movie.

51. Ask students to explain the flight of Santa Claus in scientific terms.

52. Establish a "Crazy Call" site to the Smithsonian Museum. The task of one group is to invent the call and the other group's task is to give a scientific response to the call. For example, here are some calls to the Smithsonian:
        "Where is the Ark of the Covenant?"
        "Is the Smithsonian interested in buying the carcass of Bigfoot?"
        "Could the Smithsonian take a petrified whale off my hands?"

53. Ask students to create a Periodic Table of Condiments. For example, they might include condiments that last long or those that quickly turn bad. They should give their explanation of the condiment in scientific terms.

54. Establish a "Molecules with Silly Names" contest. Students are divided into teams of two and their task is to identify a molecule with a silly name. For example:
    Arsole — arsenic equivalent to pyrrole
    Bastardane – related to admantane

55. Create a "Rubber Band Shooting Contest." Students work in teams of three. Their task is to invent a new way to shoot a rubber band.

56. Pose to students: Their task working in groups is to identify a "Physical Warning Label" for a product. For example: "This product warps space and time in its vicinity."

57. Pose to students: "Working in teams your task is to either mathematically or scientifically invent a way to catch a lion in the Sahara Desert." For example:
    Geometry Inversion Method: We place a spherical cage in the desert, enter it and lock it from the inside. We then perform an inversion with respect to the cage. Voila, the lion is inside the cage and we are on the outside.

58. Ask students to create a law that redefines the value of pi.

59. Pose to students working in groups. Their task is to identify a chemical and describe its chemical components in horrifying ways. For example, Dehydrogen monoxide (water): It contributes to erosion, is exists in tumors of patients with cancer, it is a component of acid rain. The task of the class is to guess the chemical being described.

60. Students working in group are to explain in scientific terms a common belief. For example, "When a cat is dropped it always lands on its feet."

61. Pose to students working in groups: Your group task to explain in scientific terms how I can "eat my shirt." If possible, transform the act of eating my shirt into eating a peanut butter sandwich.

62. Pose on an exam a "fractured question." For example, "Is hell exothermic (gives off heat) or endothermic (absorbs heat). Your answer must contain a logical explanation."

63. Pose the following half joke to students. Working in groups, they are to come up with a punch line:
    "A neutron walks into a bar and asks for a drink. The bartender serves the drink and says, _____."
       For example, "For you, no charge."

64. Another joke:
    Two hydrogen strings bumped into one another recently.
    One said: "Why do you look so sad?"
    Other said: "I lost an electron."
    First said: "Are you sure?"

    Other said: _____
    ("I'm positive")

65. Pose to students: "Why did the chicken cross the road?" The task of students working in pairs is to identify a scientist or scientific principle and explain the chicken crossing the road. For example: Albert Einstein. Whether the chicken crossed the road or the road crossed the chicken depends upon your frame of reference.

66. Ask students to create a scientific saying. For example: "Heisenberg may have slept here."

67. Ask students to identify a famous scientist and present their view on a current issue such as brain stem research.

68. Three men are lost in a balloon. The balloon reaches a canyon and one shouts:
    "Hellooo, where are we?" Fifteen minutes pass and then they hear a voice which says: "You're lost." One man in the balloon says, "The person who shouted must be a statistician." Ask students why they decided it was a statistician. (Possible reasons – took a long time to respond, absolutely correct in the answer, the answer is worthless.

69. Ask students to create a Recruiting Poster urging people to study science.

70. Ask students to invent crazy explanations of math formulas. For example: There once was an Indian chief who had three squaws who lived in three teepees. The Indian chief went out hunting and caught an hippotomaus, a bear, and a buffalo. He gave one squaw a bear, one a buffalo, and the other a hippo. The squaw who got the bear had a boy, the one who got a buffalo had a girl, and the one who got the hippo had twins. The mathematical explanation of this phenomenon is: "The squaw of the hippotomaus is equal to the sum of the squaws of the other two sides."

71. Ask students to create a love story about something related to chemistry. For example: Once upon a time a piece of sodium which lived in a test tube fell in love with a Bunsen burner. The sodium said, "Oh Bunsen, my flame, I melt whenever I see you..." The Bunsen replied: "My dear, it's just a phase you are going through."

72. Ask students to create one line jokes related to science. For example, "Have you heard the one about the scientist who was reading a book about helium? He just couldn't put it down."

73. Aid reluctant students who fear telling jokes by asking them to give the punch line for a joke. For example: "Where does one put the dishes? _____ (In the zinc).

74. Confusing answers that are correct. Students are to create examples. Following is one:
    Teacher: Name a unit of electrical power.
    Student: What?
    Teacher: The watt is absolutely correct.

75. The origin of life. Students are asked to give logical answers how each of the following people would explain the origin of life on Earth.
    Newton
    Britney Spears
    Harry Potter
    Adam Sandler

76. Ask students to write a rap song about some aspect of what they are studying in science.

77. Pose to students working in groups: "An alien scientist has arrived on Earth. Your task is to create a new law of physics and explain how it functions on the alien's home planet."

78. Pose to students working in groups: "Assume that dinosaurs were not wiped out and continued to exist. Present a logical explanation of a modern type dinosaur including how it functions and thinks."

79. Ask students to create a book containing sayings by famous scientists.

80. Ask students to write a science limerick. For example:
    There once was a girl named Irene
    Who lived in distilled kersone
    But, she started absorbin
    A new hydrocarbon
    And, since then has never benzene.

81. Pose to students: "Assume that humans lived at the time of dinosaurs, how would they go about killing a dinosaur only using materials available at that time period?"

82. Ask students to invent a trip through the human body in a miniaturized submarine. They are to describe what they see on the voyage.

83. Ask students to write an essay on, "The Sex Life of An Electron."

84. Have students create, "Strange Signs" about science. For example, "Man wanted to work in nuclear fission molecule reactive. High School degree required."

85. Have students pass out a petition in school to "Repeal Ohm's Law."

86. Pose to students: "What is the value of PI?"
    Mathematician – 3.1415927
    Physicist – 3.14
    Politician – 8, if it's located in my district.
    Have students add their own.

87. Ask students to write the movie review of "Lord of the Rings" as though written by a scientist.

88. Pose to students: "We are back with Adam and Eve in the Garden of Eden. What was the first scientific invention by humans?" Students provide logical answer.

89. Ask students to design a science oriented bumper sticker.

90. Ask students working in groups to explain the temperature of heaven. They can consult the Bible for assistance.

91. Ask students to identify a scientific research topic that is ridiculous.

92. Ask students working in pairs to write a science discovery story for a national scandal sheet such as the Enquirer or the Star.

93. Ask students to develop a "Cavemen List of Important Inventions."

94. Ask students working in pairs to write a Dr. Mad essay which explains the beneficial results of radiating the world.

95. Ask students working in pairs to create a list of Ten Facts about the Moon landing which includes at least one incorrect fact. Class must identify the incorrect fact.

    This activity could be weekly with different topics for each week.

96. Ask students working in groups to create a Mars Survival Kit.

97. Ask students to create a Galactic Gazette which contains stories about recent space developments. This could be a rotating assignment.

98. Ask students to make a list of mistakes in science. For example, Lord Kelvin said in the 1890s that "heavier than air machines were impossible."

99. Ask students to invent a new way of transforming garbage into something useful.

100. Ask students to create "space jokes."

101. Ask students working in pairs to describe the Moses trip from Egypt in scientific terms.

102. Ask students working in groups to develop a new scientific theory. For example: "Why Yawning is Contagious: You yawn to equalize the pressure on your eardrums. This pressure change outside your head unbalances other people's ear pressures so they yawn to even it out."

103. Ask students, using logical scientific reasoning, to write how the Earth evolved into the Planet of the Apes.

104. Ask students to write a romance story featuring chemical components.

105. Ask students working in pairs to explain how to clean the classroom in chemical terms.

106. Ask students to create a Nobel Prize for Improbable Scientific Inventions.

107. Ask students to create a new version of global warning. For example:
    Animal farts
    Human farts
    Tooth decay

108. Ask students to compose an alien transmission to planet Earth.

109. Provide students legs of animals and ask them to identify the animal.

110. Have students working in groups create Science Daffynitions:
    Q: What is one horsepower?
    A: Amount of energy it takes to drag a horse 500 ft. in one second.

111. Ask students to explain in chemical terms the benefits of a beer and ice cream diet.

POSTLUDE

A FEW LAST CHUCKLES

THE ANIMAL SCHOOL

Once upon a time, the animals decided they must do something heroic to meet the problem of the "new world" in which they lived. So, they organized a school.

They adopted an activity curriculum consisting of running, climbing, swimming, and flying. To make administration of the school easier, they decided that all students would take all subjects.

The duck was excellent in swimming, in fact, better than his instructors, but he made only a passing grade in flying, and was poor in running. Since he was slow in running, he had to stay after school and also drop swimming in order to practice running. This was kept up until his web feet were badly torn and he was only average in swimming. But, average was acceptable in the school, so nobody worried about that score, except the duck.

The rabbit began at the top of the class in running, but had a nervous breakdown due to so much make-up work in swimming.

The squirrel was excellent in climbing until he developed frustration in the flying class when his teacher made him start from the ground up instead of from the tree down. He also developed "Charlie horses" from over exertion and then got a "C" in climbing and a "D" in running.

The eagle was a problem child and was disciplined severely. In the climbing class he beat all the others to the top of the tree, but insisted on using his own way to get there.

At the end of the year, an abnormal eel that could swim exceedingly well, and also run, climb, and fly a little, had the highest average and became the class valedictorian.

The prairie dogs stayed out of school and fought the tax levy because the administration would not add digging and burrowing to the curriculum. They apprenticed their child to a badger and later joined the groundhogs and gophers to start a successful private school.

If Jesus Came To School

Then Jesus took his disciples up the mountain and gathering them around him, he taught them saying:

> *"Blessed are the poor in spirit,*
> *for theirs is the Kingdom of Heaven*
> *Blessed are the meek*
> *Blessed are they that mourn*
> *Blessed are the merciful*
> *Blessed are they who thirst for justice*
> *Blessed are you when persecuted*
> *Blessed are you when you suffer*
> *Be glad and rejoice for your reward is in heaven."*

Then Simon Peter said, "Do we have to write this down?"
And Andrew said, "Are we supposed to know this?"

And James said, "Will we have a test on this?"

And Phillip said, "What if we don't know it?"

And Bartholomew said, "Do we have to turn this in?"

And John said, "The other disciples didn't have to know this."

And Matthew said, "When do we get out of here?"

And Judas said, "What does this have to do with real life?"

And the other disciples likewise.

Then one of the Pharisees who laws present
asked to see Jesus' syllabus
and inquired of Jesus
His terminal objectives in the cognitive domain.

And, Jesus wept....

Dear Teacher, Please Excuse.......

Following are actual examples of notes sent by parents to school in order to explain why their son or daughter was absent.

Please accuse John been absent on January, 28, 29, 30, 33.

Mary could not come to school because she was bothered with very close veins.

Please escuse Gloria. She has been sick and under the doctor.

My sun is under the doctor's care and should not take P.E. Please execute him.

Lillie was absent from school yesterday. She had a gang over.

Please excuse Joe Friday. He had loose vowels.

Please excuse Joyce from Jim. She has been administrating.

Carlos was absent from school yesterday because he was playing football. He was hurt in the growing part.

Please excuse Johnny for being. It was his fathers fault.

Please excuse Diana from being absent yesterday. She was in bed with gramps.

Mary Anna was absent 11/15 because she had a fever, sore throat, headache and upset stomach. Her sister was also sick – fever, sore throat. Her brother had a low lgrade temp and a gall over. I wasn;t feeling the best either, sore throat, fever. There must be the flu going around. Even her father got hot last night.

School Cheers

Mathematics

> Pythagoras, Pythagoras, he's our man,
> If he can't prove it, nobody can.
> Learn this rule and you'll deduce
> The square of the hypotenuse
> V — I — C — T — O — R — Y
> 3.141, 3.141

English

> Two four six eight
> Now what shall we explicate?
> Shelley's ode or Shakespeare's sonnet?
> Read a line and comment on it.
> Check the meter, check that rhyme,
> We can do poems any old time.
> Quote that line.... Quote that line.

Home Economics

> Sis boom bah, sis boom bah
> Eat those carrots, raw, raw, raw
> Shun tobacco, shun the grape
> Get your body back in shape.

World History

> Harold the Saxon in a bad fix
> Battle of Hastings, 1066
> William who had conquered when the battle was done.
> What would we have called him if he hadn't won?

Librarians

> Boomalack, boomalacka, boomalacka, boom!
> Come spend some time in the reference room.
> Check the books and check the stack,
> Check them in when you bring them back.
> Five cents a day per book will accrue
> For every day that they are overdue.

Just a Minute Late ....

This piece was inspired by a phone call from a nameless high school secretary who informed me that my stepdaughter Kathy was five minutes late to school. This is dedicated to anyone and everyone who has ever been a few minutes late.

My stepdaughter brought this to school to chuckle over it with some friends. It came to the attention of the principal and the Superintendent of Schools. The next day I had to see the principal who gave me a lecture about the importance of punctuality and why making fun of lateness hurt the morale of educators. He was shocked someone in teacher education did not share his inane ideas about lateness.

Distributed by: The Minute Men of America

"Hey, Dianne, got a minute?"

"I'm in a rush. It's nearly time for the late bell to ring."

"I just wanted to tell you that I got the books from the library for our report. My brother had to go clear over to the county library to get them. I thought maybe we could get together tonight and go over the stuff. Is that OK with you?"

"Sure, thanks a lot. I'll talk to you later. Got to rush."

The Late Bell Sounds

"Oh, Mr. Wallace, could I go to my room. I'm just about a minute late. I just stopped for a second to talk about my report."

"Sorry, Diane, you know the rule. A minute late is the same as an hour late. It's the lateness that counts, not how long you're late."

"But, I just stopped to talk about schoolwork. It's not that I was doing anything wrong."

"You really miss the point, Dianne. You _did_ something wrong. You were one minute late. That minute does not belong to you. It belongs to this school. You took our minutes for your own purposes. That's, what is wrong."

"Gee, if you're that worried about the minute, I'll give it back to you this afternoon. In fact, I'll give you ten afternoon minute for the morning minute."

"Flippant talk does not excuse your behavior. How could you even think it is possible to exchange an afternoon minute for a morning minute! That's like putting a square peg in a round hole."

"Mr. Wallace, this is crazy. You make it sound as though I'm a criminal or something."

"Technically speaking, you are a criminal. You were one minute late, you broke a rule. Rules are made for everyone and once we make exceptions, then rules lose all meaning. I'll have to call your parents about this terrible infraction of school rules. They should know their daughter is a latecomer in life."

"Do you have to do that? My dad easily gets upset and he goes wild. It will mean a big hassle at home if you call. Couldn't I just take detention or something?"

"The rule is to call parents. Unless we get parents to cooperate, students will keep on coming to school late and we will lose precious minutes in the day that should be devoted to doing school work."

The Telephone Rings

"Hello, who is this?"

"Hello, who is this?"

"This is Mr. Wallace from the high school. I'm calling to let you know that Dianne was late this morning."

"Late? I saw her leave for school. She should be in school right now."

"She is in school, but she came in one minute late."

"What's wrong with that kid? Kids today don't know how to behave. I'll really give it to her when she gets home, don't worry."

"I'm just calling to let you know that she was late. After all, it's my duty to follow school rules and regulations just as it is the duty of students to obey those same rules and regulations. After all, rules are made for a purpose – to be obeyed."

"Heck, Mr. Wallace, I'm not faulting you. You're just doing your job. That's the American way. It's the kids who break the rules and waste our time. They're the criminals, not the decent folks like you who follow the rules."

"I'm glad you see it that way. We have to make special efforts these days to save every minute if we are to keep up our standards. These minutes are precious. We need those minutes or we will disintegrate into chaos."

"Well, I'm glad someone is trying to save this country. Keep up the good work. I'm one hundred percent behind your campaign to save those minutes."

The Door Opens

"Dianne, you're late. You just missed five minutes of class time. I'll have to send you to the office so they can record your lateness."

"I'm sorry, Ms. Peters, I just came from the office. Here, I have a pass explaining that I was one minute late to school."

"Oh, I see that, but what about the five minutes lateness to this class? Is that to go unrecorded?"

"But, I was talking to Mr. Wallace about the one minute lateness. That's why I'm five minutes late to class. You mean you want me to go back to the office and get another pass saying that I was five minutes late to class?"

"Dianne, I'm not trying to cause trouble for you. You are a nice girl. But, you were five minutes late to class. Those are five unreplacable minutes. After all, minutes don't grow on trees."

"But, if I go to the office to get a pass I'll never be able to finish today's test. Does that mean I'll fail?"

"Dianne, you make it sound as though I'm failing you. You're the one who is causing failure. If you came to school on time and used the precious minutes of school in a positive manner, you would never fail anything."

The Principal's Door Opens

"Dianne, come in and sit down. I have two reports about your efforts to appropriate minutes belonging to this school and using them for your own frivolous purposes."

"Sir, I was one minute late to school and then get tied up in the office talking to Mr. Wallace so I was five minutes late to social studies."

"So, you admit to stealing minutes?"

"Stealing? I was late. I didn't take any minutes or anything."

"Dianne, we aren't stupid, you know. Who are you working with to steal our minutes?"

"I'm not trying to steal anything. I was just a few minutes late, that's all."

"Yes, you were a few minutes late, and the next student is a few minutes late and ten other children are a few minutes late. Have you ever added up all those minutes? Do you know what will happen if we continue to lose those minutes?"

"I honestly don't know."

"We'll have a minute gap. The Russians will have more minutes and we will fall behind the Russians. Don't you realize the Russians insist their children come to school on time. They will get ahead of us in the minute race."

"Huh?"

"Oh, don't act so naïve. I'm quite aware that communists agents infiltrate American schools and encourage our school children to come in late. First, they want our students to be late to school, then they want to encourage our children to become poor readers and writers. The Russians are hoarding their minutes and one day they'll dump their minutes in one big push and zoom way ahead of America. Don't you realize it's your patriotic duty to come to school on time? Do you want us to fall behind the Russians in the lateness race?

"Honest Sir, I never met a Russian."

"Neither did the people of Afghanistan until the Russians came. Do you know why the Russians were able to take over Afghanistan?"

"No, sir."

"Because the people of Afghanistan are habitually late. They kept on falling further and further behind in the lateness race and the Russians won very easily. That's why every American child has to come to school on time.. Every time you are one minute late a Russian agent grabs that minute and takes it back to Russia. I hope you have some patriotism left in you."

"I'll do my best sir."

Home

"Dianne, come right in here this minute, young lady. I got a call from Mr. Wallace today saying you were late to school."

"Gee, dad, I was just one minute late."

"So, you think one minute late is nothing. Do you know what one minute can mean in life? Suppose the doctor is one minute late getting to the scene of an accident or the guy on the assembly line is one minute late doing his job? Everything gets fouled up, that's what happens."

"Dad, I'm sorry, really. I'm sorry. I'll do my best to get to school on time."

"You're not getting off so easy young lady. You did something terrible today, you were one minute late to school. If you're not punished you'll go through life thinking you can be one minute late all the time. I'm not going to be responsible for my daughter becoming a lazy one minute later."

"Dad, I told you the last time that I'm not going to get beaten. Please, let's talk. I'm warning you not to hit me."

"I'll not have my daughter stealing things that belong to others. We have always been honest people in this family. Get ready for your whipping.'

"I didn't steal anything, I was just one minute late."

"It's your duty to obey rules."

"But, what if the rules are crazy?"

"A rule is a rule. It's not the minute late that's important, it's the principle of being late and breaking rules that's important. Are you ready for your punishment?"

The Police

"Now, honey, take it easy. I'm sure you didn't mean to do it. It was just an accident, wasn't it?"

"No, that's not true. I thought about it for a minute and then I shot him."

"People don't do terrible things in a minute. They think about it for a long time."

"Oh, no, it was just a minute. Didn't you know I was the minute thief?"

"Huh? Look, honey, you're upset. I'm certain you didn't mean to kill your father. It was an accident."

"You obviously don't know who I am. I am the notorious minute thief who prowls the high school corridors stealing minutes which I carefully wrap in red packages and send to Russia. They take those minutes and give them to their school children. That's why the Russians are ahead of America in the lateness race."

"I think you had better talk to a doctor. Just wait a minute and I'll get one for you."

The Courtroom

"Dianne, you stand accused of two crimes – killing your father and stealing six minutes from your school. How do you plead?"

"I guess I'm guilty of both crimes."

"In matters where an individual is being tried on two serious counts, the more serious crime is the one the defendant must deal with. OK, you were late to school, right?"

"You mean, I won't be tried for shooting my father?"

"Not really, your lateness to school is much more serious and we have to deal with that crime. After all, society creates schools so we can have students in school who come on time. If there were no schools, how could children be late?"

"You mean the important thing in life is to get to school on time?"

"Definitely. That is the only important thing you will ever learn in school. After all, who remembers all that rubbish learned in social studies or science? What really counts is learning to be a disciplined person who obeys orders. Once you learn that every minute counts and that rules are created to that people could obey them, you'll become an outstanding student. Remember, we have rules so we can provide jobs for people like policemen or teachers. What would the principal or counselor do all day if they didn't spend time dealing with lateness? What would happen if everyone came to school on time?"

"So, it doesn't matter what I do in class so long as I get to school on time?"

"Dianne, now you are talking like an intelligent young lady. Who care what you do on the homework assignment as long as it is turned in on time?"

"I think I finally understand. Your Honor, I'm ready to be on time for school from now on."

"Excellent, excellent. I think you will become an excellent example of how we rehabilitate offenders. But, we still have to deal with the six minutes you owe the school."

"Well, judge, suppose I steal six minutes from a kid at another school and give it to my school? Is that OK?"

"Splendid, splendid. Now, that's a fine example of school spirit. I like you're attitude. Now, you are showing the spirit of patriotism and school spirit. You are ready to defend your own school. Great."

"Your Honor, from now on I shall defend my school and obey its rules, and above all, I will never be late to school."

How Long Have You Been A Teacher?

1. Do you murmur, "no cuts" when a shopper squeezes ahead of you?
2. Do you move your dinner partner's plate away from the edge of the table?
3. Do you ask if anyone needs to go to the bathroom when you enter a theater with friends?
4. Do you hand a tissue to anyone who sneezes?
5. Do you refer to "snack time" instead of "happy hour?"
6. Do you ask guests if they remembered their scarves and mittens as they leave your home?
7. Do you say "I like the way you did that" to the mechanic who repairs your car?
8. Do you say "Are you sure you did your best" to the mechanic who fails to repair you car?
9. Do you sing the Alphabet song to yourself as you look up a number in the telephone book?
10. Do you fold your spouse's fingers over the coins as you hand them over?
12. Do you ask the quiet person at a party if they have something to share with the group?

Wacky Ways To Teach For The Brave At Heart

1. Deliver your lecture in gobbledygook and insist as you talk that everyone take notes for the test at the end of the week.
2. Invite students to give a gobbledygook talk.
3. Speak so softly that no one can hear and suddenly shout: "Did everyone get that in their notes?"
4. The next time you are ready for the famous lecture on, "Why students should do their homework" invite anyone to give the lecture and promise extra credit. Students will get the point and still have fun.
5. Wear a hood with one eyehole for a period.
6. Growl and address students as "matey" when talking about something to do with sea or ocean.
7. In the middle of your talk, make a mistake, turn, shake your head, and say, "Boy, was I wrong about that. Did everyone catch my mistake?"
8. Announce that last year's students are just getting ready to submit their projects.
9. Spend a period playing your favorite music.
10. Point the overhead projector at the class as you talk. Tell them they are under the gun.
11. Announce that today is "leaf day" and that anyone in possession of a leaf will receive an "A" for the day.
12. Invite the class comic to devote one minute each day as you take attendance to tell his or her favorite jokes.
13. Role play an historical figure.
14. Teach backwards. Begin at the end of the textbook and work your way backwards.
15. Announce you will do five pushups if anyone in the class can stump you about anything in the lesson.
16. Announce you will do twenty-five pushups if the entire class passes the exam.

17. Include at least one joke on every test. The joke includes a simple question anyone can answer. This avoids having students receive a zero on your exams.
18. Spend ten minutes each week reading poetry to the class.
19. Share with students your craziest moment in teaching.
20. Read names from the absentee list and provide a wacky reason for the origin of a student's name. Begin with your own name.
21. Begin each class period with a cheer related to what is being studied. "Let's have an M, come on, let's have an A, that's it, let's have a T, and one big one for the H. Yes, today it is MATH day. Let's have a good one."
22. Read school memos to the class in a humorous tone.
23. When the class appears sluggish, invent a holiday and celebrate with the class.
24. Walk backward during the class session.
25. Arrange a schedule for calling parents during the first month of school. Tell the parent a specific wonderful thing their child did in your class. Parents love this call from a teacher.